SHAPING
A
FUTURE

The National Church Life Survey has been developed and resourced by the Uniting Church Board of Mission (NSW) and the Anglican Diocese of Sydney through its Home Mission Society. The 1991 survey involved the following denominations:

- Anglican
- Apostolic
- Assemblies of God
- Baptist
- Christian & Missionary Alliance
- Christian Revival Crusade
- Church of the Nazarene
- Churches of Christ
- Congregational
- Foursquare Gospel
- Lutheran

- Presbyterian Church in Australia
- Presbyterian Church in New Zealand
- Reformed Churches of Australia
- Salvation Army
- Seventh-day Adventist
- Uniting Church
- Wesleyan Methodist
- Westminster Presbyterian
- Some independent congregations, house churches and Christian communities

Also involved in 1996 were the following denominations:

- Christian City Churches
- Christian Life Churches

- Brethren
- Vineyard Fellowship

In 1996 the Catholic Church participated in a parallel study of Catholic parish life.

Support for the 1991 survey has come from participating denominations and Christian groups including the Bible Society, Christian Blind Mission International, the Uniting Church Investment Fund, African Enterprise, World Vision, Aware Insurance, the Leprosy Mission, Insight Books, Open Doors with Brother Andrew, Drug Awareness Council, and ANSVAR.

In 1996 the following organisations have also provided generous support:
Koorong Books, Time Magazine, Compassion Australia, Guide Dog Association of New South Wales and ACT, Scripture Union, the Salvation Army, Australian Hymn Book Committee, Uniting Church Assembly, Uniting Church Frontier Services, Uniting Church New Start Team, and Uniting Church World Mission.

Do you want further information or resources or would you like to be kept in touch? Simply use the survey hotlines or addresses:

	Uniting Church Board of Mission	**Anglican Home Mission Society**
	PO Box A2178 SYDNEY SOUTH NSW 1235	PO Box Q137 Queen Victoria Building SYDNEY NSW 1230
PHONE	(02) 9285 4594	(02) 9261 9500
FAX	(02) 9267 7316	(02) 9261 9599
E-MAIL	ncls@ozemail.com.au	

WORLD WIDE WEB http://ncls.uca.org.au/

SHAPING A FUTURE

CHARACTERISTICS OF VITAL CONGREGATIONS

PETER KALDOR
JOHN BELLAMY
RUTH POWELL

BRONWYN HUGHES
KEITH CASTLE

OPENBOOK
PUBLISHERS

Cartoons by Chris Morgan (Chris Cross Art)
Correspondence re cartoons to
PO Box 1939
ASHFIELD NSW 2131

Design by Graeme Cogdell

First printing

07 06 05 04 03 02 01 00 99 98 97   10 9 8 7 6 5 4 3 2 1

National Library of Australia
Cataloguing-in-Publication entry

National Church Life Survey: shaping a future:
characteristics of vital congregations.

   Bibliography.
   ISBN 0 85910 831 7.

   1. Protestant churches — Australia. 2. Church membership — Australia. 3. Church and the world. 4. Church work. I. Kaldor, Peter.

280.40994

Typeset in 9pt Stone Serif

Published by
Openbook Publishers
205 Halifax Street
Adelaide, South Australia   0074–97

This book is dedicated to
Florence Kaldor,
and all those praying for the NCLS,
the future of their churches
and the whole church in Australia.

ACKNOWLEDGMENTS

The National Church Life Survey is the product of the vision, energy and hard work of so many people. Thanks must go to:

- The sixty or so contact people in the participating denominations and more than a thousand people who gave feedback on survey questions, design, pilot testing, manuscripts, printouts and so on.
- The project Steering Committee — Howard Dillon, Dean Drayton, Carolyn Kitto, Geoff Huard, Reg Platt, David Manton, Phil Marshall, Silas Horton, Bob Moin — for their ongoing support at each stage of the project.
- Chris Morgan for the cartoons, which help make the issues come alive.
- Sandra Moore for her editorial help at a difficult time — the birth of this manuscript took place at the same time as that of her second child.
- Joy Sanderson, Kirsty Grugan, Kay Merriment, Lyn Marshall and Vicki Sorenson for coping with a never-ending series of edits to the emerging manuscript.
- Roslyn Simms for collecting and writing most of the stories used in this book. Unless otherwise specified, Roslyn has been the source.
- Professor George Cooney of Macquarie University for statistical advice during the study.
- Church leaders, academics and lay people who have gone to the trouble of reading various drafts of this manuscript in the midst of busy lives.
- Dean Drayton, Carolyn Kitto, Merilyn Correy, Sue Kaldor and Ian Jagelman for particular help in shaping aspects of this book or the support material that goes with it.
- Sue Kaldor, Stephen Cree, Jo Gore, Kaydee Farley, Jane Ford and Margaret Robinson for assistance in the literature review.
- Sponsors for their support.
- The thousands of congregational leaders and attenders who completed the survey — it is their efforts that have enabled the voices of attenders to be heard!

NCLS Staff Team (as at February 1997)

Peter Kaldor (Project Director)   Bronwyn Hughes
John Bellamy   Louise McLeod-Tollu
Keith Castle   Ruth Powell
                                   Joy Sanderson

SHAPING A FUTURE

CHARACTERISTICS OF VITAL CONGREGATIONS

PROLOGUE

The water and cliffs beckoned us after a long drive through the deserts of Wyoming. Far from any town, Flaming Gorge has a timeless quality, untouched by human activity. The echo of our voices off the rock face, the deep red colours of the cliff and a beautiful place to camp were an invitation to rest, but also to dream.

The issues of church life in Australia seemed far away in this place. Yet this was to be an important time of conceptualising a research strategy to explore issues which go to the heart of the mission of the church. Out of our time at Flaming Gorge came the steps which were to lead to the creation of the 1991 National Church Life Survey in Australia.

My previous research for *Who Goes Where? Who Doesn't Care?* had highlighted the importance of the make-up of the local community on the shape of church life. Yet it was clear that local context is only a part of the picture. Community context does not fully explain why some congregations are vibrant and open to their community while other congregations in the same context are stagnating or in decline. What is it about each of these congregations that has led to such different outcomes? What aspects of congregational life actually make a difference?

These are central questions for the church in Australia and beyond. I've seen many talented preachers and pastors over the years. Many wonder what difference their effort really makes. How important is their role in making their congregation more open to its surrounding community?

What about the characteristics of the church attenders themselves? Are younger congregations more likely to attract newcomers? How important are attenders' own faith journeys or experience of God? Is it a case of having the right theology?

What about the contribution of small groups or friendship networks to the vibrancy of a congregation? Or do they merely serve to make it more insular? And what about the identity and purpose of a congregation, its vision and sense of direction? What difference does that make?

As questions, ideas and issues found their way onto paper in Flaming Gorge, a central issue emerged. How might a research study evaluate the vitality or effectiveness in mission of a congregation? It is relatively easy to collect numerical growth statistics from congregational leaders. It is much more complex to explore wider questions of a congregation's openness to its community, its depth of life and faith and its care for the community.

As I pondered these things it was clear that a large survey of church life could provide answers to these questions. However, the survey needed to be more than just a survey of church leaders or of individual church attenders; it needed to depict the characteristics of congregations as well as the characteristics of the wider community they seek to serve.

Shaping a Future is the fifth publication from the 1991 National Church Life Survey. So far most of the material released in the previous NCLS publications has focused on individual attenders, their attitudes and practices. ***Shaping a Future* looks at the information from a totally different standpoint.** The responses of attenders have been combined and added to information from leaders to provide **a detailed profile of each congregation**, its life and mission.

This information has been used to identify characteristics that vibrant and effective congregations have in common. Importantly, it gives us an idea of the relative importance of each of these characteristics and, therefore, an ability to set priorities.

Shaping a Future marks an important watershed in the National Church Life Survey research. In many ways it represents a fitting culmination to what has been an extensive research program which has identified some of the great changes which are taking place in Anglican and Protestant church life in Australia.

However, this book also looks forward to the results of further research which will be carried out using the 1996 National Church Life Survey. The research covered in this publication has played an important role in framing the design of the 1996 NCLS and the printouts being provided to congregations from that survey on their life and mission.

It is our prayer that the findings of this publication will help congregations as they grapple with how to be more open to their communities. It is our hope that, while churches remain faithful to the gospel of Jesus Christ, they will discern clearer priorities for their life and ministry. When congregations take the material in this book and view it in relation to their understanding of themselves and their own unique journey, the gifts and aspirations of those who are part of their life, and the community they seek to serve, they should find that it provides useful insights that will help their congregation shape a creative and positive future.

Peter Kaldor, on behalf of the NCLS team

INTRODUCTION

As the church moves through the last decade of this century, it finds itself in a context of massive social change. Technological change, the information explosion, changing economic conditions, multiculturalism and gender issues are shaping the way Australians live. The pace of change is not slowing down.

Many people are still coming to terms with the changes of the past two decades. This is especially true in the life of the churches. There is much soul searching within the churches about future directions, as the church is stretched between the great traditions of the past and a vision not yet fully formed for the 21st century (Mead, 1991, 5).

In response to these turbulent times, many congregations are looking for new ways forward. Some have taken new initiatives in mission or refined their focus. Others have worked on how they express their faith. Some have introduced contemporary music; others have developed tailor-made programs for the young, the elderly, families, people from non-English-speaking backgrounds or other special interest groups. Underlying these changes is the assumption that churches need to be culturally relevant to communicate the gospel message to all sections of society.

Other congregations are responding to change by placing new emphasis on leadership, or on planning and setting goals. Some are refurbishing properties or relocating to new, more adaptable buildings. Still others are starting new congregations.

In contrast, some congregations are holding firmly to the traditions and models of church life handed down to them, with few changes. For many these traditions and models are filled with meaning and life. Some are concerned that too many changes may dilute the gospel message; perhaps some hope that society will come full circle and re-embrace older approaches to church life.

Complete change and holding fast to tradition are at different ends of a spectrum. Many congregations are incorporating both approaches, making changes where necessary while maintaining and communicating the essence of their traditions in their corporate life.

As congregations across Australia seek to express their faith in contemporary society, nagging questions remain: How do congregations faithfully connect the traditions of their heritage to realities of contemporary society? What should they hold on to; what needs to change? How should we shape church life for this new mission era?

WHAT THIS BOOK IS ABOUT

There is a wide array of literature and experts in Australia and overseas available to help congregations seeking to become more vital and effective. Often the wisdom offered is based purely on experience in one context, or on hunches, anecdotes or grand theories.

Shaping a Future goes beyond theories to examine vital congregations

Shaping a Future goes beyond the theories to examine vital congregations in Australia today. The purpose of this book is to outline some of the characteristics of congregations that are proving vital and effective in mission and ministry in Australia today.

This issue is explored through the 1991 Australian National Church Life Survey (NCLS), one of the most comprehensive databases on church life in any country in the world. Responses to some 200 questions were collected from 310 000 attenders and leaders in over 6500 congregations of 19 denominations. For *Shaping a Future,* 3500 congregations which provided the most comprehensive data were selected (see Appendix 1 for details).

To this was added the local demographic data from the 1991 Census, generated for each congregation. The information from both databases represents a highly detailed statistical representation of the unique features of each and every congregation and the local community within which it is located.

Australia is a good laboratory for this study: it is a prosperous English-speaking nation caught up in the global changes and social diversity that are characteristic of western nations. It is affected by similar social forces to the United States and Europe and shares a common religious heritage with Great Britain, New Zealand and, to a lesser extent, Canada. It is a country with a Christian heritage, yet one in which the churches need to adapt to being part of a diverse and changing society.

For many Australian churches the challenge is to make a major mindset shift and, as Loren Mead says, to struggle with their identity as people of God, with how they live together, and with what their environment really is (1991, 70). At the same time there is much life and growth; church life in Australia is characterised by great creativity.

While there may be databases on church life that include more congregations in other countries, there appears to be no database as comprehensive as the NCLS anywhere else in the world. The NCLS has been widely used across the church in Australia for congregational planning, denominational decision making and wider research.

All participating congregations were provided with printouts on their own life and ministry, and with resources to help them reflect on their strengths and areas for further development. Workshops helping congregations make use of NCLS material have been held across Australia. Several thousand people participated in workshop seminars between 1991 and 1996. The NCLS has proved to be a simple yet powerful tool for helping congregations start to think about their priorities and directions for the future. Printouts will again be available from the 1996 NCLS. Specific *Shaping a Future* printouts have been designed to be used in conjunction with this book.

By examining the characteristics of vital congregations, *Shaping a Future* seeks to be a resource to help congregations in mission by allowing them to gain from the experiences of churches across Australia. *Shaping a Future* is the fifth publication from the 1991 NCLS and builds upon the previous work. References are made in this book to previous publications:

- *First Look in the Mirror: Initial findings of the 1991 National Church Life Survey* (1992)
- *Winds of Change: The experience of church in a changing Australia* (1994)
- *Mission under the Microscope: Keys to effective and sustainable mission* (1995)
- *Views from the Pews: Australian church attenders speak out* (1995)

USING THIS BOOK

Learn your theories well but put them aside when you touch the miracle of a living person. Carl Jung (in Davis, Kavanagh and McGuiness, 1994, 28)

Some may be concerned that the unthinking application of general trends identified in this survey can be dangerous. NCLS staff share this concern.

The results in this book provide an overview of the experiences of churches across Australia. Readers and congregations that reflect on this overview need to bring to this reflection their own experiences and faith journeys, the passions and hopes of their attenders, the intricacies of their congregational history, and their community context. This book is designed to be a resource rather than a prescriptive manual.

This book is a resource rather than a prescriptive manual

Some have been concerned that the NCLS is, in presenting its results, reducing church life to a series of trends or formulas. 'Where is God in it?' they wonder. 'Is it not more a question of faithfulness to the biblical revelation or received tradition?'

NCLS staff are personally committed to the critical importance of faithfulness. As we understand it, faithfulness requires us to look at and listen carefully to the situations we find ourselves in, in order to live out the call to Christian discipleship effectively and in tune with gospel imperatives. It is in this context that this study seeks to make a contribution, allowing the church to see the impact of aspects of church life upon mission and congregational vitality.

Most Christian traditions assert the importance of listening. Jesus treated people differently depending upon their circumstances. How differently he related to the woman at the well, to Nicodemus, and to the woman about to be stoned. The early disciples took into account the context in which they were speaking. In Athens, Paul used as his starting point the altar to the unknown god, beginning the presentation of his message within the cultural context of the Athenians and moving on from there.

Of course there is much in church life that cannot be empirically tested. God is not bound by any rules, principles, keys, vital signs or statistical averages! Every situation is unique. We have not set out to be prescriptive or to suggest that any set of principles or priorities will automatically generate an effective and vital congregation.

God is not bound by any rules, keys or statistical averages!

This study does not suggest that faithfulness is not a critical ingredient in congregational life. Nor does the NCLS seek to replace theological reflection. Rather, it seeks to provide useful resources and insights, from the experiences of the whole church in Australia, to those who are seeking to further their understanding of how to be more faithful as Christian disciples or as a gathered body of believers. In times of continuous change it is vital to understand our congregational and community contexts, our reason for being as a congregation, and our directions for the future.

A STEP FORWARD

While it is not by any means the final word, this book takes our understanding of church life and vitality several steps forward.

- *It goes beyond numerical growth as an indicator of vitality.* In a study such as the NCLS, how might one evaluate the vitality or effectiveness in mission of a congregation? It is relatively easy to collect numerical growth statistics from congregational leaders. It is quite another thing to explore wider questions of a congregation's openness to its community.

  Numerical growth may come simply by people changing churches or it may come by outsiders with no church background choosing to become part of a gathered Christian community. Further, the vibrancy and depth of life and faith in some congregations stands in contrast to involvement that seems almost casual in others. These are difficult concepts, but they certainly need to be taken into account when considering the vitality of a congregation.

  Then there are the questions of evangelism, care and social concern and of loving our neighbour that are central to what God calls the church to be. Congregations may put much or little emphasis in these areas, or organise specific missional activities. Attenders may be doing a great deal in their everyday lives as a result of their faith.

  A study of congregational openness to the wider community needs to evaluate a range of aspects of vitality well beyond numerical growth statistics. This study uses a range of measures of congregational vitality. The seven indicators selected are detailed in Chapter 1.

- *It covers a wide range of aspects of congregational life.* The breadth of aspects of congregational life covered is outlined in summary form in Chapter 2 and detailed in Appendix 2.

- *It is based on more than the experience of larger churches in urban areas.* Much current advice relies on the experience of large urban congregations. This causes difficulties for church leaders and attenders attempting to apply the lessons in small or medium-sized congregations or in rural settings. The findings of the NCLS complement and qualify the wisdom from other sources.

- *It is based on a broad range of denominational experience.* Much previous research has been limited to the experiences of particular denominations. Nineteen denominations contributed data to the

The NCLS complements wisdom from other sources

NCLS, covering the breadth of Anglican and Protestant traditions.

- *It is based on a huge representative national sample.* Much previous work has been based on small samples, sometimes in fairly specific regions or contexts. Congregations involved in these studies may not be typical and the samples therefore may be skewed. The NCLS was national, covering all States and regions of Australia.

- *It is based on more than the leaders' perceptions.* Quite a lot of previous research has, of necessity, relied on the perceptions of leaders. The NCLS uses information primarily drawn from the perceptions of attenders, supported by data from leaders. In this way, the research is able to go beyond the experience of a few key people; it incorporates the collective experience of both leaders and attenders.

The NCLS statistics are both a blessing and a challenge. They allow this book to go beyond ideas about congregational life; they reveal cameos of Australian church life as it really is. However, it is never easy to present statistics in a reader-friendly format. To make the task as easy as possible, the book is divided into several parts.

The first two chapters explain the nature and basis of this study. They examine some of the ways vitality and effectiveness are evaluated by writers and researchers and explain the seven indicators of vitality selected by the NCLS. They also explain the statistical methodology and presentation of results used in later chapters. They set the scene and are essential background for understanding the Parts that follow.

Part 1 looks at each of the seven indicators of vitality in turn and then examines the characteristics of congregational life that are associated with each one. For instance, it looks at levels of newcomers to church life, one of the NCLS indicators of vitality, and identifies characteristics that tend to be associated with congregations with high levels of newcomers. The aim is to provide readers with a simple summary of some of the key issues in an easy-to-digest format.

Parts 2 and 3 take a more detailed look at the study from a different angle. They explore aspects of congregational life such as worship style, leadership and planning and their relationship with vitality in more depth. In what ways are these aspects related to vitality? Each chapter in Parts 2 and 3 covers a different aspect of congregational life. Readers may work through the material in the order in which it is presented, or explore areas of interest.

The NCLS offers a template for church life research. It also provides a framework to assist congregations to reflect on their mission directions. This framework is simple, sensitive and replicable in other contexts. *Shaping a Future* provides a unique opportunity for the church in Australia and beyond to take a close look at priorities for ministry, an essential task for all. It is a must for all people concerned about the shape of the church in the next millennium.

CHAPTER 1

EVALUATING CONGREGATIONAL VITALITY

A Better Way?

What are the characteristics of effective congregations? What do congregations which have a vitality that sets them apart from others around them have in common? Such questions beg a prior question: What is an effective and vital congregation anyway?

Over the last few decades many writers and researchers have asked this question. More often than not their response has come back to numerical growth. Time and again an effective, vital congregation has been defined as one that is growing numerically.

It is easy to see how such an emphasis on numerical growth has been fostered. The social changes and declines in church attendance during the 1960s and 1970s created a great deal of pessimism about the future of the church. Many commentators saw the demise of the church as imminent and inevitable.

The Church Growth Movement developed, in part, as a reaction to such pessimism. Arising out of work in the Third World of people such as Donald McGavran, it sought to develop 'scientific' principles for church growth. Its focus was on factors within the life of the congregation that could be altered in order to make a congregation more effective. Optimism was a major part of its philosophy, as can be seen from the titles of major books such as *Your Church Can Grow* (Wagner, 1976) and *Ten Steps for Church Growth* (McGavran and Arn, 1977).

Much of the work of the Church Growth Movement has come from examination of 'successful' congregations. Its work has generated both strong support and criticism. Some of that criticism has been theological; some have questioned the validity of the analysis that underpins the conclusions. Others have argued that the movement has not taken enough account of factors external to the life of the congregation, including the local community in which it is placed.

The emphasis of some within the Church Growth Movement has, intentionally or otherwise, reinforced the notion that numerical growth is the pre-eminent measure of the success of a congregation. The assumption has been made that a congregation that is growing numerically is also likely to be one that is growing and developing in other aspects as well. Even where the limitations of using numerical growth as a measure of success have been recognised, there is an absence of alternative available measures.

Further, the concepts of growth and vitality have sometimes been equated with size. 'Big' congregations must be 'growing' congregations and therefore effective congregations. Yet, while large congregations must have grown at some time, size is no guarantee that numerical growth is continuing. Some large congregations may in fact be quite stagnant. And, while they are large, they may be less effective in other ways.

Congregational vitality is clearly a multifaceted concept

The experiences of large congregations are not always directly applicable to the majority of small congregations. Congregations of different sizes may need to organise themselves in quite different ways.

Clearly there are limitations to the exclusive use of either numerical growth or size as a measure of a congregation's effectiveness or vitality.

Congregational vitality is clearly a multifaceted concept. Within the

REV McMULLAN FOUND SOME
COMFORT IN HAVING THE
TALLEST STEEPLE IN TOWN....
RIGHT UP UNTIL HIS
LAST PARISHIONER DIED.

Church Growth Movement writers sometimes point to other measures of vitality besides numerical growth. Roy Pointer (1984, 26–29), for instance, suggests these facets include: numerical growth, conceptual growth (the development of institutional aspects of a congregation's life), and incarnational growth (the congregation's contribution to the wider society in which it operates).

Others, from other traditions (eg Dietterich and Dietterich, 1989, 1), place the emphasis on providing a 'sign' and 'foretaste' of the kingdom of God. Still others are concerned about the extent to which a congregation influences the public culture of its environment, or has grown together as a community of faith, and so on.

ATTENDANCE WAS WAY UP, MORALE WAS FANTASTIC, INVOLVEMENT HAD NEVER BEEN BETTER, BUT REV. TOM STILL FELT UNEASY.....

Many observers want to emphasise the mission of the church. Callahan, for instance, suggests we need more churches of the Good Shepherd. In the biblical narrative, Jesus refers to the Good Shepherd as the one who, with 99 sheep in the fold, went out into the rough, rocky places to seek out that one sheep that was lost. 'Churches in our time are called to effective mission in sharing help with the tough hurts and hopes present among our people' (Callahan, 1983, xxii).

THE PURPOSE OF CONGREGATIONAL LIFE

While there are different understandings of the purpose of a congregation, and different traditions emphasise different priorities, there is much common ground.

Most would agree that the purpose of a congregation is to assist people both from within and beyond the congregation to worship God, to respond to the Christian faith, and to explore its implications in everyday life. Christians understand themselves to be called into a relationship with God, with others in the congregation, and with those in the wider community. They are called to be bearers of the Good News, to be signposts to God's kingdom in word and deed.

In developing indicators of congregational vitality, the NCLS sought to include some of this breadth of understanding. The NCLS was designed on the basis of a specific model of a congregation's relationship with the wider community. Three fundamental dimensions were defined as follows:

- **an attractional dimension:** drawing people into congregational life
- **an incarnational dimension:** encouraging engagement in the wider community, and
- **a faith exploration dimension:** encouraging attenders in their faith.

The indicators selected to shed light on these dimensions are described briefly here and in more detail in Appendix 1.

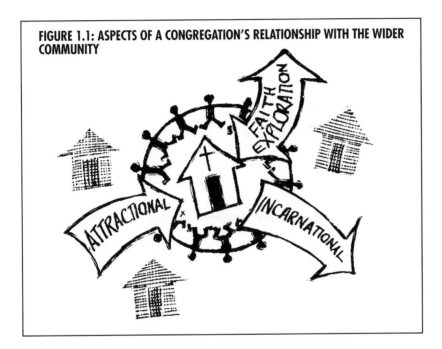

FIGURE 1.1: ASPECTS OF A CONGREGATION'S RELATIONSHIP WITH THE WIDER COMMUNITY

ATTRACTIONAL DIMENSION: DRAWING IN . . .

A congregation can encourage people to worship God, to explore and respond to the Christian faith by drawing people into its corporate life and worship.

The NCLS team selected four *attractional* indicators for this study.

Levels of newcomers: *the percentage of attenders in participating congregations who had joined that congregation in the last five years and previously were not attending church regularly anywhere else.*

One of the main objections to the church's preoccupation with numerical growth has been that it does not focus upon those who are outside of church life. The level of newcomers without a background of church attendance more closely corresponds with the gospel mandate to go into all the world and make disciples of all nations than just numerical growth, which also includes biological growth and church attenders moving between congregations. Examining the levels of newcomers in a congregation provides an indication of how well it is connecting with the wider non-churchgoing community.

The level of newcomers indicates how well a congregation is connecting with the community

Young adult retention: *the percentage of families with adolescent or adult children living at home who still attend their congregation.*

While relating to and integrating newcomers is an important aspect of mission, nurturing existing attenders and their families is also essential. The children of today's attenders will become the core of tomorrow's church; the church faces an uncertain future unless each generation can maintain and nurture the faith in the next. The transition from adolescence to young adulthood is a time where many drift away from the churches, as was shown in *Mission under the Microscope* (Chapter 9).

Numerical growth: *the growth rate of church attendance at participating congregations over the previous five years.*

While there are many who question the preoccupation with numerical growth, it nevertheless remains an important indicator for congregations. Three out of every four attenders want their congregations to get larger, and a significant proportion think their congregations will not survive unless they begin to grow *(Winds of Change,* p 306).

Levels of belonging: *the percentage of attenders in a congregation who feel a strong and growing sense of belonging to their congregation.*

This measure provides a good overall indicator of how attenders feel about involvement in their congregation and their commitment to it.

INCARNATIONAL DIMENSION: FOCUSING OUT . . .

A congregation can assist people to understand and grow in the Christian faith by encouraging its members to become involved with people in the wider community and providing, by word and actions, signposts to God's kingdom. This can be done individually or as part of corporate mission activities.

The NCLS selected two *incarnational* indicators.

A community involvement index: *this index comprises the percentage of attenders involved in community care or action groups, and the percentage of attenders involved in congregationally sponsored social care/social action activities.*

Apart from the millions of dollars administered by denominations, many congregations are involved in social welfare and social action work. Church attenders also participate in community-based groups, such as Rotary, school committees and senior citizens groups. This index provides a measure of the contribution to the well-being of the wider community from a congregation and its attenders.

A faith sharing/inviting index: *this index is made up of the percentage of attenders open to discussing their faith with others or seeking opportunities to do so, and the percentage of attenders who had invited someone to church in the last year.*

While there is often debate about the relative importance of evangelism and social concern, the NCLS has shown that the majority of attenders seek to hold a balance between the two *(Winds of Change,* p 61). It has also shown what a critical issue this is for the churches, given that 42% of attenders do not like to discuss their faith with others or have difficulty doing so in everyday language *(Mission under the Microscope,* p 59).

FAITH EXPLORATION DIMENSION: LOOKING TO GOD . . .

A congregation points people to God, to help them worship God and develop their Christian faith. Various terms are used to describe aspects of this third, central dimension. All are about a two-way relationship: human responses to God's loving intervention in the world.

A range of questions covering faith exploration were included in the NCLS. From them a single *growth in faith* index was developed.

A growth in faith index: *this comprises the percentage of attenders feeling they have grown significantly in their understanding of the Christian faith in the last year through their congregation, the percentage developing much stronger beliefs in the last year through their congregation, and the percentage making major changes in their actions and priorities as a result of their Christian faith in the last year.*

One of the central functions of the church is the nurture of faith. In the minds of many attenders this is an even more highly valued function than the opportunity for worship *(Winds of Change,* p 185). Growth in faith is seen by many as a key qualitative outcome of church involvement.

In all, the NCLS team selected seven vitality indicators for this study (see Figure 1.2). These indicators are in no way intended to be prescriptive of church life. Nevertheless, congregations that are vital and effective in their mission and ministry are likely to be growing in many of these areas.

The NCLS team selected seven indicators of vitality

FIGURE 1.2: INDICATORS OF VITALITY USED IN THIS BOOK

- Levels of Newcomers

- Young Adult Retention

- Numerical Growth

- Sense of Belonging

- Community Involvement

- Faith Sharing/Inviting

- Growth in Faith

A BETTER WAY?

The seven indicators of congregational vitality go well beyond numerical growth, providing a broader range of ways of assessing missional involvement and the openness of congregations to their communities.

Of course, indicators such as the seven selected have limits. Growth in faith, for instance, is a complex phenomenon, far broader than the simple indicator used here. There are many different points of view about what constitutes growth in faith. Similarly, there are aspects of involvement in the wider community, such as attender contributions in the workplace, which are not measured by the community involvement index used here.

Some would also want to emphasise more the significance of worship in the life and purpose of a congregation. A suitable indicator was not available from the 1991 NCLS; the 1996 NCLS will provide some options in this regard.

The seven indicators are interrelated. For instance, congregations whose members feel uncomfortable inviting others to church are unlikely to have high percentages of newcomers without a church background. Congregations whose attenders do not feel they are growing in their faith are unlikely to be motivated to mission beyond their own numbers.

Some indicators will be more important to some readers than others, depending on their backgrounds. However, while this set of indicators is not comprehensive, it does offer a broader platform for examining congregational vitality than much previous work, and should advance the church's understanding of congregational effectiveness further.

CHAPTER 2

EXPLORING CONGREGATIONAL VITALITY

How to Use this Book

The previous chapter outlined seven indicators of congregational vitality selected for this study. Having selected these indicators of congregational vitality, this study seeks to identify the characteristics of congregations that are vital and effective in each area. Specifically, what are the characteristics of congregations

- which attract high levels of newcomers to church life?
- which have higher levels of retention of children as they move into young adulthood?
- that are growing numerically?
- where high proportions of attenders have a strong sense of belonging to the congregation?
- where high proportions of attenders are involved in social concern activities in the wider community?
- where high proportions of attenders feel comfortable discussing their faith and inviting others to church?
- where high proportions of attenders feel that they are growing in their faith?

A great many factors can affect a congregation's life and relationship with the wider community. A review of the literature over the past 30 years reveals a plethora of essential priorities, important keys, core principles, central characteristics and vital signs that should be taken into account in developing the vitality and effectiveness of a congregation. As one commentator put it: 'Any meeting of church leaders in one hour could fill four walls with newsprint-size writing, listing factors and theories about church growth and decline' (Hoge, 1979a, 93)!

The NCLS project team examined international literature on congregational life and discussed the issue with consultants in Australia and overseas. The issues identified were extremely broad, ranging from worship style and patterns of nurture through to involvement in decision making, leadership style, congregational finances, the background and world view of attenders and the focus of the congregation. Figure 2.1 summarises many of the characteristics tested in the 1991 survey. For further detail on aspects of congregational life covered in this study see Appendix 2.

The NCLS thus provides a unique opportunity to explore some of these aspects of congregational life and their importance in relation to congregational vitality. Never before, to our knowledge, has the same breadth of issues been canvassed across so many denominations in a way that enables comparative study of their relative importance.

FIGURE 2.I: ASPECTS OF CONGREGATIONAL LIFE COVERED IN THIS STUDY

CONGREGATIONAL SIZE
Estimate of size
Desire for growth in size

ACTIVITIES
CHURCH WORSHIP SERVICES
Frequency of attendance
Informality/formality
Understanding language easily
Service length
Satisfaction with music
Presence of contemporary music
Satisfaction with preaching
Length of preaching
Approach to preaching

NURTURE ACTIVITIES
Involvement in groups or adult fellowships
Training attenders for ministry and mission
Dealing with everyday life issues

MISSION ACTIVITIES
Involvement in evangelistic activities
Levels of contact with outsiders
Personal evangelism/inviting to church
Links with the community
Involvement in social concern activities
Rites of passage
Other community links/advertising

GROUP LIFE
Feelings about church life
Friends/caring relationships
Friendliness to newcomers
Awareness of what is happening in congregation
Willingness to deal with hard issues
Levels and outcomes of conflict

DIRECTION SETTING
DECISION MAKING/ROLES
Levels of attenders with different types of roles
Support for those with roles
Involvement in decision making
Openness to new initiatives
Moving in new directions

LEADERSHIP ROLES & STRUCTURES
Leader background
Years in ordained ministry
Years in current congregation
Leadership structures
Main role of leader (eg pastor,
   preacher, priest, visionary, etc)
Outward focus of leader

LEADERSHIP STYLE
Leadership has vision for future
Capable of achieving goals
Directive or non-directive leadership
Takes attenders' ideas into account
Helps attenders discover their gifts

PEOPLE RESOURCES
CHARACTER
Gender
Age
Stage in life
Occupation
Education
New residents
Ethnicity
Similarity to the wider community
Homogeneity

FOCUS
Congregational catchment area
Local orientation of attenders
Specific ministry focus

PERSONAL SPIRITUAL JOURNEYS
Bible reading
Private prayer life
Decisive faith commitment
Experienced presence of God
Sense of call

OTHER RESOURCES
PROPERTY
Age of buildings
Type of building
Suitability of facilities
Visibility/accessibility
Parking
Attender attitude to property

FINANCES
Level of giving
Income from assets
Denominational support
Levels of debt

THEOLOGICAL ORIENTATION
Theological tradition
Attitude to the Bible
Evangelism or social concern emphasis
Orientation to charismatic movement
Orthodoxy of beliefs
Denomination

A CAUTIONARY WORD ON CAUSE AND EFFECT

In examining factors which may be related to vitality, it is important to understand the concept of cause and effect. Scientists often define the world in terms of cause and effect. When something happens, it is assumed that there must be some kind of rational explanation behind it. Many people even feel uncomfortable when they do not know what has caused something to happen.

There is much in the world which defies explanation. In an effort to explain things, people often attribute one primary cause to a problem. For instance they may say: 'People are unemployed because they don't really want to work' or 'Violence in society is the outcome of violence on TV'. The difficulty with these explanations is not that they are completely wrong but that they are too simplistic and overly deterministic. Too much emphasis is placed on one factor as the cause of the problem. In reality the problems described above are enormously complex and no doubt caused by many factors.

What is more, while links can be established, it is often difficult to determine which factors actually 'cause' the problem. Take the incidence of heart attack, for example. Research has found a link between heart attacks and diets high in saturated fats. By reducing the intake of saturated fat, people may reduce their risk of heart attack. Yet diet is only one part of the jigsaw puzzle. Some other factors, which may be important causes, include a lack of physical exercise, genes, age, stress levels, smoking, body weight and the presence of other medical conditions. There are probably other factors which have yet to be discovered.

The same principles need to be remembered when considering congregational life. What are the key factors which are linked with vital congregations? For some, the community context is seen as the most important factor. For others, leadership is the key, or preaching and worship style. Still others emphasise pastoral care. For others, all that seems to matter is having the right beliefs; get the theology right and all else will follow.

Many factors are related to a congregation's vitality

The reality is much more complex than this. There are many factors related to a congregation's vitality, although one factor may be more strongly related.

ANALYSIS TECHNIQUES USED IN THIS BOOK

Many of the factors listed in Figure 2.1 can contribute to or are related to each vitality indicator. For example, satisfaction with music, leaders helping attenders grow their gifts and support for those with roles are all linked to levels of belonging. But which factor is the most important?

Rather than simply listing all the factors that may be potentially important, the NCLS used an analysis technique called multiple regression, which tests the relative importance of each factor. With this technique, the strength of relationship between a particular characteristic of a congregation and an indicator of vitality can be established after taking into account the contribution of other factors. Many hundreds of regressions were carried out in the analysis for this study.

By using multiple regression, the NCLS is able to show which are the key factors in relation to each aspect of congregational vitality out of the hundreds of possible factors in the study. It is important to recognise that this technique identifies the *strength of relationship* between a particular aspect of congregational life and a vitality indicator. It does not determine which one causes the other.

Establishing the existence or otherwise of a relationship is extremely important. Another illustration from wider community life may be helpful. Take, for instance, the research into Sudden Infant Death Syndrome. Links were found between a range of factors and infant deaths long before any causality was established. Knowing the possibility of a relationship enabled people to take action even though researchers did not fully understand how these factors were related. As a consequence, hundreds of lives have been saved.

In the same way here, knowing what the key factors are in relationship to vitality will allow congregations to examine their life and reflect on priorities and future directions.

ALL JUST A MATTER OF BELIEFS OR CONTEXT?

There are many who believe that congregations are largely powerless to change their destiny. Two common reasons are given:

• *Tinkering with congregational life is of minor importance because the future of the congregation is largely determined by the context in which it finds itself.* This context can include the local community make-up or wider national trends. There is a body of sociological work which argues for the significance of contextual factors (eg Hoge and Roozen [eds], 1979; Roozen and Hadaway [eds], 1993).

• *Examining congregational life is irrelevant because the most important issue is what attenders believe.* Congregations with the right theology and beliefs will naturally be the ones that are most effective. Again, this is the subject of much debate in the light of work done by Dean Kelley in the United States (Kelley, 1972).

If either or both of these reasons is exclusively true, then there is little point in going any further in a study of congregational vitality. Therefore, these issues needed to be included in the NCLS analysis. A range of questions was included in the 1991 NCLS to describe beliefs in a congregation and its theological orientation. Similarly, data has been obtained from the 1991 Census on a wide range of demographic characteristics of local communities.

This study shows clearly that, yes, context and beliefs are important. There are strong relationships between the NCLS vitality indicators and particular local contexts on the one hand, and congregations with different belief or 'faith type' profiles on the other. These are discussed in

Context and beliefs are important

detail in Chapters 17 and 18. However, while beliefs and context are strongly related to congregational vitality, so too are other factors within congregational life.

Some may feel that relationships found between the indicators of vitality and the various aspects of church life are really due to differences in the types of communities congregations find themselves in or to differences in beliefs between congregations. For this reason, in analysis and presentation here, the strength of relationships quoted have been calculated *after* accounting for the impact of local context and beliefs. (Further details on this procedure are found in Appendix 1.)

We can learn from all congregations, regardless of their context

This means we can learn from the experience of all congregations, regardless of their context and beliefs. The conclusions can generally apply across all denominations and backgrounds. And while issues such as context and beliefs do make a significant difference, there is still much that congregations can do to grow their effectiveness in ministry and mission.

THE RATINGS SCHEME USED IN THIS BOOK

To understand the chapters that follow, it is necessary to understand the ratings scheme used in this book. The statistical techniques used provide a measure of the strength of relationship between each aspect of congregational life and the vitality indicator in question. In each table, the strength of relationship is presented in two ways. The tables include a numerical score of the strength of relationship. In technical terms this is the 'percent of variance explained by each factor after accounting for the effects of context and faith type (change in adjusted R^2)'. The larger the figure the stronger the relationship. This indicates how important a particular aspect is and allows its importance to be assessed against other aspects.

In order to simplify the presentation, a five-category rating scale, using plus signs, has been derived from this numerical score and used throughout this book. A rating of five plus signs suggests the factor is *critically* related to congregational vitality. Four plus signs indicates that the factor is *very important,* and so on down to one plus sign, which suggests the factor may be *marginal.*

Consider the example of the degree of formality in the church worship services (an aspect of congregational life) and the level of newcomers (an indicator of vitality). A high rating would mean that there is a strong relationship between the degree of formality and the level of newcomers.

In most cases the relationships noted throughout *Shaping a Future* are positive. However, in a few cases the ratings are negative. So, for example, if there is a strong negative relationship between the degree of formality and the level of newcomers, this would mean that congregations where church services are more formal would tend to have lower levels of newcomers. Where a factor is likely to have a negative impact, minus signs have been used.

A low or zero rating suggests that there is little or no relationship between the two characteristics. In such an instance, formality would have little to do with likely levels of newcomers.

FIGURE 2.2 RATING SCHEME USED IN THIS BOOK

RATING		VARIATION EXPLAINED
+++++	CRITICAL	>10%
++++	VERY IMPORTANT	5–10%
+++	IMPORTANT	3–5%
++	SOME IMPORTANCE	1–3%
+	MARGINAL	0.5–1%

PART 1

THINGS THAT MATTER

And so it is to factors in congregational life that we turn in the following chapters. What are the characteristics of congregations with a high level of newcomers or a growing sense of belonging? Or high levels of growth in faith among attenders? Or high levels of community involvement?

The seven indicators of congregational vitality which are analysed here have been described in more detail in Chapter 1. Each chapter covers one or two indicators of vitality as follows:

- Chapter 3 – Levels of newcomers and young adult retention
- Chapter 4 – Numerical growth
- Chapter 5 – Growing sense of belonging
- Chapter 6 – Wider community involvement and sharing faith with others
- Chapter 7 – Growth in faith

The chapters identify the key characteristics among congregations that are vital and effective on each of these indicators. The key characteristics are presented in each chapter in order of their strength of relationship with the vitality indicator in question. It needs to be borne in mind that these are the characteristics which have been found to be the most important in an analysis of hundreds of characteristics.

Since the purpose of this Part is to summarise the most important characteristics, they are not dealt with in any depth. More detailed discussion is found in Parts 2 and 3.

Of particular interest is the fact that while some aspects of congregational life are important in relation to several indicators, the issues differ considerably from one indicator to another. So, if a congregation is interested in attracting and retaining newcomers, for example, the issues to bear in mind are quite different from those related to growing a sense of belonging within the congregation.

As was mentioned in Chapter 2, data concerned with the theological orientation and local community context of the congregation have been treated differently. As a result, they do not appear in the list of important aspects in this Part.

It should be noted that beliefs and context do have an important impact on the seven indicators of vitality, and they are dealt with in detail in Part 3.

CHAPTER 3

THE FRONT AND BACK DOORS

Newcomers and Young Adult Retention

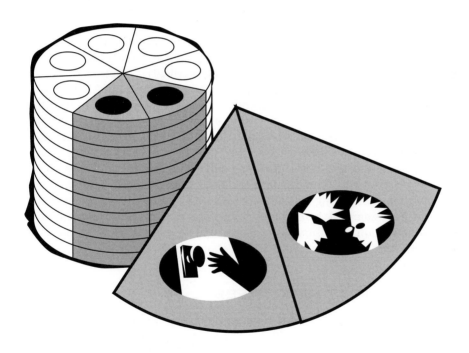

This chapter looks at the first two indicators of vitality used in this book: levels of newcomers and retention of young adults within congregational life. While on the surface the two indicators examine very different issues, the NCLS results reveal some common threads.

LEVELS OF NEWCOMERS

Congregations today are ministering in a radically different social context from the one in which many church leaders grew up. Notions of a Christian Australia, prevalent in the 1950s, were washed away with the decline in church attendance and the social revolutions of the 1960s and 1970s. Across the churches today there is talk of an emerging new paradigm for ministry. Far from maintaining and continuing a Christian society, the churches are pilgrims in a strange land. Their challenge is to communicate the essence of the faith to people who are often unaware of or distanced from Christian teaching. In effect, the churches need to rediscover their mission and their reason for being.

In such a context, the extent to which a congregation is drawing in new people from the wider community who have not previously been involved in the church is an important measure of vitality. So much growth in churches can be put down to a 'circulation of the saints', where one congregation grows because attenders have left another to join it. If the churches are to minister effectively in the diversity of Australia, there needs to be an emphasis on attracting and integrating newcomers not previously involved anywhere.

For this study, newcomers are defined as people who have been involved in their congregation for fewer than five years and were not previously attending regularly elsewhere. The indicator of congregational vitality examined here is the percentage of newcomers present in a congregation. The survey questions used to define the background of attenders, including newcomers, are shown in Appendix 3.

LOOKING AT NEWCOMERS

Newcomers have been discussed in detail in two previous NCLS publications, *Winds of Change* (Chapter 15) and *Mission under the Microscope* (Chapter 8). Some key results are summarised here.

Some 8% of attenders in church on a typical Sunday are newcomers, made up of 3% who have never attended church before (first-timers) and 5% who have returned after a long period of absence (returnees). Newcomers can be found in all denominations, although it would seem that the Pentecostal churches have drawn in more newcomers than other denominations (*Winds of Change*, p 213). About a third of all congregations in the survey recorded no newcomers.

Some key facts about newcomers include the following:

• *While newcomers may be of any age, they are much more likely to be in their 20s and 30s.* Indeed the two categories of newcomers—first-timers and returnees—have different profiles: young adults in their 20s without children form a large component of first-timers; parents in their 20s and 30s with young children comprise a nucleus of returnees.

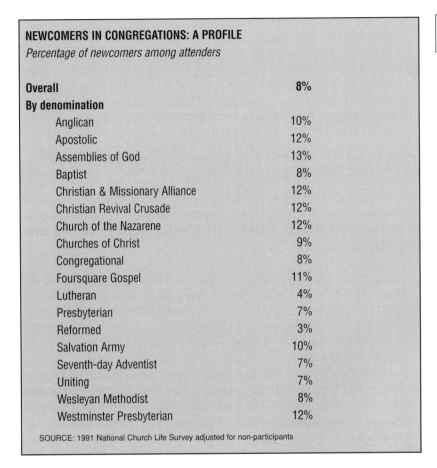

NEWCOMERS IN CONGREGATIONS: A PROFILE
Percentage of newcomers among attenders

Overall	**8%**
By denomination	
Anglican	10%
Apostolic	12%
Assemblies of God	13%
Baptist	8%
Christian & Missionary Alliance	12%
Christian Revival Crusade	12%
Church of the Nazarene	12%
Churches of Christ	9%
Congregational	8%
Foursquare Gospel	11%
Lutheran	4%
Presbyterian	7%
Reformed	3%
Salvation Army	10%
Seventh-day Adventist	7%
Uniting	7%
Wesleyan Methodist	8%
Westminster Presbyterian	12%

SOURCE: 1991 National Church Life Survey adjusted for non-participants

It is important to understand this age profile. The NCLS has highlighted the difficulties of the post-war generation in fitting into traditional church life. Yet people from the post-war generation are most likely to be newcomers. Congregations which express their faith in ways that are meaningful to the post-war generations are more likely to attract newcomers. The results in this chapter bear out this connection.

- *Newcomers are more likely to be from lower status occupations and have lower education levels* (10% have university degrees compared to 16% of all attenders).
- *Newcomers are more likely to be tentative in their church involvement.* Far from being starry-eyed enthusiasts, newcomers are more likely to feel their way gently into church life. Newcomers take longer to integrate, to feel they belong, or to have close friends in a congregation than attenders who transfer from elsewhere.

- *Newcomers are less likely to shop around for the 'right' church.* Compared to attenders as a whole, newcomers are much less likely to have looked at other congregations before joining their present one (*Mission under the Microscope*, p 110). Many newcomers either settle into the congregation they first attend or don't attend at all. This simply underscores the importance of intentionally working to welcome and integrate newcomers. There may be no second chance.
- *Newcomers tend to join congregations through a personal invitation.* More then six in ten newcomers to church life (64%) have joined through some form of personal contact, including friends, acquaintances, family, clergy or a church activity (*Winds of Change*, p 161).

CHARACTERISTICS OF VITAL CONGREGATIONS – NEWCOMERS

This study reinforces and builds on these conclusions discussed in previous NCLS publications. Figure 3.1 lists the factors in congregational life that are most strongly related to high levels of newcomers within a congregation.

- *Like attracts like.* One of the most significant characteristics of congregations with high levels of newcomers is their age profile. Newcomers are more likely to be attracted to congregations with lots of young adults or young families. Given that newcomers are themselves likely to be younger, this is a simple case of like attracting like.

Congregations should cater for younger attenders while they have a solid core in this age group

If it is an important part of their focus, congregations should think about catering for the needs and hopes of younger attenders while they have a solid core in this age group. Far too many congregations give thought to such matters only when they have lost large numbers of younger attenders and have slipped below a 'critical mass' within these age groups.

Congregations drawing in newcomers also tend to include higher levels of recent arrivals in their area. Being available to contact new residents, or intentionally doing so, may be important for a congregation wanting to connect with newcomers. New residents may be looking for friends and ways of connecting with their new community.

Congregations with higher levels of newcomers tend to include more families in their life. Many newcomers appear to be parents wanting their children to grow up in church life (*Winds of Change,* p 216). Congregations where parents find other parents or where family concerns are well catered for are more likely to be successful in integrating and retaining such people.

- *Existing attenders invite others to church.* Congregations with higher levels of newcomers are characterised by attenders being more likely to invite others to church. Such attenders are comfortable talking about their faith, have more contacts with non-churchgoers, or feel more comfortable about how outsiders will feel about their church life.

If newcomers are to be attracted, it is important that attenders feel

FIGURE 3.1: THINGS THAT MATTER — INVOLVING AND RETAINING NEWCOMERS

	STRENGTH OF RELATIONSHIP	
1. Younger age profile	++++	7.0
2. Attenders making changes in their lives as a result of faith	++++	6.9
3. Higher levels of new residents in the congregation	++++	6.0
4. Attenders ready to discuss their faith/invite others to church	++++	5.4
5. Support for those with roles	++++	5.3
6. Attenders with young families	++++	5.2
7. Contemporary styles of music and worship	+++	4.7
8. Other attenders experienced moments of decisive faith commitment	+++	4.3
9. Other attenders involved beyond worship in nurture and other activities	+++	4.3
10. Leader takes attenders' ideas into account	+++	4.2
11. Congregation has an outward focus	+++	3.9
12. Leader helps attenders discover gifts/skills	+++	3.8
13. Attenders feel they are growing in their faith	+++	3.8
14. Leader emphasis on outwardly focused roles	+++	3.7
15. Congregation has similar make-up to community	+++	3.6

NB: Strength of relationship is the percent of variance explained after accounting for local context/faith type effects
SOURCE: 1991 National Church Life Survey

comfortable to invite others to participate in congregational activities. Large buildings or flashy programs, on their own, will not draw in many newcomers, although they may encourage attenders to be more comfortable about inviting others along. Are congregations willing to make changes to their services to encourage attenders to invite their friends?

- *Attenders are growing in their faith.* Several indicators suggest that congregations with higher levels of newcomers are characterised by attenders growing in their faith in many ways. Other (non-newcomer) attenders are more likely to be growing in their faith or making changes in their actions and priorities as a result of their faith or to be comfortable discussing their faith with others. In regard to factors just outside the 15 listed in Figure 3.1, they are also more involved in private devotional practices, such as regular times of personal prayer or Bible reading, and tend to be more involved in congregational life.

Newcomers are also more likely to be found in congregations where higher proportions of other (non-newcomer) attenders have experienced a moment of conversion or decisive faith commitment. This result stands even after taking account of the theological background of the congregation. Conversion experiences imply a definite crossing of the boundary, and this may be an important ingredient in newcomers deciding to join a congregation. This result is important for all congregations, but particularly those whose traditions do not include an emphasis on such experiences or on public ownership of faith.

Again, it could be a case of like attracting like. Newcomers may well be more comfortable with others who are growing or making a fresh start in the faith or making changes in their lives.

- *Style of leadership matters.* As can be seen in Figure 3.1, several aspects of leadership style are linked to congregations with high levels of newcomers. One key characteristic of congregations with high levels of newcomers is that the leader has an outward focus to his or her ministry role, that is, the leader is committed not just to attenders within the life of the congregation but to the mission of the congregation in the wider community. Such a focus may have direct impact in terms of the leader's role and contacts. More importantly, it probably helps to focus the eyes of attenders in similar directions.

Another aspect of leadership style important in the attraction and retention of newcomers is the leader's willingness to value the contributions of attenders. This includes taking attenders' ideas into account and helping attenders discover their gifts and skills. Congregations where attenders feel that those with roles are given good support are also more likely to have higher levels of newcomers.

In short, newcomers are more likely to remain in congregations where attenders feel their contributions are valued, and where leaders demonstrate by their priorities and actions that attenders' ideas and gifts matter and are the vital building blocks upon which effective mission is built.

- *Congregation has an outward focus.* Congregations with a clear focus beyond existing attenders tend to attract higher levels of newcomers. While not as significant as attenders' openness to discussing their faith with others and inviting them to church, congregational orientation and mission activities are significant in contacting and integrating people into the life of the congregation.
- *Contemporary music and styles of worship.* Closely related to the issue of age is the style of music and worship used within a congregation. Congregations with higher levels of newcomers tend to use contemporary music in their worship.

  Congregations with higher levels of newcomers use contemporary music

  A newcomer's first contact with a congregation is most likely to be in a church worship service. For around 67% of newcomers, a church service is their first occasion at church, with 11% first attending a baptism, wedding or funeral and 6% a Christmas or Easter service. Only 4% of newcomers first go to a small group, 2% to a special outreach activity, and 2% to a social activity (*Mission under the Microscope,* p 102). Style of worship may be significant in the decision of a newcomer to continue to attend.

  As a factor, music style probably works in two ways. First, newcomers are more likely to feel comfortable in church services which include music to which they can relate. Second, existing attenders may be more comfortable to invite friends without a church background to activities that are more contemporary in nature.

YOUNG ADULT RETENTION

While integrating newcomers without a church background is a vital aspect of a congregation's mission, so too is the nurturing of existing attenders. Congregations often put a huge amount of effort into supporting attenders in their discipleship and growth in faith via small groups, Sunday schools, youth fellowships, and adult social activities.

The nurture of existing attenders of all ages and stages in life is vital. No one age group is intrinsically more important than another. At the same time, the NCLS and other research has suggested that there are high levels of drifting out of church life among adolescents and young adults (*Mission under the Microscope*, Chapter 9). For this reason, it seemed valuable to include an indicator of young adult retention in this study.

Many attenders hope and pray that their children will own Christian faith for themselves and they actively work at the faith development of their children. Congregations share this ministry by providing a range of children's and youth activities.

For the church, much depends on the continued success of this 'internal' mission. The NCLS suggests that the parents' role in this is critical. As was reported in *Mission under the Microscope* (p 114), the first contact with the Christian faith for the majority of attenders (57%) is through their parents and family.

LOOKING AT YOUNG ADULT RETENTION

To gain some indication of how effectively congregations are retaining children as they become young adults, the NCLS asked attenders whether their children were currently involved with this congregation or with another one, or were not attending church anywhere.

Which statement best describes the level of church attendance of your children?
a.   I do not currently have any children
b.   Most of my children are involved with this church
c.   Most of my children are involved with other churches
d.   Most of my children are not attending church anywhere
e.   I do not know whether my children attend church or not
f.   More than one of the above

SOURCE: 1991 National Church Life Survey adjusted for non-participants

In another question attenders were asked about the stage in life of any children still living at home. The data from both questions provides some useful insights into patterns of young adult retention. The results were detailed in Chapter 9 of *Mission under the Microscope*. Nearly all attenders with preschool and primary-aged children say that their children are involved with church activities. By the time children pass into secondary school, however, a quarter of parents report that their children have ceased to attend. The main period for drifting out of church life appears to be after children have left home, when some 40% of attenders say that their children no longer attend church.

The indicator of young adult retention used by the NCLS is the percentage of adult attenders with secondary or post-school-aged children still living at home who report that their children also attend their congregation. It is important to note that this indicator is not a measure of the retention of young adults after they have left home, but rather a measure of retention of young adults still living at home. In order to conduct a meaningful analysis, some small congregations with very few families with children in this age group were omitted from the analysis.

For further discussion on this indicator, see Appendix 1.

CHARACTERISTICS OF VITAL CONGREGATIONS — YOUNG ADULT RETENTION

The results are shown in Figure 3.2. As can be seen by the rating scores, the NCLS data is less predictive in this area than in levels of newcomers. This suggests that factors apart from those included in the NCLS are influencing decisions by young adults to remain within congregational life. Nevertheless some useful results do emerge.
- *There is strength in numbers.* Just as in the area of newcomers, the age profile of a congregation is an important predictor of levels of young

adult retention. At one level, this result is not surprising, since young adult retention and the age profile of attenders are not independent of each other. At another level, however, the data suggests that the retention of the children of attenders is related to some extent to the presence of other young people and families. In relation to young adults at least, birds of a feather do flock together. As with newcomers, this raises the question of the need for a critical mass of young attenders.

To achieve a critical mass of young adults, several congregations may need to work together. Too often congregations with only a few young attenders refuse to work together for fear of losing what they have. The NCLS results suggest that such a parochial approach may be unhelpful; congregations are more likely to lose attenders out of the church altogether. Alternatively, young adults will simply move elsewhere to find a more appropriate congregation.

As with the age profile, congregations successful with young adult retention tend to have high proportions of families. In this they tend to reflect the make-up of the community.

In relation to young adults, birds of a feather do flock together

YOUNG ADULT RETENTION IN CONGREGATIONS: A PROFILE	
The percentage of adult attenders with secondary or post-school-aged children still living at home who attend activities at their parents' congregation	
Overall	**62%**
By denomination	
Anglican	52%
Apostolic	72%
Assemblies of God	73%
Baptist	66%
Christian & Missionary Alliance	71%
Christian Revival Crusade	70%
Church of the Nazarene	73%
Churches of Christ	63%
Congregational	74%
Foursquare Gospel	65%
Lutheran	77%
Presbyterian	58%
Reformed	87%
Salvation Army	69%
Seventh-day Adventist	83%
Uniting	50%
Wesleyan Methodist	79%
Westminster Presbyterian	74%

SOURCE: 1991 National Church Life Survey adjusted for non-participants

FIGURE 3.2: THINGS THAT MATTER — YOUNG ADULT RETENTION

	STRENGTH OF RELATIONSHIP
1. Younger age profile	++++++ 10.2
2. Many families	++++ 9.3
3. Congregation has similar make-up to community	++++ 5.4
4. Local geographic focus to attenders' lives (urban areas only)	--- 4.8
5. Congregation has wider catchment (urban areas only)	+++ 4.1
6. Higher levels of new arrivals into the congregation	+++ 4.0
7. Contemporary styles of music and worship	+++ 3.8
8. Children's/youth programs are valued	+++ 3.4
9. Congregation is larger	++ 2.5
10. Attenders involved beyond worship in nurture and other activities	++ 2.5
11. Attenders ready to discuss their faith/invite others to church	++ 2.2
12. Buildings not uncomfortably empty during worship services	++ 1.7
13. Congregation is moving in new directions	++ 1.7
14. Higher proportions of attenders in roles, particularly ministry/teaching roles	++ 1.6
15. Congregation has an outward focus	++ 1.3

NB: Strength of relationship is the percent of variance explained after accounting for local context/faith type effects
SOURCE: 1991 National Church Life Survey

- *A regional focus can help.* Congregations successful in retaining young adults are more likely to have a regional focus. Most children live their lives in quite localised networks; they grow up with a geographic sense of 'community'. This often changes when they inherit the keys to their parents' car. As young adults they broaden their horizons and examine new possibilities. Until the arrival of their own children, most young adults live in dispersed interest-based networks. Congregations that are regional in nature appear to provide a comfortable home for people at such a stage in life.

  In contrast, congregations with a very local focus may be too narrow for young adults who are seeking to escape the nest. If such a congregation has been part of their childhood, it is likely to be one of the places needing to be escaped from. Likewise, congregations where attenders are more regionally focused are more likely to be retaining young adults.

A local focus may be too narrow for young adults

Denominations may need to consider a regional strategy for young adult ministry, developing congregations where young adults can gather in larger numbers and worship and participate in ways that are culturally appropriate to their generation.

- *Fresh blood is helpful.* Congregations retaining young adults are not stagnant, but have higher than average levels of new attenders joining the congregation. Not surprisingly then, another characteristic is that in these congregations attenders are more likely to invite others to church or to be open to discussing their faith with others.
- *Providing well for children and young people.* Congregations where high numbers of attenders value the children's and youth programs are more likely to be retaining young adults. Effort is apparently rewarded.
- *Contemporary music and styles of worship matter for retention as well.* Congregations that successfully retain young adults are more likely to make use of contemporary music and contemporary styles of worship. Young adults are more likely to stay where they feel that a congregation is expressing its faith and life in styles that they identify with or in which they feel comfortable.

- *Larger congregations are more likely to be retaining young adults than smaller ones.* This points again to the importance of a critical mass. Larger congregations can provide a wider range of choices (people or programs) to meet the needs of younger adults.

One of the interesting aspects of this study has been the lack of relationship between congregational size and most vitality indicators. Despite many common perceptions, smaller congregations have as much potential as larger ones (see Chapter 8 for details). The aspect of young adult retention, however, appears to be an exception.

On a similar issue, congregations that meet in buildings that feel uncomfortably empty are less likely to retain young adults. Although this situation is more common in smaller congregations, the experience can be quite dispiriting regardless of a congregation's size.

- *Encouraging involvement/ownership.* Congregations that are effective in retaining young adults are more likely to encourage attenders to be involved, to participate, and to own congregational life. As children grow up they initially have little say in whether they will attend church. As they move into young adulthood, involvement in church life has to compete with many other possibilities. A sense of involvement in and commitment to their congregation may influence their decisions.

  Congregations encouraging higher levels of attender involvement in teaching/ministry roles appear to have higher levels of young adult retention.

- *Moving in new directions.* Congregations that are willing to develop a sense of direction and, where appropriate, take risks by moving in new directions appear to retain young adults more effectively. By contrast, those congregations where attenders are uncertain about the future or where there is inflexibility are likely to lose young adults, who do not wish to be part of a congregation that does not have a positive sense of direction.

- *An outward focus.* As with newcomers, congregations with high retention of young adults also are more outwardly focused in their ministries.

CHAPTER 4

NUMERICAL GROWTH

What Makes a Difference?

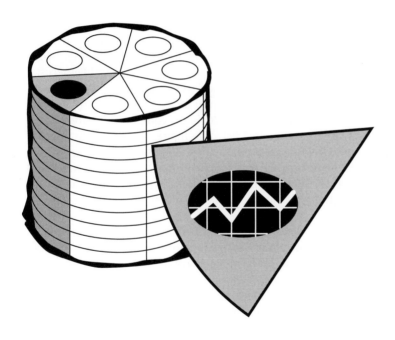

Identifying the key factors behind numerical growth in churches can be likened to the quest for the Holy Grail among some church leaders! There has been an avalanche of books on the issue. While some provide useful ideas, many have been short on research and analysis.

LOOKING AT NUMERICAL GROWTH

In order to estimate numerical growth, the NCLS asked leaders of all participating congregations for an estimate of average weekly attendance at church worship services in each of the years from 1986 to 1991 (see Appendix 1). From these figures a five-year growth rate was calculated. For congregations that had been in existence for fewer than five years, an effective growth rate was calculated for the period of time for which they had been in existence.

Analysis of these figures indicates that between 1986 and 1991 the Anglican and Protestant churches in Australia were not declining overall, but were growing roughly in line with population growth. However, individual denominational growth rates vary considerably. Mainstream denominations had an average annual growth rate of around 1.4%, while other large Protestant denominations grew at around 3% and Pentecostal churches between 5% and 6% per annum (*Winds of Change*, pp 267–268).

This data has some limitations. Because the NCLS is a study of existing congregations, no information is available on congregations that closed down in the five years prior to 1991. The figures also generally exclude non-English-speaking congregations; their inclusion may change the growth rates of some smaller denominations such as the Christian and Missionary Alliance. Despite these limitations, it is clear that the savage declines in church attendance of the 1960s and 1970s are not evident in the late 1980s and early 1990s.

In the mainstream denominations, growth has traditionally relied on the successful retention of the new generations of adherents. For other denominations, growth appears to have come through the successful incorporation of adult newcomers and switchers as well as retaining young adults. The high levels of leakage of young adults from mainstream denominations suggests that the mainstream pattern of growth is not effective and sustainable for the long term.

The mainstream pattern of growth is not sustainable for the long term

CHARACTERISTICS OF VITAL CONGREGATIONS – NUMERICAL GROWTH

The NCLS identifies a range of characteristics associated with numerically growing congregations. Taken together, these factors are more important than the local demographic context within which a congregation is placed (see Chapter 17 for more details). The most significant characteristics are highlighted in Figure 4.1.

- *Moving in new directions*. Congregations following a plan for the future, implementing new directions, or being open to new initiatives are much more likely to be growing numerically than those where the future is unclear or where attenders believe there is a need to rethink where they are heading. This result underlines one of the key findings of the NCLS: congregations willing to grapple with change, discover their purpose for being, and adopt new directions where required are much better placed to relate to the surrounding society

---

NUMERICAL GROWTH OR DECLINE 1986–1991: A PROFILE
Overall growth in church attendance 1986–91

By denomination

Anglican	8.5%
Apostolic	36.3%
Assemblies of God	37.2%
Baptist	16.8%
Christian & Missionary Alliance	9.4%
Christian Revival Crusade	13.5%
Church of the Nazarene	14.4%
Churches of Christ	13.7%
Congregational	-1.6%
Foursquare Gospel	22.5%
Lutheran	2.5%
Presbyterian	3.9%
Reformed	9.5%
Salvation Army	17.2%
Seventh-day Adventist	17.7%
Uniting	7.7%
Wesleyan Methodist	50.0%
Westminster Presbyterian	37.8%

SOURCE: 1991 National Church Life Survey adjusted for non-participants

---

It is vital that congregations develop skills in responding to change. Many congregations have recognised the need to move to a new mode of operation in a new mission era. This recognition has forced them to evaluate their directions and to discover with whom they are called to be in mission and what their sense of purpose really is. Congregations that undertake the hard work of discernment and direction setting are more likely to be growing. New attenders are more likely to stick with congregations that they feel are going somewhere.

- *Belonging and commitment are important bases from which to grow a congregation.* Congregations where high levels of attenders have a growing sense of belonging are more likely to be growing numerically. It is not clear whether numerical growth develops a sense of belonging or whether belonging and commitment encourage new arrivals to want to stay.

FIGURE 4.1: THINGS THAT MATTER — NUMERICAL GROWTH

	STRENGTH OF RELATIONSHIP	
1. Congregation is moving in new directions	++++	8.4
2. High levels of new residents in the congregation	++++	6.4
3. Serious conflict with negative outcomes	– – – –	6.0
4. Attenders committed to leader's vision for the future	++++	5.9
5. Growing sense of belonging	++++	5.7
6. Leader emphasis on outwardly focused roles	++++	5.2
7. Openness to new initiatives	+++	4.9
8. Changes in attenders' lives as a result of faith	+++	4.5
9. Congregation has an outward focus	+++	4.5
10. Facilities well utilised/worship service not uncomfortably empty	+++	4.4
11. Increasing involvement of attenders compared to last year	+++	4.4
12. General satisfaction with congregational life	+++	4.4
13. Leader helps attenders discover gifts/skills	+++	4.2
14. Attenders experienced moments of decisive faith commitment in recent years	+++	4.0
15. Younger age profile	+++	3.9

NB: Strength of relationship is the percent of variance explained after accounting for local context/faith type effects
SOURCE: 1991 National Church Life Survey

- *The congregation is connecting with new arrivals in the area.* The NCLS suggests that a characteristic of numerically growing congregations is that they have higher proportions of new residents among their number. Given that half the Australian population moves every five years, it follows that congregations not connecting with new residents will soon find themselves cut off from the wider community. This will be true in all areas, but the effect will be magnified in growth areas or areas experiencing high population turnover, such as inner city areas and some single industry or university towns.
- *Conflict does not help.* Congregations with high levels of conflict, and where there is a sense among attenders that cooperation has been diminished, or where leaders or attenders have left, are less likely to be growing numerically. While diminished growth may simply reflect people lost through conflict, it could also be that new arrivals do not want to stay in a situation of turbulence and upset.

- *Leadership style is important.* As with other indicators of vitality, several aspects of leadership style are evident in numerically growing congregations. One of the key issues is where the leader's eyes are focused: whether the leader is looking beyond the immediate congregation to those in the wider community. Such leaders keep the vision for growth before the congregation. They provide a role model and an impetus for the mission of the congregation.

  Allied to this is a vision for the future that is owned and supported by the congregation. Numerically growing congregations are more likely to have attenders who feel committed to the vision of the leader.

- *Congregation is outwardly focused.* Numerically growing congregations are more likely to be engaged in mission activities and have outwardly focused priorities.

- *Other factors.* This study reveals a range of other factors that are of less importance but are also characteristic of numerically growing congregations. They include satisfaction with congregational life, attenders growing in their faith, a younger age profile, buildings that are not uncomfortably empty for worship and attenders highly valuing the mission activities of the congregation.

A key issue is where the leader's eyes are focused

EVERYTHING WAS IN PLACE FOR MASSIVE CHURCH GROWTH, BUT STILL MAUREEN WAITED....

As will be detailed in Chapter 17, the local context in which a congregation is placed is a significant factor in determining likely numerical growth. A younger community profile, for instance, assists numerical growth. So, too, does population growth in the community.

Nevertheless, context is not the overriding determinant of numerical growth as is sometimes argued. A congregation which has a strong outward focus and sense of direction, with good leadership, and where attenders have a sense of belonging and lively faith, need not necessarily be constrained by its surrounding context. As was demonstrated in *Winds of Change,* and is discussed here in Chapter 15, attenders are often willing to travel well beyond the local area to attend the church of their choice (*Winds of Change,* p 94).

NUMERICAL GROWTH — WHAT MAKES THE DIFFERENCE?

A long-standing Lutheran congregation came to a turning point a few years ago. Situated in a rural community, the church faced all the problems affecting other rural areas — declining numbers, young people leaving for the city in droves, and a real sense of depression in the farming sector. Around them, churches were being closed or amalgamated into bigger congregations, but the Lutheran attenders were reluctant to give up their historic church and see their close-knit congregation break up.

In a mood of real crisis, the members and their leaders got together to decide what to do. The ideas that came from that meeting and subsequent workshops began to change the mood from despair into hope. The parishioners realised that they had strengths within their congregation, such as commitment to each other and their community, but that they needed to show the outside world a more welcoming face. They hoped different forms of worship would attract new people, especially the hobby farmers who visited the area at weekends.

It was suggested that the congregation reach out to the surrounding community by holding a special monthly service followed by a barbecue. This strategy was very effective, particularly with the weekend visitors, and numbers began to grow. One member observed that it was 'a remarkable change. We tried a form of contemporary worship and I'm sure that helped too.' The experiment demonstrated that tradition and new ideas could co-exist.

Probably the most satisfying aspect of the outreach was the willingness of the older, more conservative members of the congregation to try something different. They were infused with the energy to be brave and to suggest new ideas, while still feeling confident in their own strengths. Another member said: 'God has been increasing our numbers by an average of one and half new members a month and we haven't even gone looking for them'. By the simple act of turning outward, the congregation was rewarded with the sight of new faces coming in.

CHAPTER 5

A COMMUNITY TO FEEL PART OF

Growing a Sense of Belonging

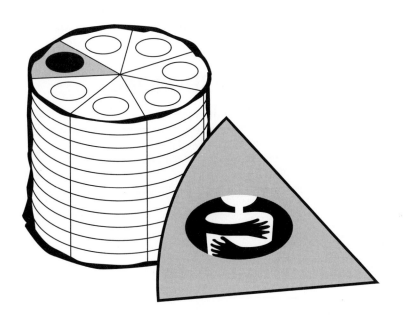

In church life there is much emphasis on community and the corporate body life of a congregation. The NCLS results demonstrate that attendance at church is far more than a spectator sport: it is about involvement, belonging, identity and sharing (*Winds of Change,* Part 3).

In contemporary society there is also much discussion about belonging and community. Society is becoming far more interest-based than locally centred, and many of the traditional forms of community and belonging have been eroded. The car has reshaped friendship networks, as have technological developments which make global communications easy. Today people may maintain friendships across a city or across the world, yet build large fences to protect their privacy in their local community.

Many commentators have suggested that as everything becomes more fragmented, the search for belonging and community increases and people become uncertain and insecure. Social commentator Hugh Mackay (1993) notes that Australians are searching for belonging and security in an era where little can be taken for granted.

The NCLS indicates that involvement in a congregation can give people that sense of identity, belonging and community to which Hugh Mackay and others refer.

LOOKING AT A SENSE OF BELONGING

Attenders were asked the following question.

Do you feel a strong sense of 'belonging' to this church?
- a. Yes, a strong sense of 'belonging', which is growing
- b. Yes, about the same as last year
- c. Yes, although perhaps not as strongly as in the past
- d. No, but I am new here
- e. No, and I wish I did by now
- f. No, but I am happy to stay on the fringe
- g. Don't know
- h Not applicable

THE CONGREGATION AT ST. MARION'S ENCOURAGED A REAL SENSE OF BELONGING .... ELSE WHERE.

Anglican and Protestant church attenders tend to feel a high level of belonging to their congregations. Overall, 61% feel a growing sense of belonging (*Winds of Change*, p 137).

Interestingly, apart from the smallest congregations, levels of belonging do not seem to be very different in congregations of different sizes. While it may be achieved in very different ways, it is possible for congregations of all sizes to create a strong sense of belonging among attenders.

SENSE OF BELONGING: A PROFILE
Percentage of attenders feeling a strong and growing sense of belonging

Overall	**61%**
By denomination	
Anglican	59%
Apostolic	76%
Assemblies of God	73%
Baptist	59%
Christian & Missionary Alliance	58%
Christian Revival Crusade	72%
Church of the Nazarene	71%
Churches of Christ	60%
Congregational	69%
Foursquare Gospel	78%
Lutheran	55%
Presbyterian	60%
Reformed	54%
Salvation Army	70%
Seventh-day Adventist	71%
Uniting	54%
Wesleyan Methodist	68%
Westminster Presbyterian	69%

NB: For further detail see *Winds of Change*, Chapter 10.

SOURCE: 1991 National Church Life Survey adjusted for non-participants

CHARACTERISTICS OF VITAL CONGREGATIONS — SENSE OF BELONGING

As can be seen in Figure 5.1 a large number of factors are strongly characteristic of congregations with high levels of belonging.

FIGURE 5.1: THINGS THAT MATTER — GROWING A SENSE OF BELONGING	STRENGTH OF RELATIONSHIP
1. General satisfaction with congregational life	✚✚✚✚✚ 29.9
2. Attenders feel they are growing in their faith	✚✚✚✚✚ 28.7
3. Congregation is moving in new directions	✚✚✚✚✚ 22.2
4. Support for those with roles	✚✚✚✚✚ 21.3
5. Leader helps attenders discover gifts/skills	✚✚✚✚✚ 20.9
6. Attenders committed to leader's vision for the future	✚✚✚✚✚ 20.5
7. Leaders capable of achieving goals	✚✚✚✚✚ 18.2
8. Satisfaction with preaching	✚✚✚✚✚ 17.1
9. Friendliness to newcomers	✚✚✚✚✚ 16.3
10. Leader takes attenders' ideas into account	✚✚✚✚✚ 16.0
11. Inspiring and directive leaders	✚✚✚✚✚ 15.8
12. Satisfaction with the music	✚✚✚✚✚ 14.6
13. Low levels of conflict	✚✚✚✚✚ 11.8
14. Increasing involvement of attenders compared to last year	✚✚✚✚✚ 11.7
15. General openness to new initiatives	✚✚✚✚✚ 10.4

NB: Strength of relationship is the percent of variance explained after accounting for local context/faith type effects
SOURCE: 1991 National Church Life Survey

- *Attenders are satisfied with or excited by their congregational life.* Several results underscore the importance of attender satisfaction with congregational life. Attenders are likely to feel a high level of belonging if they are satisfied with the music in worship, with preaching, and with congregational life in general.

Clearly, preaching and music are important to attenders. As has been documented in *Winds of Change*, a significant proportion of attenders are willing to change congregations for reasons of worship style. They will go to the church which they believe has 'got it right'. For this reason it is important for leaders to talk with and listen to attenders

**Preaching and music
are important to
attenders**

about these vital areas of worship life.

It is worth noting that satisfaction with music may mean satisfaction with traditional styles of music. If this is so, then it may be at odds with the needs of young adults and newcomers for contemporary styles of expression, which was discussed in Chapter 3. It is possible that the very factor that is promoting belonging among existing attenders is actually serving to restrict congregational development in the area of newcomers or young adult retention.

Congregations and leaders need to think carefully about such tensions as they consider competing demands and needs in congregational life.

- *Growth in faith is related to a sense of belonging.* Congregations with high levels of attenders who feel they are growing in their faith are more likely to be congregations with high levels of belonging. Such results suggest that belonging is more than a social experience. Congregations need to encourage attenders to reflect on their faith and understand their beliefs. Faith that is alive and growing is likely to lead to a stronger sense of belonging.

Belonging is more than a social experience

- *A sense of direction.* Another important factor among congregations with a strong sense of belonging is that the congregation has a clear sense of direction. Congregations in which attenders have a strong sense of belonging are congregations that are moving in new directions, where attenders are fully committed to the leader's vision for the future and perceive the leader to be capable of achieving these goals. In congregations where the future is unclear or where attenders feel there is a need to rethink directions, there tends to be less sense of belonging. In this instance, the same factors are likely to encourage both a sense of belonging and numerical growth.

- *Those with roles are given support.* It would seem that belonging in congregational life is enhanced if there is a sense among attenders that those with roles are being given good support, encouragement and care. Attenders are more likely to grow in their sense of belonging if they feel they are all being valued and are not just resources to be used up.

- *Other critical aspects of leadership.* Apart from the importance of a leader having a vision for the future and being capable of achieving the goals, several other characteristics of leadership style appear critical in relation to developing a strong sense of belonging. The results highlight an important paradox for leadership.

On the one hand, congregations with a high level of belonging are more likely to have leaders who are considered to be inspiring and directive rather than passive or acting on the goals of attenders. High-belonging congregations look for leaders to be pro-active.

On the other hand, high-belonging congregations also have leaders who take attenders' ideas into account, help attenders discover their gifts and skills, and support attenders with roles.

Herein lies a critical mix for effective leadership (see Chapter 14 for more details). Effective leaders need to blend the potentially competing demands of affirming, encouraging and empowering attenders while providing a strong sense of direction themselves.

Leaders need to empower attenders while providing a sense of direction

- *Friendliness to newcomers.* Interestingly, attenders in high-belonging congregations believe that they are very friendly to newcomers. Perhaps attenders who feel a strong passion for their congregation are more likely to work hard at welcoming and integrating new arrivals. Perhaps this result is a measure of how good attenders feel about each other in such congregations. Working on a strong sense of belonging may be an important step for congregations in seeking to welcome and integrate others.
- *Conflict does not help with belonging*! Not surprisingly, conflict has a negative impact on a sense of belonging. High-belonging congregations have little public conflict. Where attenders or members have left the congregation, or where conflict has resulted in reduced cooperation, a sense of belonging is likely to be critically reduced.

  While conflict is damaging to congregational vitality in many ways, it is essential for attenders to be willing to work through difficult issues together. Conflict, per se, is not necessarily unhealthy. But unresolved or badly resolved conflict can be unhealthy. This issue is discussed in more detail in Chapter 12.

A COMMUNITY TO FEEL PART OF: DEVELOPING A SENSE OF BELONGING

A Salvation Army Corps on the edge of Sydney took a new approach to its outreach by focusing on certain community groupings. In an area that was rapidly expanding, the church developed its worship format for Baby Boomers and their young and teenage families. The style and the times of services were changed, a morning tea was added to the end of the Sunday morning service, and modern music and prayers were introduced — and it worked, with numbers of attenders growing every week.

Members then decided that small groups were vital to reinforce a sense of belonging to the congregation. In the words of one woman: 'These are much more important now that the congregation is growing so large. I don't know everyone at a Meeting anymore, but my small group saves me from being swallowed up.'

As a further step, the congregation has set up a strong seniors program to cater for the older members, who sometimes feel 'elbowed out' by younger, more forthright members. Men are a particular concern, because 'they often see faith as the responsibility of women' and miss out on developing a spiritual life at the same pace. 'If we can correct the gender imbalance of a congregation, then it's healthier and more reflective of the community it serves', the leader said.

'Small groups work well here, too. They assimilate new people into the life of our congregation in a way that removes fear and shyness', he said. 'The best part of this whole change is that the members now feel that they own the vision themselves.'

CHAPTER 6

ON BEING SALT
AND LIGHT

**Wider Community Involvement and Discussing
Faith with Others**

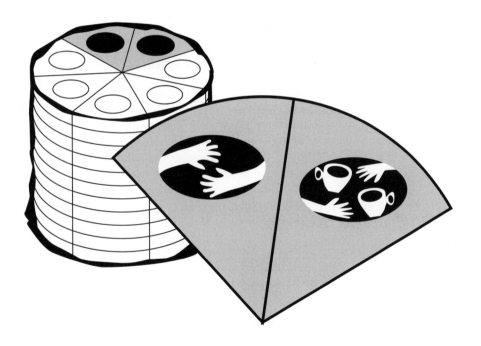

The church is called not just to minister to those who attend worship and other church activities, but to be salt and light in the wider world, to be a bearer in words and actions of the Good News of the Christian faith. Evangelism, community involvement, social action, and visitation are all ways in which Christians, individually or as part of congregational activities, seek to live out this call.

In the NCLS, this aspect of a congregation's mission has been termed the *incarnational* dimension. Two incarnational indicators of congregational vitality have been developed. The first is a measure of the extent to which congregations are involved in wider community life and in community care, welfare, or social action initiatives. The second indicator deals with how attenders feel about discussing their faith with others or inviting others into church life.

Developing adequate measures of these concepts was not easy. While the indicators selected are by no means comprehensive, they provide a useful starting point for congregations seeking to evaluate the extent to which they are being salt and light in the wider community.

WIDER COMMUNITY INVOLVEMENT

It is common for church attenders to be involved in social welfare and social action. Involvement, however, is not always through church-based activities. Many attenders also participate in community-based groups such as Lions, Rotary, school committees and senior citizens groups. The NCLS examines attender involvement in congregational-based activities as well as direct participation in wider community groups.

LOOKING AT CONGREGATIONAL CARE AND JUSTICE ACTIVITIES

Congregations are involved in wider community care activities in many ways. Around 24% of attenders are regularly involved in the social care/social justice activities run by their congregation (*Mission under the Microscope*, p 42).

Do you regularly take part in any mission activities of this church? (eg visitation, evangelism, community service/social justice/welfare)

a. No, we don't have such activities
b. No, I am not regularly involved
c. Yes, in evangelistic activities
d. Yes, in social care/social justice activities
e. Yes, both c and d above

Involvement is more common among older attenders. Those aged in their 50s and 60s are twice as likely to be involved in such activities as those in their 20s. This may be a consequence of retired attenders having more discretionary time available. It may also reflect generational changes in attitude to involvement in such activities (*Mission under the Microscope*, p 43).

Levels of involvement are similar across denominations. Attenders in Pentecostal congregations or in other large Protestant denominations have similar levels of involvement in congregational care or welfare activities as do those in mainstream denominations (*Mission under the Microscope*, p 45).

INVOLVEMENT IN CONGREGATIONAL SOCIAL CARE/SOCIAL JUSTICE ACTIVITIES: A PROFILE

Percentage of attenders involved in congregational activities of this type

Overall	**24%**
By denomination	
Anglican	20%
Apostolic	23%
Assemblies of God	21%
Baptist	22%
Christian & Missionary Alliance	18%
Christian Revival Crusade	23%
Church of the Nazarene	16%
Churches of Christ	23%
Congregational	20%
Foursquare Gospel	22%
Lutheran	19%
Presbyterian	20%
Reformed	21%
Salvation Army	28%
Seventh-day Adventist	41%
Uniting	28%
Wesleyan Methodist	18%
Westminster Presbyterian	18%

NB: For further detail see *Mission under the Microscope*, Chapter 4.

SOURCE: 1991 National Church Life Survey adjusted for non-participants

INVOLVEMENT IN WIDER COMMUNITY GROUPS

The NCLS asked several questions about attenders' involvement in wider community groups. Six out of ten attenders are involved in community organisations of some sort (*Mission under the Microscope*, p 17). The following question revealed that around 27% of attenders are involved in community care/welfare/social action groups; 24% are involved in care/welfare groups and 6% in social action groups (some are involved in both types).

Q

> **Are you involved in any community service/social action/welfare groups not connected to this church?**
>
> a. No, not really
> b. Yes, with community care/welfare groups
> c. Yes, with community action, justice or lobby groups
> d. Both b and c above

Not surprisingly, the type of group attenders become involved with is influenced by their stage in life. Attenders under 30 years of age are most likely to be involved in sporting and recreational groups, while those in their 30s and 40s tend to be involved in school organisations, mothers groups, professional associations, and sporting groups. Attenders over 60 years of age are more likely to be involved in charities and residents and leisure groups. Attenders with higher levels of education are more likely to be involved in community organisations than attenders from other socioeconomic backgrounds (*Mission under the Microscope*, pp 19, 20).

Involvement in community-based care and social action groups is much more common among attenders from the mainstream denominations. While some of this can be accounted for in the older age profile of these denominations, another important factor is the theological orientation of attenders. Those who view the Bible as the word of God to be taken literally are less likely to be involved in community-based activities than other attenders (*Mission under the Microscope*, p 22). This probably reflects a different orientation to the world between attenders with different theological understandings.

Involvement in wider community care/welfare/social action groups is also more common among attenders in smaller congregations. Again this is partly accounted for by the fact that smaller congregations have an older age profile than larger ones. However, part of the reason also would appear to be that larger congregations are more likely to run their own social action or welfare activities. Smaller congregations may find it easier and more appropriate to encourage attenders to get directly involved in community-based groups.

MEASURING WIDER COMMUNITY INVOLVEMENT

For this study, the NCLS created an overall index of wider community involvement, using measures of involvement through both congregational-based and community-based groups. An index was calculated for each congregation, comprising the percentage of attenders involved in either or both types of activity.

This index is limited in a range of ways. It cannot, for instance, measure the impact of attenders in less formal ways, such as in individual caring. Attenders may also exert significant influence through their job roles. Nor can the index measure the depth of involvement or effectiveness of attenders in these activities, only the fact that they are involved.

Nevertheless it is a useful starting point, upon which it is hoped to build with the 1996 NCLS.

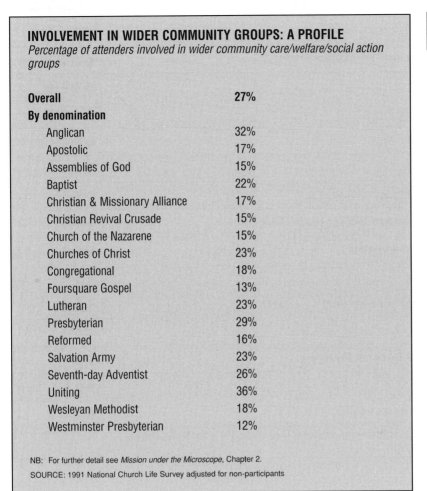

INVOLVEMENT IN WIDER COMMUNITY GROUPS: A PROFILE
Percentage of attenders involved in wider community care/welfare/social action groups

Overall	**27%**
By denomination	
Anglican	32%
Apostolic	17%
Assemblies of God	15%
Baptist	22%
Christian & Missionary Alliance	17%
Christian Revival Crusade	15%
Church of the Nazarene	15%
Churches of Christ	23%
Congregational	18%
Foursquare Gospel	13%
Lutheran	23%
Presbyterian	29%
Reformed	16%
Salvation Army	23%
Seventh-day Adventist	26%
Uniting	36%
Wesleyan Methodist	18%
Westminster Presbyterian	12%

NB: For further detail see *Mission under the Microscope*, Chapter 2.

SOURCE: 1991 National Church Life Survey adjusted for non-participants

CHARACTERISTICS OF VITAL CONGREGATIONS — WIDER COMMUNITY INVOLVEMENT

In Figure 6.1 are listed the major characteristics of congregations with high levels of wider community involvement.

- *Involvement in congregational life appears to promote involvement with the wider community.* Attenders involved in nurture activities, such as small groups, are also more likely to be involved in wider community service activities. This challenges the notion that involvement in church life isolates people from wider community affairs.

In particular, congregations with a high level of community involvement tend to have high levels of attender involvement in small groups, in congregational decision making, and in roles within the

Involvement in church life does not isolate people from community affairs

FIGURE 6.1: THINGS THAT MATTER — COMMUNITY INVOLVEMENT

	STRENGTH OF RELATIONSHIP	
1. Attenders involved beyond worship in nurture and other activities	++++	9.7
2. Higher proportions of attenders with roles, paticularly administrative roles	++++	5.8
3. Older age profile	++++	5.8
4. Local geographic focus to attenders' lives	++++	5.0
5. Attender involvement in decision making	+++	4.7
6. Low levels of conflict	+++	4.6
7. A base of attenders who have been there a long time	+++	4.6
8. Attenders value wider community involvement/care emphasis of congregation	+++	4.0
9. Attenders have close friends in the congregation	+++	3.4
10. High proportion of retired people	+++	3.2
11. Attenders ready to discuss faith/invite others to church	+++	3.1
12. Higher levels of financial giving	+++	3.0
13. High levels of devotional practice (prayer and Bible reading)	++	2.6
14. Support for those with roles	++	2.5
15. Attenders have had experiences of God's presence	++	2.0

NB: Strength of relationship is the percent of variance explained after accounting for local context/faith type effects
SOURCE: 1991 National Church Life Survey

congregation. Attenders in such congregations are more likely to be regular and generous financial contributors. Support is also more likely for those with roles.

Clearly, involvement in congregational life need not inhibit engagement in wider community concerns. Congregations that encourage involvement from their attenders appear to support involvement in many ways, including mission with the wider community.

- *Older attenders tend to be more involved.* The age profile of a congregation is related to levels of wider community involvement, with older people more likely to take part. Older people who are retired, or have reached a satisfactory plateau in their career, or who no longer have primary responsibility for children tend to be more involved in wider community affairs.

Such attenders are an important resource for congregations. While it is important to draw younger adults into the life of a congregation, the value of older attenders to the mission of a congregation should not be undervalued. Older attenders can form the backbone of a congregation's engagement with the wider community.

Older attenders can form the backbone of a mission strategy

Another possible contributing factor is a generational shift in attitudes. If there is a trend away from involvement in such activities among younger attenders, this will have significant long-term consequences for both denominational and congregational social concern activities. Older attenders currently form a large part of the voluntary workforce for social care. Who will be the future workforce?

- *Attenders with a local focus are more likely to get involved.* Another factor, not unrelated to age, is the focus of attenders in their everyday lives. Some attenders are quite locally focused, having most of their friends in the local area. Others have very little connection with the community in which they live, working in a different area and developing broader networks. Such patterns are often related to attenders' stage in life: a local focus is more common among children, among parents with a full-time responsibility for child rearing, and among those who are retired or elderly.

  Further analysis suggests that this is not purely an age effect: congregations where attenders—of any age—have a local focus are more likely to be involved in wider community groups.

- *A stable base of attenders is a useful starting point.* On a similar issue, congregations with higher levels of wider community involvement tend to have a stable base of attenders. There tends to be a core of attenders who have been with the congregation for a long time and who have strong friendship links with each other.

- *Community involvement is a known and valued aspect of the congregation.* Having a clear commitment to community involvement is linked to actual involvement in the wider community. In some cases the clear commitment may help point attenders in an outward direction; in others it may attract attenders with such passions.

- *Conflict is not helpful.* Conflict is not helpful to encouraging wider community involvement. Conflict is likely to inhibit congregational initiatives in mission activities and therefore reduce likely attender involvement. It may also sap attender energy for getting involved in community groups.

- *A lively faith.* A lively faith is a source of, and impetus for, wider community involvement. Links were found between levels of private devotional practice, experience of the presence of God and openness to discuss faith with others and wider community involvement.

* * *

Again it is important to emphasise that these indicators provide only an introduction to the issues of wider community involvement. Younger attenders no doubt engage the wider community in less formal ways or through their job roles, and this cannot be easily measured. Nevertheless, these results are an encouragement to congregations with older attenders, pointing to their potential for the mission of the church. They also demonstrate that church involvement need not cut attenders off from committed wider community involvement.

DISCUSSING FAITH/INVITING TO CHURCH

Another aspect of mission is discussing matters of faith with those in the wider community and inviting them into congregational life. The NCLS probed these issues in great detail (see *Mission under the Microscope*, Chapters 5, 6 and 7).

LOOKING AT DISCUSSING FAITH WITH OTHERS

Attenders were asked the following question about how comfortable they would be to talk to others about their faith:

> **Which of the following best describes your readiness to talk to others about your faith?**
>
> a. I lack faith, so the question is not applicable
> b. I do not like to talk about my faith; I believe my life and actions give sufficient example
> c. I find it hard to express my faith in ordinary language
> d. I mostly feel at ease about expressing my faith and do so if it comes up
> e. I feel at ease about expressing my faith and seek to find opportunities to do so

Around one half of all attenders feel ready to discuss their faith, with 43% feeling at ease about sharing their faith if the opportunity arises and another 13% intentionally seeking opportunities to do so. On the other hand, about a quarter of all attenders find it hard to express their faith in ordinary language and another 17% choose not to talk about their faith, believing that their life and actions are a sufficient example *(Mission under the Microscope*, p 59).

Older attenders are more likely to feel that their life is a sufficient example, not wanting to talk about their faith (23% of attenders in their 60s compared to only 9% of those in their 20s). Younger attenders, on the other hand, are more likely to find it difficult to talk about their faith. Those who are more involved in congregational life are more likely to be at ease about discussing their faith with others.

READINESS TO SHARE FAITH: A PROFILE
Percentage of attenders who feel comfortable discussing their faith or look for opportunities to do so

	Comfortable discussing faith	Look for opportunities	Total
Overall	**43%**	**13%**	**56%**
By denomination			
Anglican	43%	10%	53%
Apostolic	46%	27%	73%
Assemblies of God	48%	28%	76%
Baptist	45%	14%	59%
Christian & Missionary Alliance	48%	18%	66%
Christian Revival Crusade	49%	21%	70%
Church of the Nazarene	44%	21%	65%
Churches of Christ	44%	13%	57%
Congregational	49%	15%	64%
Foursquare Gospel	47%	30%	77%
Lutheran	43%	10%	53%
Presbyterian	42%	11%	53%
Reformed	47%	8%	55%
Salvation Army	42%	18%	60%
Seventh-day Adventist	45%	23%	68%
Uniting	40%	8%	48%
Wesleyan Methodist	44%	16%	60%
Westminster Presbyterian	44%	15%	59%

NB: For further detail see *Mission under the Microscope*, Chapter 5.

SOURCE: 1991 National Church Life Survey adjusted for non-participants

In a separate question, the NCLS asked attenders about issues that may inhibit their willingness to discuss their faith with others. Some important age differences were uncovered. While only 6% of attenders in their 60s fear other people's reactions, nearly a quarter of attenders in their 20s mention this as a problem. Attenders over 60 years of age, however, are more likely to feel they cannot answer difficult questions (37% of those over 60 compared to only 29% of those in their 20s). These results are discussed in more detail in Chapter 6 of *Mission under the Microscope*.

LOOKING AT INVITING OTHERS TO CHURCH

The NCLS also explored attenders' willingness to invite others to church by including the following question:

In the last year has anybody started attending church activities here or elsewhere as a result of your involvement with them?
a. Yes, as a result of discussion about the Christian faith
b. Yes, for other reasons
c. Both a and b
d. No, those with whom I have shared chose not to be involved or felt uncomfortable when they tried
e. No, I don't think I encouraged anybody to do so
f. Don't know

One in four attenders (26%) has invited somebody to attend a church activity in the last 12 months. An additional 14% of attenders have invited someone to church without success; those with whom they were involved either chose not to attend or felt uncomfortable when they tried (*Mission under the Microscope*, p 90).

Around a third of attenders have not encouraged anybody to become involved, and a further 27% do not know if they have helped anyone start attending church. Congregations need to discover why this is so.

One possibility is that attenders are unhappy with aspects of their congregational life such as the style of worship. The generational differences highlighted in the NCLS suggest this may be the case, particularly among young attenders.

Possibly some attenders feel there is no activity or context suitable to invite people to from outside of church life. They are comfortable with the style of their congregational life, but think others may find it dull or irrelevant. This may be particularly true of people without a church background or people who are part of subcultures well distanced from church life and traditions.

On the other hand, other attenders may simply lack confidence. Discovering the reason why attenders are not inviting others may unlock some key issues for congregations as they plan for effective mission in their own particular contexts.

INVITING OTHERS TO CHURCH: A PROFILE	
Percentage of attenders who successfully invited someone to church in the last year	
Overall	**26%**
By denomination	
Anglican	23%
Apostolic	40%
Assemblies of God	42%
Baptist	29%
Christian & Missionary Alliance	34%
Christian Revival Crusade	39%
Church of the Nazarene	40%
Churches of Christ	30%
Congregational	31%
Foursquare Gospel	44%
Lutheran	18%
Presbyterian	23%
Reformed	15%
Salvation Army	32%
Seventh-day Adventist	25%
Uniting	21%
Wesleyan Methodist	33%
Westminster Presbyterian	34%

NB: For further detail see *Mission under the Microscope*, Chapter 7.
SOURCE: 1991 National Church Life Survey adjusted for non-participants

An important pattern in relation to both inviting others to church and readiness to discuss faith with others is the faith type of attenders. Those with a more conservative attitude to the Bible or an openness to the charismatic movement are far more likely to be comfortable discussing their faith with others or to seek opportunities to do so. They are also far more likely to invite others to church (*Mission under the Microscope*, p 92).

AN INDICATOR FOR THIS STUDY

The NCLS shows there is a strong relationship between an attender's sense of comfort about discussing their faith with others and their willingness to invite others to church. For this reason, a composite measure was developed for use in this study. The index is made up of the percentage of attenders open to discussing their faith with others or seeking to do so and the percentage of attenders who have invited someone to church in the last year.

DAVE REALLY ENJOYED HIS CHURCH, BUT JUST COULDN'T THINK OF WHO TO INVITE.

CHARACTERISTICS OF VITAL CONGREGATIONS — DISCUSSING FAITH/INVITING OTHERS

What are the characteristics of congregations with high levels of attenders open to discussing their faith and inviting others to church? There are some important lessons to be learnt, as shown in Figure 6.2.

- *Attenders are involved in congregational mission activities.* Not surprisingly, a high level of involvement in evangelistic and mission activities is a characteristic of congregations where attenders are comfortable discussing their faith with others or inviting them to church. Such activities may provide a context for discussing faith with others; they may also help attenders gain confidence to discuss matters of faith in other contexts. Mission activities may also emphasise the importance of evangelism and outreach to attenders, even to those not involved in these activities directly.

- *A lively or developing faith is more likely to be shared with others.* Most of the characteristics of congregational life that are strongly related to high levels of faith sharing and inviting have to do with attenders' personal faith journeys. Congregations where attenders are sharing their faith tend to be made up of attenders who have active prayer lives, have a sense of God's call in their lives, feel they have experienced moments of decisive faith commitment or the presence of God in some way, or feel that they are growing in their faith or making changes to their actions or priorities as a result of their faith.

The implication is clear. If a congregation wants to encourage attenders to share their faith with others or invite them to church, a top priority is to help and encourage them in their own faith journeys.

This set of results is important. Attenders who do not have a vital and growing faith are unlikely to become active faith sharers or inviters no matter how much the leadership offers incentives or cajoles. Attenders

> **Attenders with a growing faith are likely to want to share it**

FIGURE 6.2: THINGS THAT MATTER — DISCUSSING FAITH/INVITING OTHERS TO CHURCH

	STRENGTH OF RELATIONSHIP
1. Attenders involved in congregational mission activities	✚✚✚✚✚ 21.7
2. Attenders feel they are growing in their faith	✚✚✚✚ 7.3
3. Attenders involved beyond worship in nurture and other activities	✚✚✚✚ 7.3
4. Attenders received training for mission/ministry	✚✚✚✚ 7.1
5. High levels of devotional practice (prayer and Bible reading)	✚✚✚✚ 6.5
6. Attenders have sense of God's call	✚✚✚✚ 6.5
7. Attenders making changes in their lives as a result of faith	✚✚✚✚ 5.7
8. Attenders committed to leader's vision for the future	✚✚✚✚ 5.3
9. Attenders have experiences of God's presence	✚✚✚✚ 5.2
10. Congregation has an outward focus	✚✚✚ 4.7
11. Attenders experienced moments of decisive faith commitment in recent years	✚✚✚ 4.2
12. Higher proportions of attenders with roles, particularly ministry roles	✚✚✚ 3.7
13. Growing sense of belonging	✚✚✚ 3.2
14. Leader helps attenders discover gifts/skills	✚✚✚ 3.1
15. Support for those with roles	✚✚✚ 3.0

NB: Strength of relationship is the percent of variance explained after accounting for local context/faith type effects
SOURCE: 1991 National Church Life Survey

with a growing faith are likely to want to share it with others as a natural out-flowing of the life that it provides them.

- *Small nurture groups can be helpful.* Congregations with high levels of attenders comfortable about discussing their faith or inviting others to church tend to have higher levels of involvement in nurture activities, particularly small groups. Small groups provide a forum for attenders to talk about their faith with each other. In the process, attenders can develop a clearer understanding of what their faith means to them and become more practised in talking about it with others.

Small groups provide attenders with encouragement to take risks in sharing their faith with others or inviting others to church. The sense of mutual accountability and support can be vital ingredients in activating attenders in this area.

- *Support is vital.* Not surprisingly, congregations that have high levels of attenders who feel comfortable about discussing their faith or inviting others to church have high levels of attenders being equipped for such a role. Providing support and training for attenders in evangelism is clearly vital for mobilising a congregation in this respect. It is also worth noting that high levels of a sense of belonging are also characteristic of these congregations.

  What comes first — training or faith sharing? To some extent, this is a chicken and egg dilemma. Does this link exist because attenders who look for opportunities to share their faith or invite others want training in faith sharing? Or does a congregation that works hard to emphasise the importance of faith sharing reap the dividends of such a priority? No doubt it works both ways.

- *The leader is important.* Two aspects of leadership are linked to congregations with high levels of attenders happy to share their faith or invite others to church.

  Congregations with high levels of attenders who want to share their faith are more likely to have leaders with a vision for the future, a vision that attenders are also committed to. This suggests that congregations with clear directions are likely to be congregations to which attenders are comfortable to invite others.

  Second, congregations effective in this area tend to have leaders who put an emphasis on attenders growing their gifts and skills and on ensuring that support is provided for those with roles within the

congregation. Such an emphasis is important for developing attenders' confidence and growth in faith.

- *Attenders have ministry roles within the congregation.* A high level of people with roles within the congregation is related to having attenders who are comfortable talking about their faith and for whom faith is important. Having such roles may also help attenders to be comfortable discussing their faith with others in the wider community by providing contexts for them to discuss their faith within the life of the congregation.
- *Congregations have an outward focus.* Congregations where attenders are comfortable discussing their faith tend to see their focus as being more on the wider community than on attenders within the congregation. This emphasis may help attenders recognise the importance of their role as salt and light in all aspects of their lives.

* * *

If you want to help people share their faith, make sure they have a vital faith to share. This adage is reinforced by the results from this study. At the same time, congregational leaders and support groups play a critical role in supporting and encouraging attenders in faith sharing.

CHAPTER 7

A FAITH THAT IS ALIVE

Congregations that Are Growing in Faith

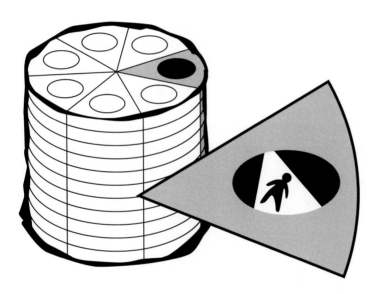

Drawing people into the life of a congregation, or encouraging them to reach out and care for the wider community, is of little value if attenders within a congregation are not being nurtured or encouraged in their faith.

Measuring nurture or growth in faith is extremely difficult. It is clear from research carried out in Australia and overseas that religious experience is multi-dimensional (*Who Goes Where?*, Chapter 3). Growth in faith can encompass a person's growth in understanding of doctrine, in their beliefs, in their experiences of God, or in the consequences of their faith in their everyday life, actions and values.

To probe these aspects in detail would require a survey in itself, far beyond the scope and purposes of this study. Instead, the NCLS selected some useful and simple indicators to create a growth in faith index.

LOOKING AT GROWTH IN FAITH

The NCLS investigated levels of faith exploration within the congregation by asking attenders for a self-assessment. Attenders were asked about the extent to which they felt they had grown in their understanding of their faith during the last year, the extent to which they felt they had developed stronger belief in or relationship with God, and the extent to which over the last year they had made changes in their actions and priorities as a result of their faith.

Over the last year, have you grown in your understanding of the Christian faith?
a. No real growth
b. Some growth
c. Much growth, mainly through this church
d. Much growth, mainly through other groups or churches
e. Much growth, mainly through my own private activity

Over the last year, have you developed a stronger belief in or relationship with God?
a. If anything I have greater doubts than before
b. No real change
c. Somewhat stronger
d. Much stronger, mainly through this church
e. Much stronger, mainly through other groups or churches
f. Much stronger, mainly through my own private activity

Over the last year, have you made changes in your actions and priorities as a result of your Christian faith?
a. No real changes
b. Some small changes
c. Some major changes
d. I do not feel I have a Christian faith

CHARACTERISTICS OF VITAL CONGREGATIONS — GROWTH IN FAITH

The results for these three questions were very similar and were included in a growth in faith index. The indicator used for this study specifically comprised: the percentage of attenders feeling they have grown significantly in their understanding of the Christian faith in the last year through their congregation, the percentage developing much stronger beliefs in the last year through their congregation, and the percentage making major changes in their actions and priorities as a result of their Christian faith in the last year.

Some 47% of attenders say that their understanding of their faith grew much over the last year. For most of these (32%), this growth was mainly through their congregation. For the remainder, growth primarily came about through involvement in other groups or their own private activity. Similar results were found in relation to the question about stronger belief.

Around 6% of attenders think that their growth in faith is due mainly to involvement in groups or churches outside their congregation. While it is positive that attenders can find such activities helpful, congregations where a high level of attenders are finding growth elsewhere may want to think about what it is they need to do to help attenders grow their faith within their own congregational context. Analysis of the NCLS results in relation to growth in faith can be found in *Views from the Pews* (p 74).

A wide range of factors are significantly related to congregations which have high levels of attenders who are growing in their faith. These factors are outlined in Figure 7.1.

- *Growth in faith is related to a positive experience of Christian community.* The most important factors which predict growth in faith are those which reflect the satisfaction of attenders with church life. A growing sense of belonging and a high level of enthusiasm among attenders are closely correlated with a sense of growing in faith. Given this, it is not surprising that factors related to growth in faith are similar to those related to belonging. A positive experience of Christian community appears to be an important ingredient of growth in faith among attenders.

- *Growth in faith is related to the empowerment of attenders.* Congregations with high levels of growth in faith tend to have leaders who put a priority on helping attenders discover and grow their gifts and skills and who take attender ideas into account in an intentional way. Leaders will also want to ensure that those with roles are given good support and encouragement.

  Attenders with roles need support and encouragement

  An environment where attenders feel valued and encouraged is conducive to growth in faith. A gospel that claims that all people are created in the image of God will be more readily understood and discovered by attenders who feel valued by their leaders.

- *Clear leadership can take attenders forward.* As with other aspects of vitality, leadership style appears critical in the area of growth in faith. Leaders in congregations with high levels of growth in faith are more likely to be visionary leaders. They are also more likely to be the kinds of leaders who instil confidence in attenders that they can achieve the goals that are set and to be inspiring attenders into action.

- *Satisfaction with worship services is important.* Satisfaction with worship services is also a characteristic of congregations with high levels of attenders growing in their faith. High-quality music and inspiring preaching are both critical aspects of congregational life in relation to growth in faith.

GROWTH IN FAITH: A PROFILE
Percentage of attenders growing significantly in their faith through congregational involvement

	Much growth in understanding through congregation	Much growth in beliefs through congregation	Major changes in actions/priorities as a result of faith
Overall	**32%**	**27%**	**23%**
By denomination			
Anglican	31%	25%	18%
Apostolic	51%	44%	45%
Assemblies of God	49%	42%	45%
Baptist	30%	25%	24%
Christian & Missionary Alliance	36%	30%	38%
Christian Revival Crusade	48%	44%	41%
Church of the Nazarene	42%	39%	34%
Churches of Christ	32%	26%	24%
Congregational	45%	36%	30%
Foursquare Gospel	54%	50%	49%
Lutheran	32%	24%	13%
Presbyterian	33%	26%	17%
Reformed	30%	24%	15%
Salvation Army	42%	36%	29%
Seventh-day Adventist	43%	39%	23%
Uniting	25%	19%	15%
Wesleyan Methodist	42%	36%	31%
Westminster Presbyterian	47%	40%	30%

NB: For further details see *Views from the Pews*, pp 74–77.
SOURCE: 1991 National Church Life Survey adjusted for non-participants

The worship service is the central component of church life for most attenders, even if it is not necessarily the thing they most value. Music, liturgy or preaching that brings attenders into a sense of the presence of God or into a critical evaluation of their own life and directions appears to be extremely important in relation to attenders who feel they are going forward in their faith. Congregations need to keep talking with attenders about these aspects of their life, paying particular attention to those who are newcomers.

Where congregations are large enough and include a diversity of attenders, there may be value in providing a range of different styles of worship and community life in which different groups can participate.

FIGURE 7.1: THINGS THAT MATTER — GROWTH IN FAITH

	STRENGTH OF RELATIONSHIP
1. Growing sense of belonging	✚✚✚✚✚ 16.4
2. Attenders committed to leader's vision for the future	✚✚✚✚✚ 14.9
3. General satisfaction with congregational life	✚✚✚✚✚ 14.6
4. Leader helps attenders discover gifts/skills	✚✚✚✚✚ 14.1
5. Inspiring and directive leaders	✚✚✚✚✚ 12.3
6. Satisfaction with preaching	✚✚✚✚✚ 11.1
7. Satisfaction with the music	✚✚✚✚✚ 10.9
8. Attenders ready to discuss faith/invite others to church	✚✚✚✚✚ 10.6
9. Support for those with roles	✚✚✚✚ 9.6
10. Leader capable of achieving goals	✚✚✚✚ 9.5
11. Attenders experienced moments of decisive faith commitment in recent years	✚✚✚✚ 9.3
12. Congregation is moving in new directions	✚✚✚✚ 8.5
13. Attenders involved in nurture activities	✚✚✚✚ 8.5
14. Congregation connects faith with attenders' lives	✚✚✚✚ 7.6
15. Leader takes attenders' ideas into account	✚✚✚✚ 7.6

NB: Strength of relationship is the percent of variance explained after accounting for local context/faith type effects
SOURCE: 1991 National Church Life Survey

- *Attenders are comfortable discussing their faith with others or inviting others to church.* Attenders growing in their faith will be more likely to want to talk about their faith. The other side of the coin is that the process of discussing their faith with others in the wider community may well be an experience that stretches attenders and helps the growth of their faith.
- *Moments of decisive faith commitment can be an impetus for growth in faith.* High growth in faith congregations tend to have high levels of attenders who have experienced moments of decisive faith commitment in recent years. Such moments can be extremely significant for attenders in their faith journey. They can also encourage other attenders. This is true for attenders of all faith types and from all denominations.

Congregations need to encourage attenders to be open to God's work in their lives. They also need to encourage attenders to talk about faith experiences with each other and publicly own the ways that God is moving them forward.

- *A sense of direction is important.* Attenders are more likely to be growing in their faith in congregations that have a sense of direction. In such congregations, there is likely to be a high level of attenders who feel the congregation is moving in new directions or think their leader has a vision for the future to which they are fully committed.

Are congregations where high levels of attenders feel they are growing in their faith more able to make critical decisions about new directions or does the act of moving in new directions require a leap of faith which stimulates growth in faith for attenders? Each factor probably influences the other.

- *Involvement in nurture activities is helpful.* Congregations with high levels of growth in faith tend to have high levels of attenders in nurture activities, particularly small groups. Such forums can be important places for attenders to wrestle with the meaning of faith in their lives. They provide a safe environment, listening ears, and a sense of accountability and mutual encouragement for attenders to move forward in their faith in a positive way.

  Congregations that want to encourage growth in faith among attenders need to ensure there is a range of forums suitable for different groups of attenders to explore what faith means to them.

- *Growth in faith involves connecting faith with life.* Congregations where attenders have high levels of growth in faith are more likely to be congregations which have an ability to help attenders connect their faith with the daily issues of life. Congregations need to encourage attenders to talk with each other about the issues they deal with in their everyday lives. Those involved in preaching or teaching roles within a congregation will need to listen carefully to attenders to discover the issues of life that are concerning them and to think through the ways that faith can help move them forward in those areas.

- *Other factors.* This study also revealed a range of other factors characteristic of congregations with high levels of growth in faith. These are presented throughout Part 2. Two other significant characteristics are a leader emphasis on outwardly focused roles and a congregational focus more on the community than on attenders.

Small groups provide a safe environment and mutual encouragement

* * *

It could be expected that growth in faith is related to issues such as the preaching and worship experience at the congregation. However, the NCLS results also show that the sense of growing in faith is more broadly related to leadership style and group processes; it is influenced by communal aspects, not just activities which have individual nurture or growth in faith as their focus.

Growth in faith has an important outward, more missional dimension to it as well. The relationship between growth in faith and high levels of attenders who are ready to share their faith with others or invite others to church bears this out.

LOOKING MORE CLOSELY

Part 2 of this book identifies and examines in more detail the relationship between the following areas of church life and the seven indicators of congregational vitality:

- Congregational size
- Worship services
- Nurture activities
- Mission activities
- Group processes
- Direction setting
- Leadership style
- Congregational focus
- Property and finances

UNDERSTANDING THE TABLES IN PART 2

The chapters in Part 2 examine each of these areas of church life in turn. The tables in Part 2 differ from those in Part 1, in that all seven indicators of congregational vitality are present, for comparison purposes.

As in the tables in Part 1, the strength of relationship between these congregational characteristics and indicators of vitality has been presented. The strength of relationship is the percent of variance, after controlling for the effect of faith type and local context. To make it simple for the reader to follow, a five category rating scale, using plus signs, has been derived from the percent of variance, in accordance with the following table:

RATING SCHEME USED IN THIS BOOK		
RATING		**VARIATION EXPLAINED**
+++++	CRITICAL	>10%
++++	VERY IMPORTANT	5–10%
+++	IMPORTANT	3–5%
++	SOME IMPORTANCE	1–3%
+	MARGINAL	0.5–1%

The larger the number of plus signs the stronger the relationship between the congregational characteristic being considered and the seven congregational vitality indicators. Where a relationship is negative, this is shown by minus signs.

A longer discussion about the tables is provided in Chapter 2 and further technical details are provided in Appendix 1.

CHAPTER 8

IS BIGGER BETTER . . . OR SMALL BEAUTIFUL?

What Difference Does Congregational Size Make?

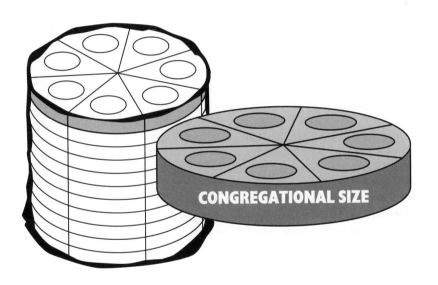

CONGREGATIONAL SIZE

The last 30 years has seen the emergence of a global youth culture. Although some aspects of that culture have changed over the years, one enduring feature is the enjoyment and sense of identity young adults get from listening to their preferred style of music in a large crowd.

In the 1960s this youth identity was shaped by the Beatles, who played at the stadium in Sydney in a tin shed more commonly used for boxing and wrestling events. In the 1990s the band U2 provided Australians with a different kind of spectacle: multi-media walls of televisions, international hook-ups and cars suspended in the air, flashing and rotating. The concert was bigger and far more sophisticated, yet the sense of celebration and identity was just as important.

So it is in some of the largest churches in Australia, particularly new churches targeting the post-war generations. There is a sense of celebration and enthusiasm, with all the dynamism which comes from being in a large crowd.

However, another equally significant movement has also emerged in recent decades. The title of E. F. Schumacher's book, *Small Is Beautiful*, captures its essence. Schumacher and many others argued that small is more accessible and allows a greater sense of involvement by ordinary people. Across the globe protest movements and dissident groups organise themselves around small cell groups and support networks.

Many social commentators have written about a deep search in contemporary society for a sense of intimacy and belonging. In a study in the United States, sociologist Robert Wuthnow showed how across America there is a search via small groups of all kinds for a place in which people can belong and feel accepted (Wuthnow, 1994).

In the churches the role of small groups is a major phenomenon, particularly among the post-war generations. House churches and intentional Christian communities, which seek to recreate the intimacy and fellowship that must have been part of the very earliest churches, have also developed. Such groups have often seen the more traditional models of church life as too institutional, impersonal and not dealing with the real issues that people are facing.

COMPETING OR COMPLEMENTARY THEMES?

So, is big better or small beautiful? On the surface these two trends would appear to be mutually exclusive and in conflict with each other.

There are some obvious advantages that could be claimed for larger congregations, mainly to do with scale: congregations need to be above a certain size in order to provide the range of worship, nurture and missional activities that may be important for an effective church. A larger congregation can provide a bigger supermarket of choices for people and therefore enable more people to find a niche in the congregation.

Attenders in smaller congregations fear losing the sense of family

Yet, despite these potential advantages, there is a fear among attenders in smaller congregations that if their congregation were to grow it would be at the cost of the sense of family that they currently experience. Is it possible that a larger congregation can deliver the same level of belonging and family that a smaller one can?

This chapter examines the relationships between congregational size and congregational vitality. The results may provide a few surprises for everyone.

CONGREGATIONAL SIZE

Just how big are Anglican and Protestant congregations in Australia? The average size of a congregation in Australia is around 70 people (*Winds of Change*, p 301). Yet on its own this figure can be misleading. More than a third of congregations have fewer than 25 attenders. More than half have fewer than 50 attenders, and only 3% of congregations exceed 300 attenders. This pattern is detailed in Figure 8.1.

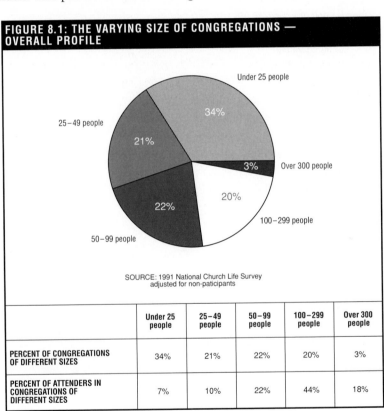

FIGURE 8.1: THE VARYING SIZE OF CONGREGATIONS — OVERALL PROFILE

Under 25 people 34%
25–49 people 21%
Over 300 people 3%
100–299 people 20%
50–99 people 22%

SOURCE: 1991 National Church Life Survey adjusted for non-paticipants

	Under 25 people	25–49 people	50–99 people	100–299 people	Over 300 people
PERCENT OF CONGREGATIONS OF DIFFERENT SIZES	34%	21%	22%	20%	3%
PERCENT OF ATTENDERS IN CONGREGATIONS OF DIFFERENT SIZES	7%	10%	22%	44%	18%

DENOMINATIONAL VARIATIONS

All told, more than 70% of congregations are from the mainstream denominations (Anglican, Lutheran, Presbyterian and Uniting). The average size of a mainstream congregation is 57 attenders. This is much lower than the other denominational groups and reflects the wide distribution of mainstream congregations across Australia, particularly in rural areas.

FIGURE 8.2: SIZE OF CONGREGATIONS BY DENOMINATION

	Average size (No. of people)
Overall	**71**
DENOMINATION	
Anglican	57
Apostolic	109
Assemblies of God	130
Baptist	124
Christian & Missionary Alliance	85
Christian Revival Crusade	100
Church of the Nazarene	41
Churches of Christ	97
Congregational	56
Foursquare Gospel	82
Lutheran	80
Presbyterian	47
Reformed	176
Salvation Army	76
Seventh-day Adventist	95
Uniting	54
Wesleyan Methodist	55
Westminster Presbyterian	91
TYPE OF DENOMINATION	
Mainstream	57
Pentecostal	122
Other large Protestant	104
Other small Protestant	87

SOURCE: 1991 National Church Life Survey adjusted for non-participants

Other than mainstream denominational groupings have higher average attendance. Large Protestant denominations, such as the Baptist and Churches of Christ denominations, have an average of 104 attenders and Pentecostal churches an average of 122 attenders. This in part reflects the tendency in these denominations to establish larger, regionally based centres.

REGIONAL VARIATIONS

Churches in rural areas are smaller on average than those in the rest of Australia. More than 70% of congregations in non-urban Australia have fewer than 50 persons. Only 12% have more than 100 attenders. Urban areas have larger congregations; only 33% have fewer than 50 attenders and 39% have more than 100 attenders.

The variations in size by community type are detailed in Figure 8.3. White-collar suburbs in major cities have the largest congregations. In contrast, congregations in blue-collar areas, growth areas and ethnic communities are significantly smaller.

Small rural communities, tourist towns and mining towns also have smaller congregations. A detailed report on regional variations has been produced by the NCLS (Kaldor and Castle, 1995).

White-collar suburbs in major cities have the largest congregations

FIGURE 8.3: REGIONAL VARIATIONS IN CONGREGATIONAL SIZE				
	CONGREGATIONAL SIZE			
	SMALL	MEDIUM	LARGE	VERY LARGE
	0–49	50–99	100–299	300+
URBAN OR RURAL				
URBAN	33%	28%	33%	6%
RURAL	72%	17%	11%	1%
AREA TYPE				
STABLE WHITE-COLLAR	21%	24%	45%	10%
NEW WHITE-COLLAR	29%	25%	40%	6%
TRANSIENT COMMUNITIES	30%	28%	33%	9%
OLDER BLUE-COLLAR	30%	29%	35%	6%
NEW BLUE-COLLAR	28%	35%	30%	7%
ETHNIC COMMUNITIES	31%	32%	31%	6%
REGIONAL CENTRES	35%	22%	39%	4%
TOURIST TOWNS	37%	37%	26%	0%
MINING TOWNS	54%	33%	31%	0%
OTHER SERVICE TOWNS	38%	28%	31%	3%
SMALL RURAL COMMUNITIES	78%	16%	6%	0%

SOURCE: 1991 National Church Life Survey adjusted for non-participants

Regional variations in congregational size partly reflect the population within each congregation's catchment. Congregations located in rural or outback areas draw from a much smaller population than urban congregations. Yet the variations in size according to community type suggest that the make-up of the community is also playing an important role. This issue is dealt with more fully in Chapter 17.

SIZE AND CONGREGATIONAL VITALITY

To what extent is congregational size related to vitality? While some aspects of vitality appear to be size related, most vary little with congregational size.

Larger congregations are more likely to be growing numerically. Congregations with fewer than 25 people tend to be in decline. Larger congregations experience higher levels of growth, with lower growth rates evident among very large congregations of more than 300 attenders. It would seem it is easier to add numbers to a congregation that is already relatively large.

Larger congregations are also more likely to be retaining young adults. Their size enables them to provide a wider range of activities and groups, and in this way they may be more able to cater for the needs of new attenders and young adults. Younger adults, for instance, may more easily find like-minded peers in a larger congregation than they would in a small one.

FIGURE 8.4: CONGREGATIONAL SIZE		
	STRENGTH OF RELATIONSHIPS	
	Congregational size	
NEWCOMERS		0.1
YOUNG ADULT RETENTION	✚✚	2.5
NUMERICAL GROWTH	✚✚	1.2
SENSE OF BELONGING		0.0
COMMUNITY INVOLVEMENT		0.1
SHARING/INVITING		0.0
GROWTH IN FAITH		0.5

NB: Strength of relationship is the percent of variance explained after accounting for local context/faith type effects

SOURCE: 1991 National Church Life Survey

Beyond these two factors, however, congregational size appears unrelated to a congregation's vitality. Size does not appear to be significant with regard to levels of growth in faith, willingness to discuss faith with others or invite others to church, and involvement in the wider community.

A similar pattern emerges in relation to belonging. Attenders in large congregations feel the same levels of belonging as those in smaller ones. This could be because of the work done by larger congregations to ensure that people don't get lost in the crowd. Or it could be that a sense of belonging is achieved through different dynamics in a larger congregation; the opportunity for interaction with a wider range of people or being part of something large or exciting may enhance a sense of belonging for many attenders.

There is no relationship between size and levels of newcomers without a church background. A larger and a smaller congregation in similar social contexts and with similar faith types among attenders (eg attitudes to Bible and theological tradition) are equally well placed to attract and retain newcomers.

As shown in Chapter 3, some denominations have higher levels of newcomers than others. This study suggests that such differences are explainable in terms of the context and particularly the faith type of their congregations rather than their size. The fact that Pentecostal churches have higher levels of newcomers, for instance, is more likely to be related to their Pentecostalism or other aspects of their worship style than their larger congregational size.

A DESIRE FOR NUMERICAL GROWTH

Three out of four attenders want their congregation to get larger (*Winds of Change*, p 306). This is made up of 58% who would like their congregation to get larger in order to be more effective and another 18% who feel their congregation will not survive unless it grows. In contrast, only 11% do not want their congregation to get larger, for a range of reasons; 13% do not know how they feel.

Yet congregations wanting to grow in order to survive have quite different levels of vitality from those wanting to grow in order to be more effective. The results are summarised in Figure 8.5.

There is a positive relationship between attenders wanting a congregation to get larger in order to be more effective and actual numerical growth. A similar relationship exists with a sense of belonging among attenders. Such an attitude towards growth appears to affect both internal congregational life and its attractiveness to outsiders. Further tests suggest that this relationship is apparent in congregations of all sizes.

On the other hand, there are significant negative relationships between vitality and wanting a congregation to grow in order to survive. Where this attitude is prevalent, there also tends to be lower levels of newcomers, young adult retention and sense of belonging. Such congregations are much less likely to be growing numerically. Further analysis suggests that,

FIGURE 8.5: DESIRE FOR GROWTH

	STRENGTH OF RELATIONSHIPS	
	Want congregation to get larger–in order to be more effective	Want congregation to get larger–in order to survive
NEWCOMERS	0.4	▬ ▬ 1.5
YOUNG ADULT RETENTION	✚ 0.5	▬ ▬ 2.9
NUMERICAL GROWTH	✚✚✚ 3.3	▬ ▬ ▬ ▬ 6.2
SENSE OF BELONGING	✚✚✚ 3.6	▬ ▬ 1.1
COMMUNITY INVOLVEMENT	0.0	✚✚ 1.2
SHARING/ INVITING	0.3	0.0
GROWTH IN FAITH	✚✚ 1.4	▬ 0.7

NB: Strength of relationship is the percent of variance explained after accounting for local context/faith type effects

SOURCE: 1991 National Church Life Survey

while this attitude is much more common in smaller congregations, the pattern holds across congregations of all sizes.

It would appear that a congregation's attitude to growth is more important than its size. A positive desire to see a congregation grow may well indicate a more outward orientation, which itself is a significant factor in relation to most aspects of vitality (see Chapter 11).

Attitude to numerical growth is more important than congregational size

Wanting a congregation to grow for its own survival is often a reflection of low vitality. While attenders in such congregations may verbalise a vague desire for growth, are they willing to count the possible costs of growth in terms of commitment, hard work and necessary changes (Wagner, 1979, 277)?

OTHER FACTORS RELATED TO SIZE

A great deal has been written on congregational size. While much of it has been preoccupied with how to increase congregational size, some has been devoted to identifying transitional stages which congregations pass through as they grow.

Arlin Rothauge, for instance, has identified four different stages in Episcopalian congregations in the United States (undated, 5–36):

- *Family church (fewer than 50 people):* characterised by intimacy and belonging where everybody knows everybody else.
- *Pastoral church (50–150 people):* increased size leads to the need for a multi-cell structure. Such a church requires a centralised authority, usually a pastor to coordinate the activities of the various clusters.

IF HE CLOSED HIS EYES DURING THE SERMON, PASTOR JIM COULD SOMETIMES IMAGINE HIS VOICE BOOMING ACROSS A CONGREGATION OF THOUSANDS... AND HE FELT A LITTLE HAPPIER.

- *Program church (150–350 people):* moving into this size category marks a change from a highly relational to an organisational style as the main mechanism for holding the congregation together. Attenders no longer find themselves automatically close to each other; opportunities for interaction need to be planned intentionally.
- *Corporation church (more than 350 people):* the congregation reaches the stage where there are many programs and separate groups. There is greater opportunity for outreach and the establishment of satellite congregations.

Other observers have developed similar typologies. They are based on an understanding that congregations of different sizes function in different ways.

How different is the functioning of different-sized congregations? In a separate analysis, the NCLS identified differences after accounting for the effects of context and faith type. Key results are summarised here; the detailed results are tabulated in Appendix 1.

- *Larger congregations have a more diverse demographic profile.* Larger congregations are more likely to include people from different age groups, or of different educational, socioeconomic, life stage and marital status, than smaller congregations. Larger congregations are also more likely to be similar in profile to the communities in which they are placed.

As congregations get larger, the leadership may need to think carefully about how to involve and value people from quite different backgrounds. This may involve specific affirmation of particular people, new styles in worship or other congregational activities, and new services or activities.

- *Larger congregations are more likely to have a range of activities.* These include activities such as Sunday schools and small groups, and facilities such as multipurpose buildings, halls and child-care facilities. It is to be expected that larger congregations will have more resources, which places them in a better position to have contact with the wider community on a range of fronts. They are also better placed to cater for particular needs, for instance, of people with disabilities or the infirm.
- *Staffing and decision making patterns appear different in congregations of different sizes.* In larger congregations there is a lower staff to attender ratio. Attenders in larger congregations are less likely to be involved in important decision making than those in smaller congregations.

  Lower levels of involvement in decision making mean an increase in the possibility of attenders losing touch with what is going on or feeling disconnected. Leaders in larger congregations need to be more intentional in communicating directions or decisions and in helping attenders to own what is happening.
- *Larger congregations are more likely to be developing contemporary styles of worship.* The worship services of large congregations are more likely to include contemporary music, informality and attender contributions within services.
- *Larger congregations are more likely to have attenders who feel the congregation is implementing new directions.* By contrast, in smaller congregations there is a higher concern about the need to rethink their directions.
- *In larger congregations higher percentages of attenders are involved in group activities.* At the same time, attenders are more concerned that their congregation may not be friendly to newcomers. Group involvement may be a key strategy to build belonging and communication in larger congregations.
- *Attenders in larger congregations are less likely to feel that their congregation needs to get larger.* The desire for growth appears to wane among larger congregations, with more attenders feeling they have reached a size which is acceptable or sustainable.
- *Attenders in larger congregations are more likely to say there is conflict present.* Given that conflict appears to inhibit numerical growth (see Chapter 12), this suggests that there are forces present within large congregations which can inhibit further growth.
- *Leadership in larger congregations needs to be different.* In larger congregations leaders are more directive and have a clear vision for the future. The process of direction setting may need to be more intentional. In larger congregations leaders are less likely to be seen primarily as pastors.
- *In larger congregations, more intentional effort needs to go into processes of communication.* Attenders in larger congregations are more likely to feel they are unaware of what committees and groups are doing.

It is important to note that the factors differentiating congregations of different sizes overlap with but are often quite different from those strongly related to numerical growth summarised in Chapter 4. This points to a common failure in some Church Growth literature to clearly distinguish between factors which are related to the *size* of congregations and those related to the *numerical growth* of congregations.

It is likely that advice on church growth which is based upon the experience of larger urban congregations runs a greater risk of confusing the two. Factors related to size and not numerical growth may be totally irrelevant to the fortunes of smaller congregations.

WHAT DIFFERENCE DOES SIZE MAKE?

Congregational size generally has little overall relationship with congregational vitality. There is a place for both the big and the small. Indeed, even in the very largest congregations there is an emphasis on the small via small groups and other networks. The seemingly contradictory desires for large celebrations and intimacy are not so much competing as complementary.

There is a place for both large and small congregations

It is important that leaders understand the make-up and nature of their congregation and its style of operation. Congregational vitality may be affected if a congregation's style of operation does not grow and develop as the congregation increases in size. Further research into such issues will be possible from the 1996 NCLS.

Larger congregations are more attractive to younger adults; the age profiles of larger congregations tend to be younger than those of smaller congregations. Such a pattern is true for all major denominational groupings (*Winds of Change*, p 305) and is in keeping with the desire in these generations to be part of a large celebratory, enthusiastic crowd. Opportunities for sharing and belonging are provided through small groups and other activities.

Smaller congregations will find it more difficult to grow numerically and retain younger attenders. Post-war attenders have lower levels of denominational loyalty and are more likely to move to a congregation that is attractive to them or meets their needs.

Yet smaller congregations have an equally important role in relating to newcomers. Clearly size is not a major obstacle to newcomers joining a congregation. Smaller congregations can play a very important role in the life of the church by inviting and integrating friends and contacts into their life.

Smaller congregations have an important role in the front line of mission in Australia. They are the normal expression of church life in rural areas and in many suburban situations. They can be particularly significant in serving a special-interest group and in pioneering new styles of ministry. They can be important in drawing in people who are more comfortable in small groups, who are broken or need high levels of care, or who have a strong commitment to particular values and traditions (Robinson and Yarnell, 1993, 212–216).

Smaller congregations often have a low corporate self-esteem, which can hinder their mission. There may be a single cause for this, but often it is due to a range of factors, possibly exacerbated by a history of frustration or a society that celebrates the large (Burt and Roper, 1992, 73).

Patient and careful leadership will be required to move a small congregation forward, given their often limited resources. This study offers small congregations a hope that vitality is possible and achievable no matter what their size. It also points to the importance of the role of smaller congregations alongside larger ones in mission in contemporary society.

CHAPTER 9

MATTERS OF WORSHIP

Where Culture Collides with Tradition

WORSHIP SERVICES

At the heart of most congregations are the services of worship. They are usually the main gathering for attenders and the first entry point for the majority of new attenders. Worship services are where the gathered congregation offers praise to God, receives teaching and the sacraments, and offers prayers for corporate and individual needs.

The significance and meaning of these meetings varies greatly. Attenders have different hopes and expectations, different preferences in music, prayer and preaching. Some want a lively service, others time for silence and contemplation. Some want a service that their children can participate in, others a service full of the symbols and traditions they have known all their life.

There is much discussion within the churches about appropriate styles of worship. There is discussion about the place of a written liturgy, of experiential worship, of 'seeker-friendly' services for people with non-church backgrounds, and of services for particular age, ethnic or interest groups. There is the need for worship involving the wider community, such as services marking important community events. In the area of worship, some parts of the church are undergoing a radical transformation.

The NCLS included a range of questions to explore the relationship between worship styles and congregational vitality. Since many congregations run multiple services, the NCLS asked leaders to provide information about the style of each service. In addition, attenders were asked their feelings about the preaching, music and language used in the worship services they attend.

This chapter deals in turn with overall approaches to worship, musical style and preaching.

OVERALL APPROACHES TO WORSHIP

Many have argued that the post-war generations find involvement and informality helpful to their worship experience and that newcomers will be more comfortable with language they can readily understand or services that are not too long.

In some denominations, however, leaders are arguing for higher levels of liturgical order. Some may feel that denominations risk losing attenders by abandoning a more traditional order in worship. There may be great value in order and style that is constant in an era where so much else is uncertain.

ATTENDER PARTICIPATION WITHIN SERVICES

Leaders were asked about the roles played by attenders in worship services and whether spontaneous contributions from attenders are encouraged during the services. How do levels of attender participation relate to congregational vitality?

As can be seen in Figure 9.1, greater participation by attenders is of *some importance* in relation to a sense of belonging, numerical growth, and attenders discussing their faith and inviting others to church. It is *marginally* related to attracting and retaining newcomers, encouraging wider community involvement, and growth in faith.

FIGURE 9.1: APPROACH TO WORSHIP

	STRENGTH OF RELATIONSHIPS			
	Attender participation within services	Informality of worship style	Ease of understanding the language used in services	A short service
NEWCOMERS	+ 0.7	++ 1.6	0.0	+ 0.6
YOUNG ADULT RETENTION	0.2	0.1	0.0	0.0
NUMERICAL GROWTH	++ 1.3	+++ 3.0	++ 1.0	0.4
SENSE OF BELONGING	++ 1.0	++ 1.0	+++ 3.1	0.5
COMMUNITY INVOLVEMENT	+ 0.6	++ 2.0	0.3	0.1
SHARING/ INVITING	++ 1.2	+ 0.7	0.1	0.2
GROWTH IN FAITH	+ 0.5	++ 1.8	+ 0.8	− 0.8

NB: Strength of relationship is the percent of variance explained after accounting for local context/faith type effects
SOURCE: 1991 National Church Life Survey

Some writers have stressed the importance of active attender involvement in worship services. Lyle Schaller, for instance, suggests that worship which is appealing to 20 to 40 year olds must evoke a sense of active involvement, rather than encouraging a spectator role (Anderson, 1990, 97). The NCLS results suggest that giving attenders a greater role, whether in the running of the service or preaching, as well as opportunities for sharing or open prayer, are generally positive in relation to congregational vitality.

FORMALITY

In a study of Southern Baptist churches in the United States, C. Kirk Hadaway concluded that formal liturgy is more characteristic of churches that have plateaued numerically than those that are growing (1991, 66).

The NCLS asked leaders about levels of formality in services, about the use of written liturgy and traditional symbols or rituals, and the dress of the worship leader. This study suggests that informality in both worship style and the dress of the worship leader is of *some importance* or is *marginally* related to most aspects of vitality. Informality is part of the culture of post-war generations; congregations which opt for an informal style are more likely to be growing numerically or attracting newcomers.

Congregations which opt for an informal style are more likely to be growing numerically

APPROACHES TO WORSHIP: A PROFILE

- 40% of all church services are described by congregational leaders as formal, 42% as semi-formal and 18% as informal.
- Written liturgy is used in 39% of church services; a further 12% use a written service outline. In 32% of church services, a standard approach is used (no written outline), and in 17% the approach varies from week to week.
- Written liturgy is most often used in Anglican (91%) services.
- Robes and vestments are worn by worship leaders at 47% of church services and formal clothing at 28% of services. More casual wear is worn at 25% of services.
- Robes and vestments are virtually confined to mainstream denominations; they are worn at most Anglican (88%) and Lutheran (86%) services, and some Presbyterian (27%) and Uniting (36%) services.
- Traditional symbols and rituals play an important part in 21% of church services. They are of some importance in 20% and of little or no importance in 59% of services.

SOURCE: 1991 National Church Life Survey adjusted for non-participants

Some might be concerned by such a finding, particularly those from denominations that place a high value on received tradition. They may feel that such traditions are not to be altered lightly, based on how attenders feel.

However, there would appear to be clear shifts in how different generations most comfortably express their faith (*Winds of Change*, Chapter 19). Perhaps this result should not be seen as a rejection of order or reverence, but rather a change in the way it is expressed. The richness and authenticity of worship can be maintained, even if it is expressed in a different way.

LANGUAGE

Attenders were asked whether they had any difficulty understanding the language used in their congregation, such as in hymns or preaching. Figure 9.1 shows that congregations with a high level of attenders experiencing language difficulties are a little less likely to be growing numerically. The use of clear and simple language in the church service appears *important* in relation to a sense of belonging among attenders.

In a society where fewer people understand the symbols, traditions and teachings of the Christian churches it is important to communicate and celebrate in ways that are as jargon-free as possible.

Historically there has been a major emphasis on the written word. Yet television has reshaped communication. Australian author Bill Lawton argues that most mainline denominations place too high a value on literacy: in church the Bible is read, the prayers are read, the hymns are read — a 'gospel of Word by words'. Lawton suggests the church needs to explore how far it can utilise oral and visual forms of communication (1988, 23).

SERVICE LENGTH

Some feel that if a church service runs too long attenders will lose interest and it will be unattractive to newcomers. However, some large and numerically growing congregations, particularly Pentecostal churches, hold quite lengthy services.

The NCLS does not reveal any strong relationship between service length and congregational vitality (see Figure 9.1). However, the 1993 National Social Science Survey found that the major criticism of church services among the general population is that they are too long, although this does not appear to affect actual attendance levels (Hughes, Thompson, Pryor and Bouma, 1995, 48). It could be that the length of a service is not a barrier to newcomers if other aspects of their experience are positive.

MUSICAL STYLE

A central aspect of most worship services is the music. Hymns and other sacred songs remain important, although during the past two decades there has been a move towards using contemporary music.

SATISFACTION WITH MUSIC

Attender satisfaction with music is critical in relation to a sense of belonging

As can be seen in Figure 9.2, attender satisfaction with music at church is a *critical* factor in relation to attenders' growth in faith and sense of belonging. Music is a major vehicle for the expression of ideas and feelings. Attenders who are uncomfortable with the music are less likely to feel a sense of belonging.

FIGURE 9.2: MUSIC IN WORSHIP

	STRENGTH OF RELATIONSHIPS		
	Satisfaction with music	Use of contemporary music	Contemporary styles of worship
NEWCOMERS	− − − 3.2	+++ 4.1	+++ 4.7
YOUNG ADULT RETENTION	0.4	++ 2.3	+++ 3.8
NUMERICAL GROWTH	+ 0.7	++ 1.2	++ 1.7
SENSE OF BELONGING	+++++ 14.6	0.0	++ 1.0
COMMUNITY INVOLVEMENT	0.0	− − 1.7	++ 2.8
SHARING/ INVITING	++ 2.2	+ 0.9	++ 1.8
GROWTH IN FAITH	+++++ 10.9	++ 2.0	++ 2.2

NB: Strength of relationship is the percent of variance explained after accounting for local context/faith type effects
SOURCE: 1991 National Church Life Survey

Congregations need to ensure that attenders are generally satisfied with the style of music encountered. However, this is easier said than done. Music is a key way in which people from different generations, ethnic or interest groups express their culture and identity and differentiate themselves from other groups. Congregations which include a wide diversity of attenders may well find music issues difficult.

Satisfaction with music among attenders is negatively related to the flow of newcomers. In other words, as the proportion of newcomers in a congregation increases, the overall satisfaction with the music among attenders generally decreases. Further analysis suggests that this pattern is due to lower satisfaction with the music among newcomers themselves rather than any dissatisfaction among other attenders.

The implication of this result is quite important. It cannot be assumed that newcomers are happy with the music they are encountering. They may well be putting up with the music for the sake of other benefits they receive from their involvement.

Hadaway suggests that the musical styles in a congregation should reflect the musical tastes of those in the wider community around it (1991, 69). Attenders from a particular background or generation may be very comfortable with their music, while those in the wider community or visitors to the congregation may find it quite alienating. Congregations that want to attract others from the wider community will need to reflect carefully on their choice of music.

CONTEMPORARY MUSIC

There has been much debate among churches here and overseas about appropriate styles of music. This debate has been prompted by a shift towards the use of popular music styles in worship services, a trend which has been generally supported by advocates of church growth. White lists four major trends in music in the worship of numerically growing churches in the United States. These trends are that music is contemporary and upbeat, high quality, presented in innovative ways, and there is lots of it (1992, 82). In some congregations the pace of worship is faster, and contemporary music is one of the most distinctive characteristics. Gospel songs are more numerous than hymns; the songs include recent compositions and some compositions from within the congregation, and there is more active participation by the congregation (Schaller, 1987a, 67).

Easum suggests that music is *the* major vehicle for celebration and communication and therefore music in worship must be culturally relevant. A culture defined generationally will require expressions of faith within the style, sounds and symbols of that culture. Synthesiser, drums, flute, electric guitar, tambourine, bass and piano should be the basic instruments of worship today, backed up with electronic and lighting supports (Easum, 1993, 85, 86).

MUSICAL STYLE: A PROFILE

- Traditional hymns are mostly sung at 41% of services and mainly choruses or other contemporary songs at 20% of services. An equal mix is sung at 29% of services, while in 10% of services no songs are sung.

- Traditional hymns predominate at Presbyterian (73%), and Uniting (57%) worship services. Pentecostal services use mainly choruses and other contemporary music (94%) while an equal mix of songs is most common among Baptists (51%), Salvation Army (72%) and the smaller denominations.

- Although in practice there may be a range of instruments used, organs or pianos are the primary form of musical accompaniment (83% of services). Electrified instruments are mainly used at 8% of services, and non-electric instruments such as acoustic guitars at another 9% of services. Organs or pianos are the main form of accompaniment across all denominations, except Pentecostal, where mainly electrified instruments are used (52% of services).

SOURCE: 1991 National Church Life Survey adjusted for non-participants

WHERE MEREDITH WAS

WHAT MEREDITH REMEMBERED.

Not everybody is enamoured of contemporary music and its potential in worship. One stream of thinking has seen rock music as of the devil. One pastor of a large Baptist church in the United States, Homer Lindsay, notes that 'Gospel Rock is a contradiction of Christianity. It's against all that is holy and spiritual. I am not going to use worldly means to reach lost people' (Towns, 1990, 112).

Others are concerned for different reasons. They prefer a more formal liturgy, of which solemnity is an important ingredient. The sound and movement of rock music runs counter to this requirement.

Contemporary music is important in attracting newcomers

Are congregations which use contemporary music more vital and effective? The answer appears to be, in some areas, yes. Figure 9.2 shows that using contemporary music in church services is *important* in relation to attracting newcomers and of *some importance* in relation to numerical growth, young adult retention, and growth in faith. There is, however, no relationship with attenders' sense of belonging.

It is interesting to contrast this result with the previous one for satisfaction with music. There is a strong relationship between satisfaction and a sense of belonging or growth in faith. Clearly, music is an important factor in providing an environment conducive to belonging and growth in faith. Yet it is the presence of contemporary music, not widespread satisfaction, that is more strongly linked to newcomers, young adult retention and numerical growth.

This tension is difficult, but is not to be avoided by congregational leaders as they set priorities for the future. A large proportion of church attenders were born in the pre-war era. For these attenders, contemporary music is often quite difficult and unhelpful to their worship experience (*Winds of Change*, p 169) and may adversely affect their sense of belonging. Providing a worship context helpful to outsiders is clearly important; it is important, too, for existing attenders to find life and meaning in the worship style.

Responding to this tension may take different forms in different contexts. Some congregations have wholeheartedly embraced contemporary styles to the exclusion of traditional styles. Others maintain traditional styles. Still others have sought to mix them, sometimes creating a useful compromise, at other times creating a worship style that is unsatisfactory to all parties. Many congregations offer different styles in different worship services.

Yet there can be no doubt about the direction of the trend. Congregations that look only to the desires of existing attenders may find themselves in decline. Avoiding the issue is likely to prove to be unhelpful.

GETTING WORSHIP RIGHT — WHERE CULTURE COLLIDES WITH TRADITION

A Uniting Church in regional Queensland found itself in the middle of a developing suburb full of young families. The church's minister 'borrowed' six key members of a nearby parish to assist in commencing a new ministry and then began to develop a mission plan appropriate to this young community. Their energetic youth worker concentrated his efforts at the local primary school, talking with children and making contact with families.

Both the minister and youth worker realised that music and movement in the worship services would be helpful and were able to persuade church leaders to agree to a new style of worship. 'The music band that we have now is made up of musicians who'd never had anything to do with a church before', said a member of the congregation.

'We found that service times were important too — services begin at 6.30 pm on a Saturday evening, followed by refreshments. This really fits with the lifestyle of the young families in our area.'

Inspired by growing numbers at the Saturday services, the leaders tapped into the creative energy of the congregation, encouraging them in music and drama, stretching and developing their talents. It helped make worship exciting and relevant.

While it is often the case that new congregations go through many changes before finding their own style of worship, this particular model has proved very durable. In fact, it is still in place even though the original minister and youth worker have both now moved on.

CONTEMPORARY STYLES OF WORSHIP

The word 'contemporary' will doubtless mean different things to different people. Some may, for instance, see services based on the traditions of the Taizè community in France as contemporary. It will be important to develop styles that are meaningful and appropriate to particular contexts and cultural groups.

Nevertheless, across the church in Australia there has been a growing emphasis on styles of worship that have an outward informality, that incorporate rhythm and a range of musical instruments, notably the guitar, that rely on contemporary symbols and that invite attenders' contributions and participation.

The NCLS shows that such an orientation tends to be characteristic of more vital and effective congregations. The positive relationship between a contemporary style of worship which incorporates these aspects and most congregational vitality indicators is also presented in Figure 9.2.

WHAT ABOUT THE PREACHING?

SATISFACTION WITH PREACHING

Many see the quality of preaching as an essential ingredient of congregational life. A study of Episcopalian congregations in the United States found that good preaching plus warmth and the spiritual depth of the minister/pastor/priest is related to church growth; being ignored by the leader, poor sermons, and difficulty in following services are barriers to joining a new church (Oswald and Leas, 1987, 26). Thompson, Carroll and Hoge, in a study of Presbyterian congregations in the United States, found that the quality of preaching attracts new members (Thompson *et al*, 1993, 197). From a study of churches in New Zealand, Ray Muller found that responsive preaching was included in a secondary list of factors contributing to the numerical growth of churches (Muller, 1993, 232). May is more eloquent: 'Church history shows us again and again that in times of great revivals and spiritual renewals, powerful preaching has been a vital part of the movement' (May, 1986, 210).

Others are less positive. In his study of Southern Baptist churches, Hadaway concludes that there is a weak correlation between growth and 'dynamic preacher/exciting sermon'. Some pastors may be able to cause a church to grow by the quality of their preaching, but, for most, the objective quality of sermons has little to do with growth (1991, 67). In another study, Rauff concluded that few newcomers to church life ascribed extraordinary preaching skills to the pastors of the churches they joined (1979, 204).

As can be seen in Figure 9.3, the NCLS shows that, as with music, attenders' satisfaction with the preaching is seen as a *critical* factor in relation to a sense of belonging and growth in faith among existing attenders. It is positively related to numerical growth, though perhaps not to the extent some may expect.

It has less relationship with other aspects of vitality, confirming some of the more cautionary comments of Hadaway and Rauff. Satisfaction with preaching is *marginally* related to the flow of newcomers.

APPROACH TO PREACHING

It has been suggested that sermons need to be short and simple in order to be understood. Anderson, for instance, suggests that preachers need to strive for simplicity, with stories to aid listening, and not preach for longer than 25 minutes (1992, 218). Likewise, Morris suggests that sermons

FIGURE 9.3: PREACHING

	STRENGTH OF RELATIONSHIPS		
	Satisfaction with preaching	Brevity of preaching	Type of sermon preached
NEWCOMERS	**+** 0.8	0.0	0.0
YOUNG ADULT RETENTION	0.0	0.1	0.0
NUMERICAL GROWTH	**++** 3.0	0.4	0.0
SENSE OF BELONGING	**+++++** 17.1	0.0	0.0
COMMUNITY INVOLVEMENT	0.0	0.2	0.2
SHARING/ INVITING	**+** 0.7	0.0	0.2
GROWTH IN FAITH	**+++++** 11.1	**—** 0.5	0.0

NB: Strength of relationship is the percent of variance explained after accounting for local context/faith type effects
SOURCE: 1991 National Church Life Survey

should be short and succinct, since most people's attention span is about 15 to 30 minutes (1993, 228).

The growth of many Pentecostal churches, where preaching is often much longer, counters this logic. Indeed, the NCLS suggests that sermon length has little overall relationship with a congregation's vitality. The length of the sermon is not a significant factor, particularly if preachers have a good communication style. Good preachers can hold the attention of attenders for reasonable periods of time; poor preachers may not hold their attention for even a short time!

Sermon length is not a significant factor

These findings are paralleled in another Australian study. The 1993 National Social Science Survey also found that concerns about the length of sermons as well as other aspects of preaching appear to have little impact on actual church attendance (Hughes, Thompson, Pryor and Bouma, 1995, 48).

Leaders were also asked what type of sermon they usually preached — one which explained a passage of the Bible in detail, or one which was more topical in approach, using the Bible as support. The NCLS shows no relationship between the type of sermon preached and congregational vitality.

Preachers need to get feedback from attenders to develop a realistic appraisal of their giftedness in preaching and what is being gained from it. Given that communication involves both speaker and hearers, it is important for each congregation to develop patterns that are right for their situation.

GETTING WORSHIP RIGHT

The church service is a central event in the life of a congregation. In worship a congregation defines its ethos and identity, builds community and establishes a common language and history. It can be a prime time for nurturing among attenders the connection between faith and life (Crabtree, 1989, 17–18). The worship experience can inspire attenders, launching them into a new week in hope and confidence. For the clergy it is a major time of contact with attenders and an opportunity to build faith and lead people in worship (Hughes, 1989, 59).

Attender satisfaction with worship style is strongly related to congregational vitality, particularly in the areas of sense of belonging and growth in faith. Its impact, in the main, is on building up and renewing existing attenders, rather than on attracting newcomers. The use of contemporary music, attender involvement in worship, and informality have a greater impact in relation to numerical growth, the attraction of newcomers, and the retention of young adults.

In these results, the NCLS points the church to the shape of its worship in the future. There is a revolution going on in the churches over matters of worship style. Congregations cannot afford to ignore such issues.

Denominations with centuries of worship heritage and tradition will need to explore how to connect those traditions with contemporary styles of expression. It will be inadequate to give mere lip-service to this matter or to take only token steps in this direction. The levels of denominational switching among young adults, discussed in *Winds of Change* (p 230), underscore the need to be relevant to the post-war generations if congregations want to have young adults in their churches. Many congregations, particularly in mainstream denominations, will be faced with a severe tension between the demands of a changing community culture and the needs and demands of older attenders.

The discussion here has largely been cast in generational terms. Yet in Australia there are many different cultural groups, differentiated not only by generation but also by ethnicity, socioeconomic status or interests. Many have argued for the importance of worship styles that are culturally appropriate (eg Millikan, 1981). Studies such as *Who Goes Where?* (Kaldor, 1987) highlight the need for the church to minister in different ways to different subcultures. As Ed Vaughan has noted in an analysis of the issues facing the Anglican Church in Sydney, a congregation sensitive to the subcultures in its community will know their language (Vaughan, 1988).

Responding to diversity is not straightforward and there is no one formula for relating to all the different cultural groups that make up the Australian community. Churches will need to understand with whom they are in mission and develop styles of worship that resonate with the culture of that group. While this is often an extremely touchy issue, it is one that must not be avoided.

CHAPTER 10

NURTURE ACTIVITIES

Growing the Christian Body

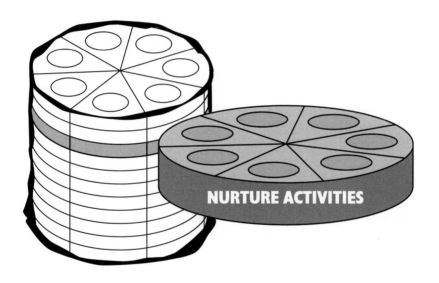

NURTURE ACTIVITIES

People attend churches for many different reasons. One of the main expectations people have of church attendance is spiritual nurture, which can occur through a variety of avenues including teaching programs, small groups, Sunday school, youth groups, and personal interaction between attenders.

This chapter identifies some of the resources which are commonly committed to spiritual nurture and their relationship with congregational vitality. The resources identified include both *corporate* resources, such as group prayer, Bible study and discussion groups, and *private* ones, such as private Bible reading and prayer.

CORPORATE NURTURE ACTIVITY

In most congregations, the church worship service is the central corporate activity of congregational life. In worship services attenders pray and worship together, receive teaching, share in communion and enjoy fellowship. The church service is an important time which contributes greatly to the nurture of attenders' faith.

However, for many attenders it is not the only form of involvement. About a third of attenders at church on an average Sunday are regularly involved in mission activities connected with their congregation. Still more are regularly involved in small groups or church social activities. In some congregations weekday ministries can be more important to some attenders than the Sunday services.

INVOLVEMENT IN CONGREGATIONAL ACTIVITIES

Does a high level of attender involvement in congregational activities have any relationship with vitality? Involvement in mission activities is dealt with in the next chapter. Aspects of involvement considered here include
- frequency of worship service attendance
- frequency of attendance at small groups or other social or group activities
- hours involved in congregational activities.

The NCLS suggests that the overall level of attender involvement in congregational activities is strongly related to congregational vitality. Figure 10.1 shows that a high level of involvement is *very important* in relation to growth in faith and a sense of belonging. It is also *very important* in relation to the involvement of attenders in wider community groups and in sharing faith and inviting others to church, *important* in relation to levels of newcomers, and of *some importance* in retaining young adults. There is, however, little relationship with the numerical growth of a congregation.

The relationship between levels of newcomers and involvement is quite complex. Newcomers themselves have lower levels of involvement and tend to remain more on the fringes of congregational life (*Winds of*

Change, p 114). Non-newcomers in high newcomer congregations, however, tend to be more involved in congregational life than their counterparts in other congregations. It is this relationship that is shown in Figure 10.1.

FIGURE 10.1: INVOLVEMENT IN CONGREGATIONAL ACTIVITIES	STRENGTH OF RELATIONSHIPS	
	Overall level of involvement in congregational activities	Involvement in small groups in the congregation
NEWCOMERS	+++ 4.3	++ 1.5
YOUNG ADULT RETENTION	++ 2.5	++ 1.7
NUMERICAL GROWTH	+ 0.8	+ 0.6
SENSE OF BELONGING	++++ 7.5	+++ 4.7
COMMUNITY INVOLVEMENT	++++ 9.7	+++ 3.9
SHARING/ INVITING	++++ 7.3	++++ 5.2
GROWTH IN FAITH	++++ 8.5	++++ 6.5

NB: Strength of relationship is the percent of variance explained after accounting for local context/faith type effects

SOURCE: 1991 National Church Life Survey

Clearly involvement is positively related to vitality. The NCLS also asked attenders whether their levels of involvement had increased or decreased in the previous year. Although not reported here, increasing levels of involvement is a characteristic of congregations with high levels of belonging or growth in faith. A positive church experience is likely to heighten a desire among attenders to be involved.

It is also positively related to numerical growth, suggesting that numerical growth occurs not only through the addition of new attenders but in the increasing frequency of involvement of fringe and core attenders.

John Bodycomb provides an important insight by suggesting that an effective congregation will be drawing attenders into its life primarily from among fringe attenders and contacts and encouraging greater involvement of fringe attenders. (Bodycomb, 1986, 14–16).

Interestingly, of the three aspects included in overall level of involvement — church services, small groups, and hours of involvement — the most strongly related to vitality is the involvement of attenders in small groups.

SMALL GROUPS

One of the major developments in church life in recent decades has been the growth of small group networks within the life of congregations. Small groups can take a variety of forms. Bible study groups or cell groups are common in churches today, as are prayer groups.

John Mallison has been a key advocate of small groups in Australia. He considers the small group to be the basic building block in congregational life, fostering discipleship and spiritual growth and allowing attenders to care for one another, to serve, and to prepare each other for mission in the world (Mallison, 1996, 7–12).

Some 22% of attenders are involved in small groups for study, prayer or sharing, another 22% are involved in fellowship or social groups, and a further 19% are involved in both types of group. In total, then, 63%, or nearly two-thirds of attenders, are involved in some kind of group outside of the worship service (*Winds of Change*, pp 107, 108).

Some 77% of Anglican and Protestant congregations in Australia have groups which are used for Christian nurture, which indicates just how widespread they have become. Some 61% of congregations indicate that prayer meetings are also a regular feature of their congregational life.

CORPORATE NURTURE: A PROFILE

- 77% of congregations have small groups for Christian nurture; of these, 48% consider their small groups to be central to the congregational nurture strategy.

- Small groups are of central importance to most congregations in Pentecostal (82%), Baptist (75%), Churches of Christ (66%), Salvation Army (67%) and most small Protestant denominations (77%).

- 61% of congregations have regular prayer meetings; 22% of these are separate prayer meetings and 36% are part of small groups. Just 3% have half or full days of prayer in addition to other prayer meetings.

- Separate regular prayer meetings are characteristic of most Pentecostal congregations(76%).

SOURCE: 1991 National Church Life Survey adjusted for non-participants

Some studies have found a relationship between the involvement of attenders in small groups and the numerical growth of churches. Klopp's study of some churches in the United States found the small-group experience to be a significant factor contributing to numerical growth (1982, 68). In a New Zealand study, Ray Muller also found that small groups were a significant factor contributing to numerical growth (Muller, 1993, 231).

The NCLS shows that there are some strong relationships between the proportion of people involved in the group life of a congregation and congregational vitality. Figure 10.1 shows that being involved in groups can be *very important* in relation to growth in faith and attenders discussing their faith or inviting others to church. It is *important* regarding wider community involvement and growing a sense of belonging. Small-group involvement is helpful not only in nurturing the inward life, but also in promoting a more outward focus among attenders.

In further analysis not presented here, it is evident that involvement in small groups for sharing, prayer or Bible study rather than in social or fellowship groups is the key factor in relationship to growth in faith. In addition, the proportion of attenders involved in small groups rather than social or fellowship groups is important in relation to sharing faith and inviting others to church as well as to developing a sense of belonging.

Higher levels of involvement in small groups is also a characteristic of congregations retaining young adults. At the same time, further analysis also revealed a significant relationship between retention and children's and youth programs being valued highly by attenders. The effort put into this area can have a significant effect in integrating young adults.

Small groups are a significant part of the social landscape in contemporary society. Robert Wuthnow cites research suggesting that 40% of adults in the United States claim to be involved in 'a small group that meets regularly and provides caring and support for those who participate in it' (Wuthnow, 1994, 45). Such groups include the many small groups connected with churches or organised independently by Christian people, as well as self-help groups, Alcoholics Anonymous and similar groups, therapy sessions and recovery groups.

Small groups are a significant part of the social landscape in society

Critics sometimes suggest that support groups are quite artificial, encouraging those involved to focus more on themselves. Indeed, Wuthnow suggests that this kind of group may be at a crossroads. It can continue on its present course, helping make people feel good about themselves and encouraging a pragmatic spirituality. Alternatively, it could focus more on challenging people at deeper levels to make a more serious commitment to the wider community and to those in need (Wuthnow, 1994, 27).

Casual observation of small-group life in Australia would suggest that such comments could well apply here too. Many groups connected with New Age spirituality as well as many church-based small groups appear quite inward-looking and self-focused. On the other hand, there are many Christian small groups or intentional communities making a significant contribution to the wider society. Some examples can be found in *Where the River Flows* (Kaldor and Kaldor, 1988).

TRAINING FOR MINISTRY AND MISSION

Some congregations offer training programs in aspects of ministry or mission. Informal training or instruction may also be given without a structured course. Are congregations which provide training of some kind more vital and effective?

Some studies have found a relationship between the training of attenders and congregational vitality. Ray Muller, for instance, found that evangelism training was included in a secondary grouping of factors which contributed to numerical growth in New Zealand congregations (Muller, 1993, 232).

Many would see that offering training is, in fact, part of the church's true mandate. They argue that the whole people of God share in ministry, and clergy and lay people together must be trained for this shared ministry. It should not be merely for a spiritual elite but for everyone (Hesselgrave, 1980, 69).

The NCLS shows that there are links between receiving training and sharing faith. Some 78% of attenders who look for opportunities to share their faith have had training, compared to only 30% who do not like to talk about their faith. In addition, attenders who have undertaken training are more likely to say that they are growing in their faith. More than 52% of attenders who have had training in mission have grown much in their faith, compared to 31% of attenders who have not had such training (*Mission under the Microscope,* pp 76–78).

These results are confirmed for congregations as well as for individual attenders. Figure 10.2 shows that training is *very important* in relation to attenders sharing their faith and inviting others into church life and also in relation to growth in faith. It is also *important* in promoting a sense of belonging and of *some importance* in relation to most other areas.

FIGURE 10.2: FAITH AND LIFE

	STRENGTH OF RELATIONSHIPS	
	Training for mission and ministry	Discussion of important life issues
NEWCOMERS	✚✚ 1.2	✚ 0.7
YOUNG ADULT RETENTION	✚✚ 1.3	✚✚ 1.0
NUMERICAL GROWTH	✚ 0.9	✚ 0.5
SENSE OF BELONGING	✚✚✚ 3.5	✚✚✚✚ 6.9
COMMUNITY INVOLVEMENT	✚✚ 1.8	✚ 0.9
SHARING/ INVITING	✚✚✚✚ 7.1	✚✚ 2.8
GROWTH IN FAITH	✚✚✚✚ 5.9	✚✚✚✚ 7.6

NB: Strength of relationship is the percent of variance explained after accounting for local context/faith type effects

SOURCE: 1991 National Church Life Survey

Connecting faith to daily life is very important for growth in faith

CONNECTING FAITH TO LIFE

Australian author Robert Banks believes that the church must make a greater effort to link the faith to the concerns of everyday life (Banks, 1987). How important is it for attenders to feel that their congregation

EGBERT SPECIALISED
IN CONNECTING FAITH
TO LIFE. SO IT WAS A
SHOCK TO EVERYONE
WHEN, AFTER FOUR SOLID
WEEKS, EGBERT HADN'T
WORKED OUT A CHRISTIAN
WAY OF TYING UP SHOES.

helps them connect their faith with the daily issues of their lives?

Some 71% feel that the important issues of their daily lives are being addressed in their congregations. For most (41%), this occurs through informal discussion of issues with other attenders. Only 30% feel that important issues are discussed through the formal activities of their congregation; these are made up of 22% who feel that their concerns are discussed in sharing groups or other activities, and 8% who feel that their concerns are addressed in other ways, such as through the preaching (*Winds of Change*, p 143).

Figure 10.2 shows that congregations where a high proportion of attenders believe that everyday issues are discussed in their congregations also tend to be more vital and effective. Helping attenders to connect their faith with daily life is *very important* in relation to both growth in faith and a sense of belonging among attenders. It is of *some importance* in relation to attenders sharing their faith with others and in retaining young adults in congregational life.

It is important to note that the key factor is that attenders are encouraged to discuss the issues affecting them. Congregations which only address these issues in the preaching or do not address them at all are less likely to be effective.

Clearly there can be more to spiritual nurture than just listening to a sermon. This is a challenge for many congregations, since only a minority of attenders feel they are being given opportunities to discuss the concerns of their everyday lives within the formal activities of their congregation. Many congregations may need to be more intentional about providing opportunities for this to occur.

PRIVATE DEVOTIONAL PRACTICES

Private devotional practices are encouraged across the church as an important Christian discipline and way of focusing on God. There are many such practices, including meditation, prayer, fasting, solitude and simple living. The NCLS focused on just two of the most commonly practised disciplines: prayer and Bible reading. Some 64% of attenders read the Bible on their own at least once a week or more often, while 68% pray frequently or habitually (*Views from the Pews*, pp 86–89).

Bible reading and prayer are closely related to the qualitative aspects of congregational vitality. The results are shown in Figure 10.3.

FIGURE 10.3: PRIVATE DEVOTIONAL PRACTICES

	STRENGTH OF RELATIONSHIPS		
	Bible reading	Private prayer	Devotional practices (Bible and prayer)
NEWCOMERS	✚✚ 1.2	✚✚ 2.3	✚✚ 2.9
YOUNG ADULT RETENTION	0.0	0.3	0.3
NUMERICAL GROWTH	0.0	0.0	0.0
SENSE OF BELONGING	✚✚✚ 3.8	✚✚✚ 3.3	✚✚✚ 4.9
COMMUNITY INVOLVEMENT	✚✚ 2.4	✚✚ 1.3	✚✚ 2.6
SHARING/ INVITING	✚✚✚✚ 5.0	✚✚✚ 4.9	✚✚✚✚ 6.5
GROWTH IN FAITH	✚✚✚ 3.9	✚✚✚ 3.1	✚✚✚ 4.7

NB: Strength of relationship is the percent of variance explained after accounting for local context/faith type effects

SOURCE: 1991 National Church Life Survey

Congregations where high proportions of attenders undertake regular Bible reading and prayer also tend to have higher levels of attenders who are growing in faith, are sharing their faith, have a sense of belonging, and are involved in the wider community. Bible reading and prayer are unrelated to numerical growth and the retention of young adults.

Newcomers to congregational life tend to have lower levels of Bible reading or private prayer (*Views from the Pews*, pp 86–89). But the opposite is true of non-newcomers in high newcomer congregations, who have more active devotional lives than their counterparts in other congregations. It is this positive relationship that has been presented in Figure 10.3.

PERSONAL SPIRITUAL JOURNEYS

Much time is devoted in church life to preaching and teaching, to pastoral work and encouragement in the faith. Attenders work together to build one another up in love and to encourage one another in discipleship.

Each person can be said to be on a spiritual journey, which has both individual and corporate aspects. This journey also has many milestones, which likewise can be intensely private or can occur in a corporate setting.

Probing aspects of attenders' spiritual journeys is very difficult. The NCLS included several questions, the results of which are examined here.

GROWTH IN FAITH

Attenders were asked to assess whether they felt they had grown in beliefs or understanding of their faith and whether they had made changes in their actions or priorities in the previous year. These have been combined into the growth in faith vitality indicator and were the subject of Chapter 7.

The relationship of these indicators to other aspects of vitality are shown in Figure 10.4. The strong relationship with a sense of belonging and discussing one's faith with others is evident. Likewise, growth in faith is a characteristic of congregations that are growing numerically or drawing in newcomers.

Growth in faith is a characteristic of congregations that are growing numerically

DECISIVE FAITH COMMITMENT

Christian commitment can take place in many different ways. For some people, commitment is a gradual journey of acceptance and discovery of faith. They look back and cannot name a point at which they crossed from unbelief to belief. Others are able to identify a specific moment of decisive conversion or commitment.

In some denominations, making a decisive faith commitment is encouraged as the critical first step or first sign of growth in faith. It is so valued that attenders are frequently encouraged to make a specific, public commitment. Other denominations place less emphasis on a public faith commitment, encouraging attenders to find God in the everyday events and rhythms of life.

While some denominations place more emphasis upon conversion experiences than others, many attenders in all denominations have experienced a time when God became very real and their lives took a new

FIGURE 10.4: PERSONAL SPIRITUAL JOURNEYS

	STRENGTH OF RELATIONSHIPS		
	Significant growth in beliefs or understanding	Made major changes in life as a result of faith	Decisive faith commitment
NEWCOMERS	+++ 3.8	++++ 6.9	++++ 8.9
YOUNG ADULT RETENTION	+ 0.5	+ 0.9	++ 1.2
NUMERICAL GROWTH	++ 2.7	+++ 4.5	+++ 4.0
SENSE OF BELONGING	+++++ 28.7	++++ 8.8	+++ 4.9
COMMUNITY INVOLVEMENT	+ 0.7	0.2	++ 1.7
SHARING/ INVITING	++++ 7.3	++++ 5.7	+++ 4.2
GROWTH IN FAITH	N/A	N/A	++++ 9.3

1. NB: Strength of relationship is the percent of variance explained after accounting for local context/faith type effects
2. N/A: Not Applicable

SOURCE: 1991 National Church Life Survey

course. Sometimes these experiences are so vivid and dramatic that the details can be remembered years later. At other times they are much less dramatic.

Attenders who make public professions of faith see them as highly significant to their faith journey. The majority of attenders (56%) can pinpoint a specific moment of conversion or faith commitment in their lives, while a further 33% say that their faith has grown gradually (*Mission under the Microscope*, pp 128–139).

Congregations with higher proportions of attenders who have experienced definite moments of faith commitment tend to have higher proportions who feel they are growing in their faith. They also have higher levels of a sense of belonging.

There is a significant relationship between experiences of decisive faith commitment and the flow of newcomers into a congregation. This may reflect the enthusiasm for evangelism of congregations with many attenders who have experienced decisive faith commitment. It also suggests that being brought to a point of decisive faith commitment is an important part of the process of integration for newcomers into church life.

It is important to remember when examining these results that they are not simply a product of the theological orientation of attenders. The results show the relationship with the seven vitality measures *after* taking into account the effect of faith type and context.

Attenders were also asked whether they had a strong sense of what God was calling them to do in their lives and about their experiences of the presence of God in their lives. Although the results are not presented here, a strong sense among attenders of what God is calling them to do in their lives is positively associated with most aspects of vitality. Likewise, having some kind of experience of God's presence is strongly related to most aspects of vitality.

GROWING THE CHRISTIAN BODY

There are great dangers in carrying out research into the life of the churches. Researchers must tread warily. There is the danger of reductionism — the attempt to explain everything in church life in human terms. Attenders often point to the spiritual or the divine as having a major impact in their lives. They become unhappy when they perceive that research is trying to reduce the fortunes of congregations to a matter of technique. Do it this way and everything will be well; do it that way and your church will not prosper. 'Where is God in all this?' they ask.

Then there are the dangers associated with each aspect of religious experience. High levels of Bible reading or prayer can be symptomatic of legalism rather than of a living faith. Experiences of God can become an end in themselves, to be pursued to the exclusion of right living or issues of justice and need. An over-emphasis on conversion can lead to a denial of the faith of others whose growth in faith has been more gradual.

The NCLS recognises these dangers. Yet there can be no denying the relationship between religious practices and congregational vitality. Congregations where attenders are frequent in attendance at church services and small groups, where there are high levels of devotional practice, and where attenders are open to experiencing God's presence in their lives are also more likely to be vital and effective.

Not surprisingly, high levels of small-group involvement and devotional practice are strongly related to attenders' growth in faith. These results confirm what many believe about the importance of nurture activities beyond attendance at worship services.

Small-group involvement is also strongly related to a sense of belonging to the congregation, as well as to involvement in community care activities, sharing faith, or inviting others to church. Small-group involvement is helpful not only in nurturing the inward life, but also in promoting a more outward focus among attenders.

Congregational vitality is more than a matter of having the right activities. Congregations where there are high proportions of attenders who have active personal devotional lives and who have made decisive faith commitments and where the issues of daily life are readily discussed also tend to have higher levels of both belonging and growth in faith.

CHAPTER 11

MISSION ACTIVITIES

An Optional Extra?

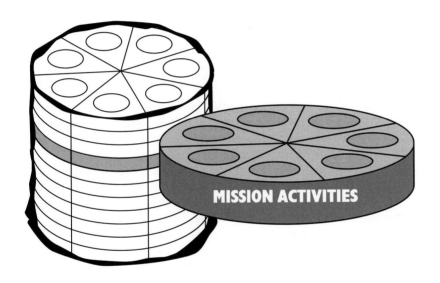

MISSION ACTIVITIES

While different traditions may express it differently, nearly all traditions have a strong outward focus. The Great Commission and Great Commandment call Christians to be salt and light in word and deed in the wider community.

The wider church has a strong commitment to social concern and welfare. The churches are major contributors to the welfare effort in Australia and are responsible for administering large amounts of government funding as well as their own contributions.

In the media church leaders are sometimes called on to comment on events in society, and in some places clergy have regular radio spots or columns in local newspapers. Most churches advertise through the use of signs, newsletters or letterbox drops.

Congregations may organise specific evangelistic activities or programs to meet community needs. They may have contact with the community through baptisms, marriages and funerals or by allowing community groups to use their property. Churches are often called upon to conduct services to commemorate major moments in history, human tragedies or other significant events.

Individual attenders have networks of family, friends and acquaintances within which they live out the gospel. Attenders can also influence important decisions in their workplace and by participation in the public realm.

Yet in practice many congregations appear to be insular and inward-looking, quite the reverse of the rhetoric of their message. How important is an outward focus to the vitality of a congregation?

Different traditions place different emphases on particular aspects of mission. For many, the essence of mission is evangelism: to communicate the good news about Jesus to all. For others, mission is about living for the good of other people and society, caring for or standing with the poor, the disadvantaged or the hurting. Most attenders seek to hold these different aspects in tension: 16% of church attenders place their priority on evangelism alone, 5% on social action alone and 53% on a mixture of both (Winds of Change, p 61). This chapter explores the relationship between both kinds of activity and congregational vitality.

AN OUTWARD FOCUS

The NCLS asked several questions about the outward focus of congregations. Leaders were asked about the mission activities of their congregation. Attenders were asked about the extent to which their congregation was focused on serving its members or the wider community and the aspects of congregational life they most valued, including outreach and community service activities. From these, some measures of outward focus were developed.

Leaders were also asked about the primary focus of their congregations. Nearly a quarter of leaders (23%) say the focus is on church attenders. Around 50% of leaders see their congregation as having a parish or regional focus. Finally, 27% of leaders see the focus of their congregation as being to all people with whom they come in contact.

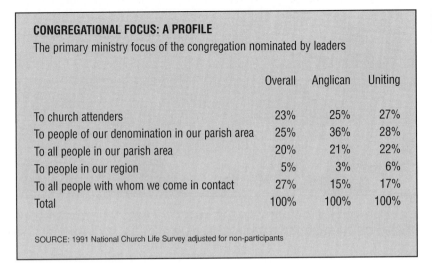

CONGREGATIONAL FOCUS: A PROFILE
The primary ministry focus of the congregation nominated by leaders

	Overall	Anglican	Uniting
To church attenders	23%	25%	27%
To people of our denomination in our parish area	25%	36%	28%
To all people in our parish area	20%	21%	22%
To people in our region	5%	3%	6%
To all people with whom we come in contact	27%	15%	17%
Total	100%	100%	100%

SOURCE: 1991 National Church Life Survey adjusted for non-participants

The relationship between outward focus and vitality is summarised in Figure 11.1. As can be seen, an outward focus is strongly related to most vitality measures. An outward focus is significant in relation to wider community involvement, drawing in newcomers, numerical growth and

FIGURE 11.1: OUTWARD FOCUS OF CONGREGATION

	STRENGTH OF RELATIONSHIPS		
	Focus beyond congregation	Focus on attenders or denominational affiliates	Congregation has an 'activist' orientation
NEWCOMERS	+++ 3.9	− 0.9	++ 1.8
YOUNG ADULT RETENTION	++ 1.3	0.2	+ 0.5
NUMERICAL GROWTH	+++ 4.5	− − 1.7	++ 1.0
SENSE OF BELONGING	+++ 3.3	− 0.9	++ 1.3
COMMUNITY INVOLVEMENT	+++ 4.0	0.0	++ 2.3
SHARING/ INVITING	+++ 4.7	− 0.8	++ 1.8
GROWTH IN FAITH	++++ 7.1	− − 1.1	+++ 3.2

NB: Strength of relationship is the percent of variance explained after accounting for local context/faith type effects
SOURCE: 1991 National Church Life Survey

REVEREND!! SIR! WE CAUGHT THIS YOUNG CHRISTIAN FROM ALL SAINTS CHURCH MINISTERING IN OUR PARISH BOUNDARIES...SIR!!

attender openness to discussing their faith with others or inviting them to church. What is equally significant is the positive relationship with belonging and growth in faith. A focus beyond oneself would appear to result in a more positive experience of congregational life; growth in faith appears related to looking beyond oneself to the needs of others.

As can be seen in Figure 11.1, while the figures are not large, congregations with a primary focus on church attenders or denominational affiliates are less likely to be effective across most indicators. The most significant impact is with numerical growth. Congregations that focus only on church attenders or on affiliates of the same denomination within a parish area are less likely to grow numerically than other congregations. Attenders who are growing in their faith are more likely to be found in congregations which focus on all contacts and less likely to be in those which focus on church attenders or denominational affiliates.

> **Congregations that focus only on church attenders are less likely to grow**

The Anglican and Uniting Churches are two major denominations with parish structures. Further analysis was carried out on these denominations. As with the wider sample, congregations in these denominations which focus on church attenders or the people of their denomination in their parish area are less likely to be growing numerically.

The study also sought to probe the nature of congregational involvement in the wider community by asking attenders to evaluate whether their congregation was 'activist' in orientation (often taking a stand on issues) or more 'educational' (more about providing a forum for the discussion of issues, leaving attenders to get involved as appropriate).

The results are also provided in Figure 11.1. Across nearly all aspects there appears to be a positive relationship between 'activism' and vitality. The educational model appears less likely to promote growth in faith and wider community engagement or to be attractive to newcomers.

EVANGELISTIC ACTIVITIES

Congregations run a wide range of evangelistic activities. The NCLS collected data from leaders about the types of activities being run. It also probed whether attenders value such activities more than other aspects of congregational life and the proportion of attenders involved in these activities.

Some previous research has highlighted the relationship between evangelistic activity and church growth. In a study of Southern Baptists in the United States, Hadaway found that, among a range of factors, evangelistic outreach and recruitment were the most important things churches could do to promote growth (Hadaway, 1991, 192).

EVANGELISTIC ACTIVITIES: A PROFILE
A range of mission activities are run by congregations each year.

- 23% hold evangelistic services or crusades of some kind
- 26% hold evangelistic Bible studies
- 13% have mission activities in schools
- 9% conduct visitation programs
- 8% do street evangelism
- 6% run drop-in centres

See *Mission under the Microscope* p 41 for further details
SOURCE: 1991 National Church Life Survey adjusted for non-participants

Figure 11.2 indicates that the existence of evangelistic activities is less important than the level of attenders being involved in and valuing them.

Not surprisingly, the proportion of attenders who are regularly involved in evangelistic activities is closely related to the proportion of attenders who feel confident to share their faith and invite others to church.

Those at ease discussing their faith may be more likely to get involved in evangelistic activities. Evangelistic activities may also provide a supportive forum for attenders to talk about their faith. In addition, such activities may provide an impetus for attenders to invite others along or to discuss matters of faith.

The involvement of attenders in the evangelistic activities of their congregations is also related to their involvement in the wider community. While this may simply reflect the fact that some activities have both an evangelistic and a community care focus, the result is an interesting one, suggesting that many congregations are broadly 'activist' rather than being exclusively concerned with just social welfare or evangelism.

FIGURE 11.2: EVANGELISTIC ACTIVITIES

	STRENGTH OF RELATIONSHIPS		
	Existence of evangelistic activities	Attender involvement in and valuing of evangelistic activities	Overall impact
NEWCOMERS	++ 1.5	++ 1.7	++ 2.1
YOUNG ADULT RETENTION	0.3	0.0	+ 0.7
NUMERICAL GROWTH	+ 0.9	++ 2.1	++ 2.9
SENSE OF BELONGING	0.4	+++ 3.1	+++ 3.7
COMMUNITY INVOLVEMENT	− 0.7	++++ 6.6	++++ 7.3
SHARING/ INVITING	++ 1.5	+++++ 21.1	+++++ 21.5
GROWTH IN FAITH	++ 2.0	+++ 3.9	+++ 4.8

NB: Strength of relationship is the percent of variance explained after accounting for local context/faith type effects

SOURCE: 1991 National Church Life Survey

Some may also be surprised at the relatively small relationship between evangelistic activities and both numerical growth and levels of newcomers. Other aspects of church life may be more important when planning for mission, even though on the surface they may be less directly related to the mission task.

ST. JUDES EVANGELISM MONTH WAS A GREAT SUCCESS.
THERE WERE NO CONVERTS, BUT THE MEMBERS FELT BETTER AFTERWARDS.

Indeed, it is illuminating to re-examine the conclusions in Chapters 3 and 4 regarding the aspects of congregational life most related to the flow of newcomers and to numerical growth. Many may not be commonly thought of as priorities in planning for mission.

This result also suggests that more newcomers may join through invitations from attenders met in the course of everyday life than through congregational mission activities.

PERSONAL CONTACT

Congregations can be in contact with the wider community through formal events, such as mission activities and Sunday schools, and informally through contact between attenders and other people in their everyday lives. While measuring the levels of contact between attenders and those in the wider community is difficult, the NCLS sought to explore the issue by asking attenders how many non-churchgoers they talked with individually for at least 15 minutes during the past week.

Generally, the levels of everyday contact between attenders and the wider community is not significant to congregational vitality; there is, however, a relationship between levels of contact and the attraction of newcomers.

FIGURE 11.3: CONTACT BEYOND CHURCH

	STRENGTH OF RELATIONSHIPS
	Levels of significant contact with people beyond church life
NEWCOMERS	✚✚ 1.3
YOUNG ADULT RETENTION	✚ 0.5
NUMERICAL GROWTH	✚ 0.8
SENSE OF BELONGING	0.2
COMMUNITY INVOLVEMENT	0.4
SHARING/INVITING	✚ 0.6
GROWTH IN FAITH	0.2

NB: Strength of relationship is the percent of variance explained after accounting for local context/faith type effects

SOURCE: 1991 National Church Life Survey

The number of contacts attenders have with those in the community will not promote congregational vitality. Far more important is what attenders do with the contacts they have. Attenders who have many community contacts are no more or less likely to feel comfortable discussing their faith. However, those with more contacts are more likely to have actually shared their faith with others (*Mission under the Microscope*, p 11). A wide range of contacts may be a helpful asset in evangelism; encouraging personal contacts without helping attenders to be comfortable discussing their faith is unlikely to be an effective mission strategy.

PERSONAL EVANGELISM

Many congregations encourage attenders to 'bloom where they are planted'. Rather than relying on 'cold contact' evangelism of strangers, congregations encourage attenders to share their faith with their families, friends, neighbours and colleagues. The key to numerical growth is often seen as the willingness of attenders to invite people with whom they have built relationships into the life of the church.

More newcomers join through personal invitation than through congregational mission activities

As can be seen in Figure 11.4, sharing faith and inviting others to church is related to congregational vitality. A comparison with the data in Figure 11.2 shows that readiness to share faith and invite others to church appear to be more important than regular involvement in the mission

FIGURE 11.4: DISCUSSION OF FAITH/INVITING TO CHURCH

	STRENGTH OF RELATIONSHIPS		
	Readiness to share faith with others	Inviting others to church	Overall impact
NEWCOMERS	✚✚ 2.7	✚✚✚ 3.5	✚✚✚✚ 5.4
YOUNG ADULT RETENTION	✚✚ 1.6	✚ 0.7	✚✚ 2.2
NUMERICAL GROWTH	✚ 0.6	✚✚✚ 3.5	✚✚✚ 3.6
SENSE OF BELONGING	✚✚✚ 3.4	✚✚✚✚ 6.5	✚✚✚✚ 8.0
COMMUNITY INVOLVEMENT	✚✚ 1.9	✚✚ 1.6	✚✚✚ 3.1
SHARING/ INVITING	N/A	N/A	N/A
GROWTH IN FAITH	✚✚✚✚ 5.3	✚✚✚✚ 8.7	✚✚✚✚✚ 10.6

1. NB: Strength of relationship is the percent of variance explained after accounting for local context/faith type effects
2. N/A: Not Applicable

SOURCE: 1991 National Church Life Survey

activities of the congregation in relation to levels of newcomers and numerical growth.

Willingness to share faith and invite others to church are *important* in relation to numerical growth and *very important* in regard to the flow of newcomers. Taken together, a willingness to share faith and invite others to church is one of the most important factors in this survey in predicting the flow of newcomers.

As significant as congregational evangelistic activities may be, this study suggests that, for most congregations, personal evangelism may be of greater significance. It will be essential for congregational leaders to address the issues of helping attenders to be comfortable discussing their faith with others, given that 25% find it hard to do so and another 17% feel their life and actions are sufficient (see Chapter 6). It will also be important to have frank discussions about how attenders feel about inviting others to church.

Leaders need to help attenders be comfortable discussing their faith

There also is a strong link between being comfortable about discussing faith with others and a sense of belonging and growth in faith. No doubt each reinforces the other.

SOCIAL CONCERN ACTIVITIES

Congregations engage in a wide range of community care and service activities. Almost half of all congregations (46%) allow community groups to use congregational property. About 35% of congregations are directly involved in providing welfare services such as counselling or opportunity shops, 32% run mothers groups, play groups, craft groups and so on and 27% participate in special community activities such as peace marches and community fairs. Around 45% of all congregations have representatives on community groups or committees.

Because it is based on a survey of attenders, the NCLS has no way of hearing the voice of people served by the mission activities of a congregation but not actively involved in its life. Further, most social care or social action activities arise from compassion for others in response to a perceived need or injustice. Their value needs to be understood from that perspective.

What is being evaluated here is the benefit to a congregation of social care activities rather than their overall merit.

Raymond Fung argues that Christians who become partners with people in the community, working together to meet their needs, will communicate the church's vision more effectively and lead others to join the Christian community (Fung, 1992, 39–41). The church's message will be more credible in the community as a result of the church caring for people in need and actively pursuing public policies which affect the welfare of all Australians (Nichols, 1984, 71).

The NCLS results provide some support for these views. Involvement in wider community care activities is related to numerical growth, evidence that an activity which is not overtly evangelistic may still assist growth.

Such activities may relate to numerical growth in several ways. They may provide forums for relationships to develop and invitations to church to be extended, they may give a congregation a higher profile in the community, or they may help attenders to feel more at ease inviting others to join.

COMMUNITY LINKS: A PROFILE

Congregations make links with the wider community in a variety of ways:
- 46% allow community groups to use their property
- 45% are represented on community groups/committees
- 35% provide welfare services or facilities to meet needs
- 32% provide for common interest groups (eg playgroups, adult education, etc)
- 27% participate in community activities (eg community fairs, peace marches)
- 11% run aged-care activities or schools for seniors

See *Mission under the Microscope* p 39 for further details.

SOURCE: 1991 National Church Life Survey adjusted for non-participants

Focusing on the needs of others may be a key to personal growth for attenders

Community links are also related to growth in faith and are *important* in relation to sharing faith and inviting others to church. Focusing on the needs and concerns of others may well be a key to personal growth for many attenders; in serving others attenders may themselves be transformed.

FIGURE 11.5: SOCIAL CONCERN ACTIVITIES

	STRENGTH OF RELATIONSHIPS		
	Existence of links with the wider community	Attender involvement in and valuing of community care activities	Overall impact
NEWCOMERS	0.3	0.0	✚ 0.5
YOUNG ADULT RETENTION	✚ 0.5	0.3	✚ 0.7
NUMERICAL GROWTH	✚ 0.9	✚✚ 1.9	✚✚ 2.4
SENSE OF BELONGING	0.4	✚✚ 2.2	✚✚ 2.4
COMMUNITY INVOLVEMENT	✚✚ 1.4	N/A	N/A
SHARING/ INVITING	✚ 0.7	✚✚✚ 3.6	✚✚✚ 3.8
GROWTH IN FAITH	✚✚ 1.0	✚✚ 1.3	✚✚ 2.1

1. NB: Strength of relationship is the percent of variance explained after accounting for local context/faith type effects
2. N/A: Not Applicable

SOURCE: 1991 National Church Life Survey

RITES OF PASSAGE

It is common for people to want to have children baptised or to want to be married in church, irrespective of whether or not they attend church. The majority of funerals are also carried out by clergy. About 11% of all newcomers first go to a baptism, wedding or funeral connected with the congregation that they now attend (*Mission under the Microscope*, p 102).

Are congregations which perform higher numbers of baptisms, marriages or funerals for those not involved in congregational life likely to have more newcomers? Detailed analysis not presented here suggests the flow of newcomers into church life is not connected to the number of such ceremonies performed. Neither is the number of ceremonies related to other measures of vitality. Perhaps it is more a question of the way these opportunities are handled and the relationships that are built up during the preparation.

ADVERTISING

The majority of congregations in Australia pursue some form of advertising: 69% advertise their activities through a newsletter, form letter or letterbox drop; 53% use signboards, posters or community notice boards; and 61% use magazine or newspaper advertisements. Some 17% use radio or other media.

Some writers claim that advertising campaigns can make a difference to the effectiveness of a congregation (eg Schaller, 1987, 220). Others are less convinced of its value. Barna notes that while newspaper advertisements can be effective to some extent, a personal invitation is far more effective in attracting newcomers. He suggests that, unless professionally developed and placed, advertising has little impact (1988, 53 and 108).

The NCLS shows that what Barna says is also true in Australia, where just 1% of attenders began at their current congregation as a result of seeing a newsletter, advertisement, or signboard (*Winds of Change*, p 155). This study found little relationship between advertising and congregational vitality.

AN OPTIONAL EXTRA?

It is important to acknowledge the limitations of this study in relation to evaluating the impact of mission activities in the wider community. The NCLS examines the impact of mission activities on congregations; it does not examine their contribution to the well-being of the community itself.

Clearly an outward focus is an important characteristic of vital congregations. An outward focus is important in relation to most indicators, including those concerned with the building up of existing attenders. A congregation seeking to become more effective would do well to look beyond itself to the needs and aspirations of those around them. Far from being an optional extra, an outward focus is a core characteristic of effective congregations.

While congregational mission activities can be important in relation to numerical growth and levels of newcomers, the willingness of individual attenders to invite others into church life is more important. Attenders need to be helped to discover how to live out and express their faith in all aspects of their lives. The role of the congregation is not necessarily to provide its own mission activities, but to support and foster the individual endeavours of its attenders in their daily lives.

This is not to say that congregational mission activities are unimportant, since they are positively related to vitality, particularly a readiness among attenders to share their faith and invite others to church. Such activities may help reinforce an outward focus. They may provide an important avenue for attenders to express their faith in actions and gain confidence in sharing their faith with integrity.

BEING INTENTIONAL ABOUT MISSION

This chapter suggests that not only the extent of but also the nature of an outward focus is important to the vitality of a congregation. Simply educating attenders and leaving responses up to the individual appears inadequate; a more active outward orientation is positively related to all aspects of vitality.

In a study of church life in Hartford in the United States, congregations were classified in terms of the way each defined its relationship with its community:

- *Activist:* Congregations actively engaged in wider community life, often with high levels of social action, both as a congregation and by individual attenders.
- *Civic:* Congregations which are outwardly focused but place more emphasis on individual Christian responsibility. These tend to be more affirming of dominant community values and structures, and take a more educational role, leaving the individual to shape his or her own response.
- *Sanctuary:* Such congregations are more focused internally on providing attenders with a refuge from the world rather than encouraging outward engagement.
- *Evangelistic:* Having much in common with the sanctuary model, these congregations are, however, more activist in the wider community in the area of verbal proclamation of the gospel message (Roozen, McKinney and Carroll, 1984, 34–36).

The Urban Church Project in London created a similar typology of congregations, categorising them in terms of 'introverted isolation' through 'caring activism' or 'aggressive evangelism' to 'incarnational mission'. This final category involves an activist approach, incorporating both social concern and evangelism (Browning, 1986, 83).

Reflecting on experiences in inner-city Melbourne, Australian priest Ron Browning finds a movement towards 'incarnational mission' is desirable and the most faithful form of Christian mission. Members of the congregation seek, unjudgingly, to be part of the lives of others and to communicate their motivation for that involvement. Those outside of the church life develop a sense of belonging to the church through their association with the church members, though they may themselves rarely attend the worship services (1986, 84, 85).

Not everybody would agree with Browning's position. In practice many congregations operate from quite a different model that Martin Robinson describes as 'growth by attractive worship theory' (1992, 44). This approach is often practised by churches of a Pentecostal or charismatic background and relies on attenders being committed and excited enough about congregational life to invite others to participate.

In practice the two approaches need not be seen as mutually exclusive, and congregations would do well to consider both the extent to which attenders are earthed in the life of the wider community and the extent to which they are excited enough and comfortable about inviting friends and contacts to come along to church activities.

CHAPTER 12

BODY LIFE THAT WORKS

A Congregation that Plays Together Stays Together!

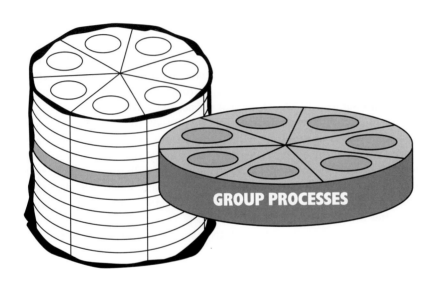

GROUP PROCESSES

One of the issues facing Australian society in the 1990s is a redefinition of community. Some remember with nostalgia local communities where agreed values were upheld and local institutions such as the church were the focus of community life.

Much has changed in the last 40 years. Local communities in urban areas have become dormitory suburbs, where people eat and sleep but may have little to do with their neighbour. Many people spend much of their time associating with workmates and friends who live in entirely different regions.

For some, the glittering face of the city masks a sense of loneliness created by a lack of sufficient relationships. Many Australians are searching for community and for meaning. Social commentator Hugh Mackay suggests that churches should become places of community at a time when community identification had declined (*The Australian* 23/6/94).

Defining exactly what is meant by 'community' is fraught with difficulty. However, one important point of consensus is that community involves some sense of belonging and identification with an area or group of people.

Most attenders feel a strong and growing sense of belonging to their congregation. Overall, 81% of attenders have high levels of belonging. This comprises 61% of attenders who have a strong sense of belonging which is growing, and 20% who have a strong sense of belonging which is about the same as the previous year (*Winds of Change*, p 137).

Community also encompasses the quality of interactions between attenders. Will congregations where interactions between attenders are positive also be more open to the wider community in word and deed, will more attenders be growing in their faith, and will they be better at drawing in newcomers or retaining existing attenders? Or do such congregations become insular and inward looking, where new arrivals leave after finding it too hard to break in?

This chapter focuses on various aspects of the group life of congregations. In particular, it examines
- feelings about congregational involvement
- caring relationships within the congregation
- friends and communication within the congregation, and levels of conflict.

FEELINGS ABOUT INVOLVEMENT

Attenders were asked how they were feeling about their congregation. Possible responses included 'excited', 'positive', 'apathetic', 'over-extended' and 'discouraged'.

Figure 12.1 also includes, for completeness, the relationship between patterns of belonging in a congregation and other indicators of vitality.

Attenders' feelings about congregational life are related to congregational vitality, particularly to a sense of belonging and growth in faith, but also to the flow of newcomers and numerical growth. Congregations which have high proportions of attenders who feel discouraged, apathetic or over-extended tend to have lower proportions of newcomers. Similarly, congregations with high proportions of discouraged attenders are less likely to be growing numerically.

Congregations with discouraged attenders are less likely to be growing numerically

These findings are quite important. Exhorting attenders to do more may not result in either numerical growth or an increase in the proportion of newcomers. It could be that attenders become so fatigued that they are unable to engage in the life and mission of the congregation with any enthusiasm.

Newcomers are more likely to be in congregations where attenders invite others to participate in congregational life. Attenders who are discouraged or negative about their congregation will be less likely to invite others, resulting in an inevitable decline in the level of newcomers.

Congregations with high levels of newcomers tend to have higher levels of attenders feeling excited or positive about congregational life. Also, as is shown in Figure 12.1, while it takes newcomers time to grow a sense of belonging, non-newcomers in high newcomer congregations in fact tend to have higher levels of belonging than is the case in other congregations.

FIGURE 12.1: FEELINGS ABOUT CONGREGATIONAL INVOLVEMENT

	STRENGTH OF RELATIONSHIPS	
	Attenders feel positive about involvement	Sense of belonging
NEWCOMERS	++ 2.2	++ 2.9
YOUNG ADULT RETENTION	++ 1.5	0.0
NUMERICAL GROWTH	+++ 4.4	++++ 5.7
SENSE OF BELONGING	+++++ 29.9	N/A
COMMUNITY INVOLVEMENT	– – 1.1	++ 1.6
SHARING/ INVITING	++ 2.8	+++ 3.2
GROWTH IN FAITH	+++++ 14.6	+++++ 16.4

1. NB: Strength of relationship is the percent of variance explained after accounting for local context/faith type effects
2. N/A: Not Applicable

SOURCE: 1991 National Church Life Survey

Congregations with high levels of wider community involvement tend to have higher levels of belonging but also higher levels of attenders feeling discouraged with congregational life. While such community group involvement may be positive, it may also be a warning signal to some congregations; attenders may have become disillusioned enough with their congregation that they are detaching from it and seeking fulfilment in outside community groups.

Congregations that want to be vital and effective will need to explore why attenders feel over-extended, apathetic or discouraged. Understanding may be a first step to moving forward.

FEELINGS ABOUT CHURCH: A PROFILE

- 66% of attenders feel positive about their congregations; but only 13% feel excited.
- 14% feel apathetic, over-extended or discouraged and 7% are unsure how they feel.
- Attenders at Pentecostal congregations are the most likely to feel excited about church (34%).
- 61% of attenders have a growing sense of belonging to their congregation, while 15% feel it is declining or they do not feel as though they belong.

SOURCE: 1991 National Church Life Survey adjusted for non-participants

FRIENDS AND CARING RELATIONSHIPS

The Bible likens the Christian church to a body made up of many parts. When one part of the body suffers all the other parts suffer with it. This implies a high level of personal interaction, that attenders are in such close relationship that what affects one affects the rest.

Whitehead and Whitehead (1982, 54) observe that personal communication should not be left to chance. Many congregations fail to provide opportunities for members to share with and offer each other mutual support. Congregations that do not do this, they conclude, will not survive long as communities. In order to realise their potential for community, people need an openness towards others, a capacity for commitment, and some tolerance for the ambiguities both in themselves and in other people (Whitehead and Whitehead, 1982, 114, 121).

Mallison (1996, 9,10) feels that small groups are essential for giving people an opportunity to love one another. For Christians, being involved intimately with others is not an optional extra. Callahan suggests that many congregations are ineffective because they become preoccupied with programs and lose sight of the people whose needs the programs are intended to meet (1983, 39).

Around 70% of attenders have some or all of their closest friends in their congregation. Only 9% have little relationship with others in their congregation (*Winds of Change*, p 132).

Attenders were also asked to select two aspects of congregational life they most valued. Some 34% selected being part of a caring congregation, a further 4% enjoyable social activities, and another 5% the chance to meet new people (*Winds of Change*, p 185). For many church attenders, their congregation is more than just a place to go for worship and other programs; it is also a social unit where they have close friendships with others.

CONGREGATIONAL VITALITY AND RELATIONSHIPS

Research overseas suggests that friendship is a significant factor in congregational vitality. Is the same true in Australian congregations?

As shown in Figure 12.2, being part of a caring congregation and having friends in the congregation are *very important* when it comes to developing a sense of belonging. This result is not surprising, but it does underline the need for relationships with others if a person is going to feel part of a congregation.

Congregations with higher levels of wider community involvement also tend to have more close friendships between attenders. Again, wider community involvement does not appear to be hampered by close friendship bonds within the congregation. Rather, the reverse seems to be true.

Friendship and being in a caring congregation has less impact on other measures of vitality. Being part of a caring congregation is only *marginally* related to numerical growth and of *some importance* to growth in faith. Overall, it appears that the relational aspects of church life, while important in themselves and a critical ingredient of belonging, are of less importance in distinguishing congregations on other aspects of vitality.

Friendship has less impact on most measures of vitality

FRIENDLINESS TOWARDS NEWCOMERS

Whatever the reality, the majority of attenders think that their congregation is friendly to new arrivals at church. Effective congregations are, however, more likely to have a higher proportion of attenders who feel

FIGURE 12.2: FRIENDS IN THE CONGREGATION

	STRENGTH OF RELATIONSHIPS	
	Levels of close friendship/being in a caring congregation	Friendliness towards newcomers
NEWCOMERS	0.3	0.2
YOUNG ADULT RETENTION	0.3	0.5
NUMERICAL GROWTH	✚ 0.6	✚✚ 2.4
SENSE OF BELONGING	✚✚✚✚ 5.6	✚✚✚✚✚ 16.3
COMMUNITY INVOLVEMENT	✚✚✚ 3.4	✚ 0.6
SHARING/ INVITING	0.4	✚✚ 1.1
GROWTH IN FAITH	✚✚ 1.6	✚✚ 2.8

NB: Strength of relationship is the percent of variance explained after accounting for local context/faith type effects

SOURCE: 1991 National Church Life Survey

this way. Figure 12.2 shows that friendliness to newcomers is *critical* in regard to a strong sense of belonging and of *some importance* in several other areas.

Interestingly, while perceived friendliness to new arrivals is related to numerical growth, it is not related to the flow of newcomers into congregational life. Is it because 'welcoming churches' are more welcoming towards people who are like themselves, that is, people who are switching or transferring from another congregation? Or is it because newcomers to church life prefer anonymity or are sometimes uncomfortable about the welcome they receive?

A key part of growing the Christian body is the integration of new arrivals into the life of the congregation. Of all new arrivals (switchers, transfers and newcomers) around 80% first attend a worship service. Another 5% first attend a baptism, wedding or funeral at their congregation, and a further 3% first attend a Christmas or Easter service. In total, nine out of every ten attenders attend a church service of some kind as their first contact with their congregation (*Mission under the Microscope*, p 102).

It would seem important, then, that new arrivals are made to feel welcome at the worship service. Some congregations opt for intentional welcoming programs, rostering regular attenders to be on the lookout for new arrivals and to make them welcome. As Peter Corney notes in *The Welcoming Church*: 'Jobs that are everybody's tend to be left to everybody else, and therefore don't get done' (1992, 20). Schaller considers a 'cadre'

MARGARET BECAME THE FIRST PARISHIONER TO BE ASKED **NOT** TO WELCOME PEOPLE.

of greeters to be an 'essential, but often ignored, component of the church growth strategy' (1983, 74).

However, others emphasise widespread congregational commitment to welcoming new arrivals. The existence of a welcoming party or even a defined process of integration into the congregation is not as important as the members of the church being friendly, open, and wanting to include new members in what they are doing (Oswald and Leas, 1987, 17, 18; Johnson, 1989, 56). In his study of previously unchurched Christians, Rauff found that the warm welcome given by the congregation, and the confidence of attenders in the worth of their congregation, were important factors in conveying benefits of church attendance to outsiders (Rauff, 1979, 201).

While friendliness towards new arrivals is positively related to congregational vitality, it is, in fact, negatively related to congregational size. In other words, as congregations grow larger they are perceived by their attenders to be less and less friendly towards newcomers. Given that there is a relationship between friendliness and numerical growth, this suggests that congregations need to work harder and more intentionally on friendliness as they become larger.

In around 30% of congregations, integration generally happens in informal ways. The remaining 70% make use of a range of strategies, including follow-up visits, hospitality, orientation programs and groups of various types. Larger congregations are more likely to use groups or courses to promote integration; the larger the congregation the more they need formal ways to make others welcome.

Congregational leaders may find it helpful to talk to newcomers about their experience in joining the congregation. This will throw light on the effectiveness of existing approaches towards helping newcomers to fit into the congregation (Oswald and Leas, 1987, 78).

ABIGAIL FIRMLY BELIEVED THAT A THRIVING CHURCH COMMUNITY NEEDED EFFECTIVE COMMUNICATION.

COMMUNICATION WITHIN THE CONGREGATION

Many writers agree that, of all group processes, communication is one of the most critical to the effective functioning of a congregation. Croucher (1991, 23–25) suggests that congregational leaders should create a number of communication channels to allow attenders to know more of what happens at leaders meetings. Feedback by way of formal and informal means should also be encouraged.

Clear and open communication channels involve careful listening as well as clear expression of a point of view. Feelings as well as content need to be both expressed and heard. Openness and honesty in communication are required if sound decisions are to result. Proper communication channels must be established so that everyone knows whom to talk to about what.

To evaluate how open the channels of communication within congregational life are, the NCLS asked attenders whether they felt that people in their congregation were often unaware of what committees and groups in the congregation were doing.

As can be seen in Figure 12.3, good communication is *very important* for promoting a sense of belonging and of *some importance* in some other areas.

Another aspect of communication is the degree to which conflict is open or hidden. Finney contrasts unhealthy churches, where issues are buried and fester, with healthy churches, where tensions are out in the

FIGURE 12.3: COMMUNICATION				
	STRENGTH OF RELATIONSHIPS			
	Awareness of what committees/groups are doing		Attenders ready to confront each other	
NEWCOMERS	✚	0.7	✚	0.9
YOUNG ADULT RETENTION		0.0		0.0
NUMERICAL GROWTH	✚✚	1.6	✚✚	1.5
SENSE OF BELONGING	✚✚✚✚	5.0	✚✚✚	4.2
COMMUNITY INVOLVEMENT		0.0	✚✚	2.2
SHARING/ INVITING		0.3	✚✚	2.1
GROWTH IN FAITH	✚✚	1.1	✚✚✚	3.5

NB: Strength of relationship is the percent of variance explained after accounting for local context/faith type effects

SOURCE: 1991 National Church Life Survey

open (Finney, 1991, 18). Honesty with one another is a key aspect of community, including agreeing to disagree or pointing out where behaviour has been inappropriate.

The NCLS asked attenders whether people at their congregation are generally willing to confront or correct one another where necessary. A willingness to confront others with concerns is of *some importance* or *marginal* in relation to most aspects of congregational vitality and *important* for developing a sense of belonging and growth in faith. However, as will be seen in the next section, willingness to confront others does not generally outweigh the negative impacts of conflict.

LEVELS OF CONFLICT

If friendship and being part of a caring congregation enhance congregational vitality and effectiveness, what is the effect of conflict?

In the United States, Olson found that congregations which had experienced serious conflict over theological, social, financial or other issues in the previous ten years were less likely to grow numerically than churches which had not experienced such conflicts (Olson, 1993, 219). A study of Episcopalian congregations found that those which were successfully assimilating new members had low levels of conflict and disunity (Oswald and Leas, 1987, 25).

FIGURE 12.4: THE IMPACT OF CONFLICT

	STRENGTH OF RELATIONSHIPS	
	Conflict currently exists	Previous conflict had negative results
NEWCOMERS	0.0	0.0
YOUNG ADULT RETENTION	▬ ▬ 1.4	0.5
NUMERICAL GROWTH	▬ ▬ ▬ 4.1	▬ ▬ ▬ ▬ 6.0
SENSE OF BELONGING	▬ ▬ ▬ ▬ ▬ 11.8	▬ ▬ ▬ ▬ 9.3
COMMUNITY INVOLVEMENT	▬ ▬ ▬ 4.6	▬ ▬ 2.8
SHARING/ INVITING	0.1	0.3
GROWTH IN FAITH	▬ 0.7	▬ ▬ 2.4

NB: Strength of relationship is the percent of variance explained after accounting for local context/faith type effects

SOURCE: 1991 National Church Life Survey

The NCLS found that 13% of congregational leaders reported that people or the minister had left their congregation over the past two years because of conflict. A further 13% said that reduced communication or cooperation had resulted from conflict.

In congregations where serious conflict existed, the major consequences had been evenly spread between the minister or people leaving and between reduced cooperation/communication and improved co-operation/communication. While good can come from serious conflict, there had clearly also been significant damage.

The presence of ongoing conflict is strongly detrimental to congregational vitality. Conflict is particularly detrimental to growth in numbers, to attenders feeling a strong sense of belonging, and to encouraging wider community involvement. This suggests that it is in the best interests of congregations to resolve conflict quickly and amicably.

Ongoing conflict is strongly detrimental to congregational vitality

While a history of conflict is not as strongly related to congregational vitality as current conflict, it does have some impact. Although congregational effectiveness need not be permanently dulled by conflict, congregations can carry the legacy of conflict for some time. This reinforces the need to get conflict resolved.

Interestingly, further analysis suggests that the cause of the conflict does not appear to make a difference. The existence of conflict is damaging to congregations regardless of the issue at stake.

CONFLICT IN THE CHURCH : A PROFILE

- How much conflict is there in our churches?

  44% of leaders feel conflict has been evident in their congregation in the past two years made up of
  - 25% where it is easily resolved
  - 16% where it can only be resolved with much effort
  - 4% where there appears to be no clear solution

  On this basis, serious conflict exists in one in every five congregations.

- Serious conflict is most evident to the congregational leaders of large Protestant denominations (28%) — Baptist, Churches of Christ, and Salvation Army — as well as some small Protestant denominations. It is least evident to congregational leaders of mainstream and Pentecostal denominations.

- What type of conflict is evident in congregations? Leaders, who could select two, cite the following conflicts:
  - 45% because of differences in personality
  - 33% over procedures or ways of doing things
  - 23% over goals, purpose or vision of the church
  - 21% about power and control
  - 14% differences in theology/doctrine
  - 9% role conflict

SOURCE: 1991 National Church Life Survey adjusted for non-participants

PASTOR!! SIR!! THE MANAGEMENT COMMITTEE SUGGEST THAT WE AREN'T IN A GOOD POSITION TO BARGAIN, BUT THEY WILL CONSIDER MOVING THE COMMUNION TABLE ... IF WE CEASE HOSTILITIES.

BODY LIFE THAT WORKS

A living congregation is not programmatic in character but is a 'highly relational organism that stems from a person-to-person kind of ministry' (George 1994, 71). The NCLS results presented here support such a statement. Relational concerns such as friendship, communication, being part of a caring congregation, and developing a sense of belonging are all associated with congregational vitality.

In seeking to develop effective congregations, leaders may want to encourage attenders to be more involved in congregational activities. Yet there is a need for balance. Congregations where attenders feel over-extended, apathetic or discouraged will be less effective in mission. In some circumstances, leaders may need to rationalise activities and find ways to renew and refresh attenders.

Several of the aspects of group life examined here tend to be hard to maintain with increasing congregational size. As congregations grow numerically, it is especially important for them to review how best to encourage a positive group life. People can feel part of the bigger entity if the leaders continue to explain how each aspect of congregational life fits into the whole. 'People don't mind being cogs if they have an understanding of the whole machine' (Finney 1991, 77).

One of the sad facts of church life is that congregations are damaged by conflict. Relationships can break down and an irretrievable split can occur. Often the split is along generational lines or is a result of strong factions. Irrespective of the issues at stake, such conflict is detrimental to congregational vitality unless it is carefully worked through, and even then it may take time to grow beyond the hurts of the experience.

It may not be the presence or absence of conflict that is the key issue but how conflict is handled. An absence of conflict may simply be a sign of domineering leadership (Callahan, 1983, 58) or of a lack of real vision over which disagreement could take place (Herald, 1989, 12).

This is not to suggest that difficult issues should be avoided at all costs or swept under the carpet. Indeed, congregations where attenders are willing to confront each other where necessary are more likely to be vital and effective than those where issues are suppressed or hidden. It is important for congregations to weigh up the benefits of confronting issues against the negative impact of open conflict. This suggests that it is important for congregations to manage differences well, create positive processes for communication and discussion and, where possible, avoid sliding into open conflict. There is much good literature on working through conflict, and leaders in congregations would be well advised to be familiar with it.

MANAGING CONFLICT: SOME ISSUES TO BEAR IN MIND
- Keep channels of communication open
- Depersonalise dissent
- Look inside the other person's frame of reference
- Allow the opportunity for creative and meaningful participation by every person
- Keep opening new opportunities for people to invest themselves in ministry
- Seek agreement on short-term goals
- Study 1 Corinthians 12
- Build mutual trust
- Establish a grievance committee
- Recognise events or facts that paralyse the congregation

(Schaller, 1986, 169–172)

CHAPTER 13

MOVING FORWARD TOGETHER

Lay Leadership, Decision Making and Change

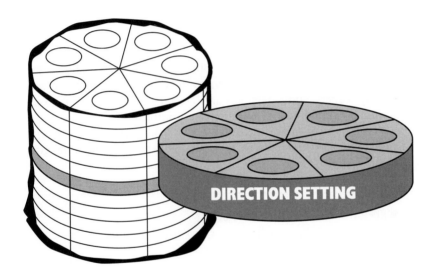

DIRECTION SETTING

135

The previous chapter examined some key aspects of group life within a congregation. This chapter focuses on some other aspects of congregational life: roles in leadership, congregational direction setting and decision making.

These are important issues: holding roles indicates the degree to which leadership responsibility is distributed, direction setting indicates a level of intentionality about congregational life, while involvement in decision making indicates how authority is distributed.

Many writers on congregational vitality and growth suggest there is a need for congregations to plan more intentionally for their future and to move in new directions. How important is it for a congregation to have a vision for where it is heading and for that vision to be owned and capable of being achieved?

ATTENDERS IN LEADERSHIP

ATTENDERS WITH ROLES

Many roles in congregational life are filled by attenders. There are lay preachers and administrators, elders and Sunday school teachers, servers and worship leaders, choir members and greeters. There are small-group leaders, property committees, treasurers, and outreach leaders. Many see the spreading of roles among attenders as an outworking of the teaching in the Bible about spiritual gifts: each person in the body of Christ has gifts to offer the church.

ATTENDERS' ROLES AT CHURCH: A PROFILE

- 37% of attenders have official roles of some kind (12% in teaching/ministry, 10% administrative, 5% both, 1% employed, 9% other) while 13% have an informal or unofficial role. About half of all attenders (50%) think they do not have a role.

- There is a high degree of uniformity across denominations regarding the proportion of attenders with roles. The Seventh-day Adventist church has the highest proportion of attenders with roles of some kind (65%).

- In Pentecostal denominations the proportion of attenders with teaching/ministry roles (20%) is three times higher than those with administrative roles (7%).

- In Uniting, Presbyterian and Seventh-day Adventist churches at least 20% of attenders have administrative roles.

SOURCE: 1991 National Church Life Survey adjusted for non-participants

Half of all attenders have some kind of role in their congregation (*Winds of Change*, pp 118, 119). It might be expected that in numerically growing congregations higher proportions of attenders have some kind of role; the more hands there are, the more work that can be done.

However, as can be seen in Figure 13.1, there is only a *marginal* relationship between the proportion of attenders with roles and the numerical growth of the congregation. Furthermore, this relationship is negative in that congregations which are growing are likely to have lower levels of attenders with roles. Presumably many new attenders in growing congregations have not taken on specific roles.

The proportion of attenders with roles is strongly linked to the proportion involved in community service activities. It would appear that high levels of ministry in the congregation and mission in the wider community are complementary rather than competing agendas.

Ministry in the congregation and mission in the wider community are complementary agendas

FIGURE 13.1: ATTENDER ROLES IN CONGREGATIONAL LIFE

	STRENGTH OF RELATIONSHIPS		
	Levels of attenders with roles	More attenders in teaching/ministry roles than administrative roles	Support for those with roles
NEWCOMERS	━ ━ ━ 3.9	✚✚ 1.7	✚✚ 1.1
YOUNG ADULT RETENTION	✚✚ 1.6	✚✚ 1.2	0.4
NUMERICAL GROWTH	━ 1.0	✚ 0.8	✚✚ 2.0
SENSE OF BELONGING	✚ 0.8	0.2	✚✚✚✚✚ 21.3
COMMUNITY INVOLVEMENT	✚✚✚✚ 5.8	━ ━ 1.1	✚✚ 2.5
SHARING/ INVITING	✚✚✚ 3.7	✚ 0.7	✚✚✚ 3.0
GROWTH IN FAITH	━ 1.0	✚ 0.6	✚✚✚✚ 9.6

NB: Strength of relationship is the percent of variance explained after accounting for local context/faith type effects

SOURCE: 1991 National Church Life Survey

Other relationships are not as strong; some are positive, some negative. The proportion of attenders with roles is negatively related to the proportion of newcomers in the congregation. Further analysis suggests that this is because newcomers themselves, who tend to be young or may be on the fringe of congregational life, are less likely to have a role in the congregation, rather than this being a general congregational characteristic.

It has sometimes been said that it is more important for attenders to be involved in teaching and ministry roles than to hold church offices or carry out administrative tasks. This study suggests there is some truth to this. As can be seen in Figure 13.1 congregations where there is a higher proportion of attenders in teaching or ministry roles than in administrative roles tend to be more vital in all aspects except wider community involvement.

SUPPORT FOR THOSE WITH ROLES

Attenders were asked whether they believe that people with particular responsibilities and roles in their congregation receive adequate support. The results are also shown in Figure 13.1. There is a *critical* relationship between having a sense of belonging and believing that people with roles are given adequate support. There is also a relationship with nearly all other aspects of vitality.

If the results in regard to roles are mixed, in regard to support for people in roles they are clear-cut. Support for those with roles would seem to be more important to congregations than the actual levels of attenders with roles.

Attenders with leadership roles require support for what they do. This support can take a number of forms: affirmation by the congregation and its leaders, financial or administrative assistance, or hands-on help with the tasks being undertaken.

Even permission to be adventurous in a role may be a significant form of support. Kennon Callahan stresses the need for congregations to encourage improvisation, even if mistakes are made. If the atmosphere is one of blame, attenders may be frustrated in their roles (Callahan, 1990, 220). On the other hand, support may involve setting boundaries for roles, helping attenders to be more focused, and preventing roles becoming so large that attenders experience burnout.

MOVING IN NEW DIRECTIONS

Denominations and congregations are being challenged to plan creatively for the future while preserving the core values and traditions of their heritage. Rising to this challenge can create tensions within congregations as conflicting priorities and preferences are expressed. Just how important is it for congregations to be open to new directions or to be actively pursuing new directions?

AN OPENNESS TO NEW INITIATIVES

The NCLS underlines the importance of openness to new initiatives. Figure 13.2 shows that an openness to new initiatives is *critical* in relation to developing a sense of belonging. Where a mistrust of new initiatives exists, attenders are less likely to feel that they belong. This could indicate a breakdown in communication and relationships more generally.

An openness to new initiatives is *important* in relation to numerical growth and the level of newcomers. Again, the study suggests that an openness to new ideas and new directions is an important part of the

FIGURE 13.2: OPENNESS TO NEW INITIATIVES

	STRENGTH OF RELATIONSHIPS	
	Congregation is open to new initiatives	Congregation is moving in new directions
NEWCOMERS	+++ 3.2	++ 2.8
YOUNG ADULT RETENTION	+ 0.6	++ 1.7
NUMERICAL GROWTH	+++ 4.9	++++ 8.4
SENSE OF BELONGING	+++++ 10.4	+++++ 22.2
COMMUNITY INVOLVEMENT	▬▬ 2.2	▬▬ 1.4
SHARING/ INVITING	++ 2.4	++ 1.5
GROWTH IN FAITH	++++ 5.4	++++ 8.5

NB: Strength of relationship is the percent of variance explained after accounting for local context/faith type effects

SOURCE: 1991 National Church Life Survey

environment within which a congregation can grow numerically. Rigid adherence to traditions, holding on to power, or a refusal to even contemplate change can stifle growth. These attitudes and behaviour convey an expectation that visitors and newcomers must fit into established patterns.

A refusal to contemplate change can stifle growth

Openness to new initiatives is also a *very important* characteristic of congregations where attenders are growing in faith. In such congregations, attenders may feel less attached to existing programs, to the buildings, or to other aspects of congregational life about which changes may be proposed. Possibly growth in faith has been a product of being stretched by going in new directions. Many attenders attest to how their faith grows when they move in new directions and are forced to depend on God.

Several writers have suggested that openness to new initiatives is an important characteristic of vital congregations. Some suggest that effective congregations are always adventurous; they are prepared to risk failure (Moyes, 1975, 41). Others suggest that congregations which are open to new initiatives will assess carefully whether existing practices actually prevent the congregation fulfilling its vision and purpose (Anderson, 1990, 167).

Such flexibility is not always easy to maintain. A congregation's response to change needs to be skilfully managed to ensure that the congregation does not become a casualty of change (Gibbs, 1987, 185).

While it is not as strong, there is also a link between a congregation's openness to new initiatives and the readiness of attenders to discuss their

faith or invite others to church. In contrast, an openness to new initiatives is negatively related to wider community involvement. This negative relationship is largely a function of the age of attenders. In *Mission under the Microscope* it was noted that involvement in community groups is more common for older attenders, who may also be more likely to resist change (p 19).

MOVING IN NEW DIRECTIONS

It is one thing to be open to new initiatives and another to be actually pursuing new directions.

Congregational leaders were asked whether, over the past two years, plans had emerged for changes or new directions in the outreach or wider community involvement of their congregations. Attenders were asked about their view of future directions for their congregation.

> **NEW DIRECTIONS: A PROFILE**
> - In 40% of congregations, new plans were adopted and implemented in the past two years for outreach or wider community involvement. In a further 39% of congregations, there have been some ideas which have yet to be further developed or formally adopted. In the remaining 21% of congregations, no such plans have surfaced.
> - Congregations in Pentecostal (69%) and some of the small Protestant denominations are the most likely to have adopted and implemented new directions.

A sense of direction in congregational life is strongly related to vitality. Congregations where a high proportion of attenders feel that their congregation is moving in new directions are more likely to be going forward on nearly all of the indicators in this study. In contrast, congregations where attenders believe there is a need to rethink what is being done or are uncertain the congregation can survive are less likely to be effective.

It is interesting to note that having a sense of direction, whether that is staying on a steady course or implementing new directions, is *critical* in relation to a sense of belonging.

The relationship between new directions and vitality is one of the strongest in this study. It is *very important* in relation to numerical growth and growth in faith, and of *some importance* in other areas.

VISION AND DIRECTION

Attenders were asked whether their senior minister/pastor/priest has a vision for the growth of the congregation and its members to which they are fully committed. The results suggest the existence and ownership of a vision for the future are key ingredients of an effective congregation.

A vision is *critical* for both developing a sense of belonging and encouraging growth in faith among attenders. It is a *very important* characteristic of numerically growing congregations and those encouraging attenders in sharing and discussing matters of faith with others. It is *important* in relation to newcomers and of *some importance* in relation to wider community involvement. The results are shown in Figure 13.3.

FIGURE 13.3: VISION FOR GROWTH			
	STRENGTH OF RELATIONSHIPS		
	Leader has a vision for growth to which attenders are committed	Attenders confident the leader can achieve goals	Attender involvement in important decision making
NEWCOMERS	+++ 3.1	++ 1.2	▬ ▬ 1.4
YOUNG ADULT RETENTION	0.4	+ 0.5	▬ 0.7
NUMERICAL GROWTH	++++ 5.9	++ 2.7	▬ ▬ 1.5
SENSE OF BELONGING	+++++ 20.5	+++++ 18.2	++ 1.4
COMMUNITY INVOLVEMENT	++ 2.1	+ 0.9	+++ 4.7
SHARING/ INVITING	++++ 5.3	+ 0.9	++ 2.5
GROWTH IN FAITH	+++++ 14.9	++++ 9.5	0.3

NB: Strength of relationship is the percent of variance explained after accounting for local context/faith type effects

SOURCE: 1991 National Church Life Survey

Many Australian authors have written on the importance of church leaders having a vision for the future direction of their congregation (eg Corney, 1991, 55; Moyes, 1975, 31; Croucher, 1991, 60). Internationally, there is an almost unanimous emphasis on this aspect of leadership among leading American and British church growth writers. In a study of the Church Growth Movement, Rainer suggests that one of the most frequently mentioned characteristics of 'good' leaders is that they have vision (1993, 186). The visionary leader plays the role of a catalyst, providing encouragement to those who can see the vision and are willing to work for it (Hadaway, 1991, 91).

Developing a vision is vital at the outset of a ministry; reviewing and maintaining it may well be an ongoing priority. Such a process is not always easy, particularly when large amounts of information are increasingly available and need to be assessed. A leader's ability to gather, analyse and understand information, and then to discern new directions, requires considerable skill. Many would agree with Lee that vision needs to be earthed in biblical truth and take into account unique congregational and community characteristics (Lee, 1989,133–138).

Confidence in the leader's ability to achieve goals is critical to belonging

Having a vision may be of little use if the congregation does not believe the leader can achieve goals that are set. The NCLS shows attenders' confidence in their leader's ability to achieve goals is *critical* in the area of belonging and *very important* in relation to growth in faith.

INVOLVEMENT IN DECISION MAKING

This raises a critical question: does a vision need to emerge from the employed leader of a congregation or can it just as effectively come from those in the wider congregation? Many commentators assume that the vision is formulated by the leader. C. Kirk Hadaway, however, suggests from his study of Southern Baptist churches that a vision imposed on a congregation only seems to work where it taps a previously accepted vision or latent sense of purpose. In other cases, the pastor had to successfully lead the congregation to formulate a new vision themselves (Hadaway, 1991, 84).

The 1991 NCLS cannot directly answer this question; the 1996 NCLS may provide insights in this area. Attenders were, however, asked about their involvement in important decision making within their congregation.

Many have seen attender involvement in decision making as being crucial to the ownership of new directions. Decisions reached by consensus may promote the achievement of goals and help assure group harmony in pursuit of these goals. If decision making is not participatory, ownership may be absent and decisions will be resented or will lack real impact. If church members are not involved in the process of change, they may resist the change being pushed on them (Callahan 1983, 56; Maxwell in Towns, 1990, 30).

The involvement of attenders in decision making is related to congregational vitality in different ways (see Figure 13.3). A high level of involvement in decision making appears to be an *important* characteristic of congregations with a high level of wider community involvement. Involvement in decision making is also positively related to some other areas, including developing a sense of belonging and the involvement of attenders in sharing the faith and inviting others into church life. Congregations where attenders have been offered the opportunity to get involved but have chosen not to appear less effective in these areas.

INVOLVEMENT IN DECISION MAKING: A PROFILE
- 66% of attenders feel they have the opportunity to participate in the important decision making of their congregation. 34% often participate in such decision making.
- Attenders at Pentecostal congregations (49%) are the least likely to say they have been given the opportunity to participate in important decision making.

SOURCE: 1991 National Church Life Survey adjusted for non-participants

As with roles, the involvement of attenders in important decision making in the congregation is negatively related to the flow of newcomers and numerical growth.

Several factors appear to be operating in these results. First, new arrivals in numerically growing congregations tend to be less involved in decision making. Second, the negative relationship between young adult retention and numerical growth is a reflection of lower levels of involvement in decision making in larger congregations, as noted in Chapter 8.

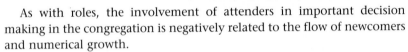

FOR BETTER OR FOR WORSE, EVERYBODY AT ST. MARK'S HAD A SAY IN EVERY DECISION MADE.

MOVING FORWARD TOGETHER — LAY LEADERSHIP, DECISION MAKING AND CHANGE

An Anglican congregation in Brisbane faced a challenge as a result of stagnation. Although only 15 years old and attracting new people, this congregation was losing them just as quickly. Action was needed to combat an inward-looking attitude that had crept into the congregation.

Several futile attempts were made by a steering committee to plan a new approach. A breakthrough came with information from the 1991 NCLS printout on their congregation's life. There was a lot of interest and discussion about the issues raised by the printouts. According to the minister, the resulting burst of energy gave people a real sense of direction and purpose.

More attenders became involved in decision making. They looked at areas such as worship, welcoming, and the education and nurture of members. The energy didn't stop at the church door. Several of the congregation, wanting to help members of their own family, became involved in a local mental health self-help group that was part of a government program. Their involvement was very significant to the group, and helped give the congregation an outward focus and a sense of purpose that had been lacking.

What can be made of these results? Involvement in decision making has a positive relationship with some aspects of vitality, although it is nowhere near as important as attenders' commitment to the vision for the congregation. While democratic, attenders' participation in decision making may not result in clear directions or a vision for the future.

Involvement in decision making depends on the context and size of the congregation as well as the nature of the issues to be solved. Effective decision making encourages everybody to participate at appropriate levels in important decisions. This is not to say that all decisions need to be made by everybody in the congregation. Beyond procedures for making important decisions there needs to be a streamlined structure for making minor decisions or carrying out administrative tasks. Congregations also need to trust those in leadership.

Encouraging involvement in decision making may require longer term or older members to be prepared to relinquish positions of power and to encourage younger and new attenders to be involved. The involvement of younger attenders in decision making will make it easier for leadership to be passed from generation to generation.

RESPONDING TO A CHANGING SOCIETY

So much church life and tradition has been based on the assumption that society and its institutions will change very little, if at all. This era of rapid, continuous change has created a crisis for a great many congregations and their leadership (Walrath, 1979, 248).

If a congregation is to be vital and effective, it will need to be able to adapt to change and chart new directions. This process is not always easy, and many leaders have received little training in this area.

This chapter suggests some critical aspects of effective leadership. Effective leaders need to help a congregation develop and own a vision. They need to develop confidence among attenders that goals can be achieved. Effective leaders help their congregation through the sometimes difficult process of change.

Effective leaders need to help a congregation develop and own a vision

These results provide little comfort for congregations where initiative is stifled, where there is excessive focus on their heritage, or where people preserve the old ways of doing things for their own sake. Such congregations may well have a firm sense of direction, but it comes at a price.

Openness to change, by itself, is not enough. Congregations without a sense of who they are will most likely be blown where the wind takes them. There may be congregations who are very open to new initiatives but who lack a firm direction or a strong sense of core values.

Clearly congregations need to hold the issues of new directions and their identity in tension. While remaining faithful to the gospel and core values, they need to be open to new directions, eager to develop a vision for how they can respond to the needs and culture of those in the community they seek to serve.

PLANNING FOR CHANGE

The results in this chapter point towards the importance of an openness to new initiatives, a positive sense among attenders about the directions of their congregation, a vision for the mission and ministry of the congregation, and a confidence that goals can be achieved.

All these elements need to be embodied in the planning processes adopted by congregations. Planning has become an increasingly important aspect of congregational life. Some 71% of congregations have some kind of plan, although the percentage engaging in detailed planning, including goals and strategies, is about half this number. Planning is more common in larger congregations.

PLANNING IN THE CHURCHES: A PROFILE

In relation to the level of planning in congregations
- 16% have a formal long-range plan with specific strategies to achieve goals;
- 21% have a formal medium-term plan with specific strategies;
- 34% have an informal plan reflecting overall vision and directions;
- 11% have short-term plans such as a preaching roster;
- 18% have no overall plan.

SOURCE: 1991 National Church Life Survey adjusted for non-participants

---

Planning helps congregations make the best use of limited resources. Defining a mission focus and ministry or mission goals helps congregations to be faithful and good stewards of the resources at their disposal.

Planning also allows congregations to be pro-active rather than reactive to situations. Instead of simply being buffeted by changes in the community and in church life, congregations are able to come to grips more quickly with what is happening and make the necessary changes to minister more effectively in a new situation.

CHAPTER 14

DICTATOR OR TEAM PLAYER?

Styles of Leadership

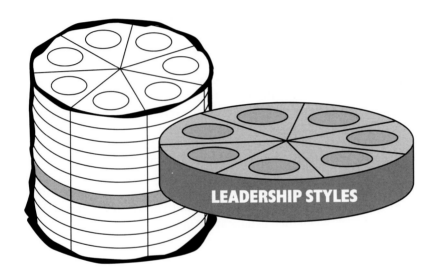

LEADERSHIP STYLES

Being a minister, pastor or priest is a tough job in any generation, but in the 1990s many leaders are finding the role particularly taxing. Not only are society and church life changing, but there are conflicting expectations about the role of the clergy.

For some attenders, it is important that their minister/pastor/priest has well-honed pastoral skills; what matters is making sure that people feel cared for. Other attenders think it is more important that he or she has good preaching skills and a charismatic personality and can deliver a message from the pulpit that holds everybody's attention. Expectations in the 1990s may also include corporate management skills: the ability to enunciate a vision, to organise people to carry it out and to encourage young leaders.

What does it take to be an effective leader? Finding reliable answers to this question is imperative if today's church leaders are to be equipped to help create vital and effective congregations for tomorrow.

BACKGROUND OF LEADERS

One of the most important decisions made by congregations and denominations is the appointment of clergy. Often lengthy discussions take place between prospective candidates and congregation as each assesses their compatibility and the minister's suitability for the task.

Some writers consider the background of leaders to be very important. Eddie Gibbs draws attention to the combined effects of experience and age on leadership style. He notes that youthful enthusiasm and experimentation are often linked. 'The older we get the more conservative we tend to become' (Gibbs, 1987, 93,94). Bill Hybels believes that pastors are most effective when their demographic profile is similar to that of their target audience (Towns, 1990, 48). There is a conviction among many that ministry to an urban subculture is best carried out by a person of the same subculture (Tiller, 1983, 43,44).

The NCLS included a number of questions which probed the background of the senior minister/pastor/priest of each congregation. Information which was collected included

- age
- occupational and educational background
- highest theological qualification
- sense of call to ministry and aspects of motivation for involvement with their current congregation
- distance of their current congregation from where they grew up
- number of years in ordained ministry
- number of years with their current congregation.

PROFILE OF A TYPICAL SENIOR MINISTER / PASTOR / PRIEST

- The average age of a senior minister is 47 years.
- About half of all senior ministers in the Anglican (50%) and Uniting (56%) churches are aged 50 years or more. This compares to less than a third in most other denominations.
- 96% of senior ministers/pastors/priests are males.
- 80% believe that the Bible is the word of God to be read in the context of the times, while a further 17% believe that the Bible is the literal word of God.
- 14% have no formal theological qualification, while 46% have a degree in theology or higher.
- 53% have a sense of call to ministry at their congregation, and 45% have a more general sense of call.
- The average length of time they have been at their current congregation is about four years.
- The average length of time they have been in the ordained/paid ministry is 16 years.
- 37% were senior managers or professionals before they joined the ministry; only 5% were machine operators or labourers.

SOURCE: 1991 National Church Life Survey adjusted for non-participants

The effect of gender could not be tested because there were insufficient female senior ministers across the denominations. Overall, this study found few links between congregational vitality and these aspects of staff background. The links that were found are shown in Figure 14.1.

FIGURE 14.1: SENIOR LEADER BACKGROUND

	STRENGTH OF RELATIONSHIPS		
	Age	No. of years in ordained ministry	No. of years at current congregation
NEWCOMERS	0.4	▬ 0.7	0.1
YOUNG ADULT RETENTION	0.4	0.0	0.1
NUMERICAL GROWTH	▬ 0.8	▬ ▬ 1.3	0.3
SENSE OF BELONGING	0.2	0.4	▬ 0.8
COMMUNITY INVOLVEMENT	0.1	0.0	0.1
SHARING/ INVITING	0.1	0.2	0.4
GROWTH IN FAITH	▬ 0.6	▬ 0.6	0.1

NB: Strength of relationship is the percent of variance explained after accounting for local context/faith type effects

SOURCE: 1991 National Church Life Survey

One element of the senior pastor's or minister's background which is related to congregational vitality is the number of years in the ordained ministry. The longer a person has been in the ordained ministry the less likely their congregation is to be growing numerically. Although this relationship is relatively minor, it does suggest that the flexibility and enthusiasm brought to the clerical role by new ministers/pastors/priests has some impact. At the same time, it should be noted that there appears to be little association between the age of the senior minister and congregational vitality. The key is years actually in ministry.

The number of years that a person is with a congregation has become an important issue for some. In some denominations, ministers can stay for as long as they choose, and it is not unusual to find ministers who have been with one congregation for many years. In other denominations there are limitations on length of tenure. For instance, the Salvation Army often moves officers from one corps to another after short periods of time. In the Uniting church there has generally been a ten-year limit on the length of time a minister can stay in the one parish.

There is conflicting evidence regarding the effect of the length of tenure. Hadaway's study of Southern Baptist pastors concludes that they are generally at their most productive in years three to six in their congregation (Hadaway, 1991, 75–78). Schaller considers years five to eight to be the most productive (Schaller, 1975a, 96). Many authors agree with Schaller, favouring longer-term pastorates (eg Wagner, 1984, 69; Pointer, 1984, 82; Gibbs, 1987, 89).

Other writers favour still longer periods of tenure. Reeves and Jenson suggest that it takes seven to 12 years for a pastor to have a wide impact on an established congregation (Reeves and Jenson, 1984, 24). Vaughan says that in the world's largest churches, the average tenure of the senior pastor is 20 years, with the minimum being ten years (Vaughan, 1986, 131). Easum predicts pastorates among congregations with an emphasis on equipping laity for ministry to average 20 to 30 years in the 21st century, because of the importance of strongly developed relationships between clergy and lay people (Easum, 1993, 78).

The NCLS has found very little relationship between the length of tenure of clergy and congregational vitality. This suggests that the issue of tenure is complex; no doubt clergy burnout, stress, role expectations, personality, stage in life and so on interplay with length of tenure in ways beyond the scope of this study.

It is important to see the limitations of these findings in relation to the staff selection process. They do not mean that congregations should not bother about the backgrounds of prospective ministers. It will always be necessary to consider carefully the background of ministers, their experience, qualifications, personality and so on. As Chapter 12 shows, it is important that staff and attenders are able to work together well, since conflict is highly detrimental to congregational vitality.

LEADERSHIP STRUCTURES

The organisational structure of congregations varies significantly. Clergy may find that the structures and consequent responsibilities in one congregation or parish are very different from those in the next, even within the same denomination. Structural models include

- one minister, one congregation
- one minister, multiple congregations
- multiple leaders, one congregation
- multiple leaders, multiple congregations
- a leadership team with or without a team leader.

There are advantages and disadvantages to each ministry model. Team ministry has appeal for some. A mix of leadership styles or gifts can model the interdependence of the body of Christ. The range of personalities on the team may appeal to different people. More staff time can be made available for particular projects or priorities. On the other hand, a team that is not working well can use a huge amount of energy maintaining communication and resolving conflict.

Ministry to multiple congregations has it own unique challenges. Staff who are responsible for multiple congregations may find themselves spread too thinly. Different congregations can have distinct corporate identities, making it difficult for the clergy to be well matched to all congregations (Schaller, 1984, 88).

FIGURE 14.2: LEADERSHIP STRUCTURES			
	STRENGTH OF RELATIONSHIPS		
	Women are senior or assistant ministers	Higher ratio of staff to attenders	Staff working with more than one congregation
NEWCOMERS	+ 0.6	0.0	▬ ▬ 1.5
YOUNG ADULT RETENTION	0.0	▬ 0.6	0.3
NUMERICAL GROWTH	0.2	▬ 0.7	▬ 0.6
SENSE OF BELONGING	+ 0.5	0.0	0.4
COMMUNITY INVOLVEMENT	0.2	0.1	0.0
SHARING/ INVITING	++ 1.1	0.0	▬ 0.7
GROWTH IN FAITH	++ 1.6	0.0	▬ ▬ 1.4

NB: Strength of relationship is the percent of variance explained after accounting for local context/faith type effects

SOURCE: 1991 National Church Life Survey

A congregation may become too large for one person to handle. Win Arn contends that there should be no more than 150 attenders for any one full-time staff person; if this ratio is exceeded very little growth can be expected (Arn, 1986, 100,101).

The NCLS suggests that these structural issues are only mildly related to congregational vitality. Variables in the analysis included
- ratio of staff to attenders
- number of congregations for which staff are responsible
- existence of multiple staffing at the congregation
- mix of roles within the staff team
- length of time the staff team has been together
- ratio of ordained to non-ordained people on the staff team
- employment of women as clergy in the congregation
- increase in staff numbers in the last few years.

Significant relationships with congregational vitality are shown in Figure 14.2.

The presence of one or more women on the staff of a congregation appears to be of *some importance* or *marginal* in relation to several aspects of vitality. Larger congregations provide more opportunities for females to be employed in leadership positions.

Working with more than one congregation appears unhelpful in a range of aspects of vitality, particularly growth in faith and levels of newcomers. Presumably it is a case of staff being spread too thinly and not having the time to deal with the pastoral and ministry needs of each congregation.

LEADERSHIP ROLES

Senior ministers/pastors/priests usually have a range of roles. Preaching, leading worship and administering the sacraments are public roles which are commonly carried out. In some congregations the leader's role may extend to being an evangelist as well as a teacher. During the week the senior minister may carry out a pastoral role as well as attending to a host of administrative duties.

Clergy are often required to balance different priorities in fulfilling each of these roles. The priority attached to each is not simply a matter of time management but may reflect specific theological understandings, the minister's job description, and his or her gifts and skills.

Does the priority given to particular roles impact on the vitality of a congregation? The NCLS asked senior leaders what they see ideally as the two most important tasks from the following list for a minister/pastor/priest in a congregation.

a. **Educator** — teaching people about the Christian faith
b. **Equipper** — trains laity for ministry and mission
c. **Evangelist** — converting others to the faith
d. **Organiser** — supervising the work of the church or parish
e. **Pastor** — visiting, counselling and helping people
f. **Priest** — conducting worship and administering the sacraments
g. **Social reformer** — tackling social injustices
h. **Visionary** — providing directions for the future
i. **Other**

FIGURE 14.3: HOW SENIOR LEADERS SEE THEIR ROLE

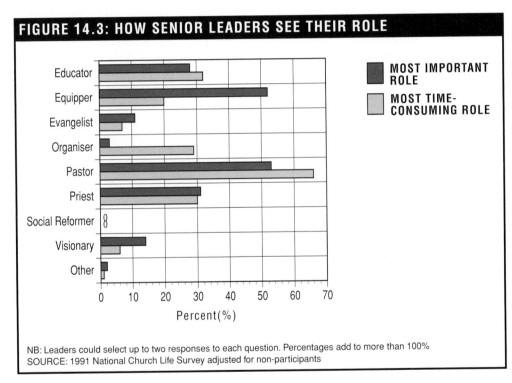

NB: Leaders could select up to two responses to each question. Percentages add to more than 100%
SOURCE: 1991 National Church Life Survey adjusted for non-participants

Some 53% of senior ministers see one of the two most important tasks to be that of a pastor. About half (52%) see equipping lay people for ministry and mission as important. Other important roles are as an educator (28%) or as a priest (31%).

Senior ministers were also asked what roles they spend most time on in their congregation. Being a pastor (66%), priest (30%) or educator (32%) are among the top responses. Only 20% believe they spend large amounts of time being an equipper, despite the importance of the role. By contrast, 29% find most of their time being taken up as an organiser, although only 3% think this is an important role.

There are some major discrepancies between how time is spent and how leaders think it ought to be spent. Many leaders are clearly caught up in high levels of organisational activity that they do not consider to be a priority. Some also feel overburdened with pastoral responsibilities, although it is accepted as a major job role. Many would feel they are not giving the equipping of attenders for ministry and mission the attention it deserves.

LEADER ROLE AND VITALITY

The role of pastor is seen as important by both senior leaders and attenders. However, there is virtually no relationship between the importance placed on this role by leaders or attenders and congregational vitality. Similarly, there appears to be no relationship between congregational vitality and a priority on the minister's teaching role. There is a small negative link between congregational vitality and attenders identifying the major role of their leaders as being a priest. Such results may surprise many, since the above roles are regarded by many as foundational aspects of effective leadership.

This is not the case in relation to priority being given to some other roles. Vital congregations tend to have a higher proportion of attenders who believe that the most important role of their minister is that of an equipper or an evangelist. It is interesting to note that the role of equipping lay people for ministry and mission is seen as one of their most important roles by 52% of senior ministers, even though for many it occupies far less of their time than they would like. Senior leaders who see themselves as being effective in evangelism or in motivating the lay people to achieve goals in ministry also tend to be associated with more vital congregations. The strength of relationship between the vitality measures and such an outwardly focused role mix can be seen in Figure 14.4.

An outward focus is important to all aspects of vitality

The NCLS shows that an outward focus by the senior minister is *very important* in relation to a growth in faith of attenders and numerical growth. An outward focus is *important* to attracting and retaining newcomers without a church background and to a sense of belonging among attenders.

Similar results have been found in overseas research. Hadaway found that Southern Baptist pastors of growing churches stood out from other pastors in their commitment to evangelism. The pastor's commitment to and involvement in evangelistic visitation and encouragement of evangelism through preaching, training and mobilising lay people were all important for a church to grow (Hadaway 1991, 79, 80).

In the past few decades there has been increasing emphasis on the role of lay people. Although they may still have some way to go in putting it into practice, most denominations acknowledge that the mission of the church is only achievable through the mobilisation of the whole body of believers. The NCLS indicates that evangelism and equipping lay people for ministry needs to be a priority; leaders need to be given the space and skills to put more time into this role.

Does this mean that teaching, pastoral or priestly roles (where applicable) are not significant or important? Far from it. The importance of such roles can be accepted as a given and a necessary prerequisite for effective ministry. However, where they are not accompanied by an emphasis on equipping attenders for mission or by a leader modeling an outward focus, a congregation is less likely to be vital and effective.

FIGURE 14.4: LEADER ROLES	STRENGTH OF RELATIONSHIPS	
	Leader emphasis on outwardly focused roles	
NEWCOMERS	+++	3.7
YOUNG ADULT RETENTION	+	0.7
NUMERICAL GROWTH	++++	5.2
SENSE OF BELONGING	+++	4.8
COMMUNITY INVOLVEMENT	++	1.6
SHARING/INVITING	++	2.9
GROWTH IN FAITH	++++	6.2

NB: Strength of relationship is the percent of variance explained after accounting for local context/faith type effects

SOURCE: 1991 National Church Life Survey

APPROACH TO LEADERSHIP

There has been much debate in recent years about appropriate styles of leadership. Should leaders be highly directive or, in this era of empowerment, should leaders primarily support the goals and directions of attenders? The NCLS provides some important insights in this area.

In the light of criticism that leaders have been too dogmatic, dictatorial or directive, many congregations have moved to a more consensual team approach. However, some sense that the pendulum has swung too far in the direction of consensus in leadership. If this is correct, leaders who take a supportive role are less likely to be in effective congregations than those who take a lead in developing visions and priorities for their congregation. The NCLS asked attenders to assess the style of their senior leaders by nominating which of the following four approaches is most characteristic of them:

- bold strong leaders who are clearly in charge
- leadership that inspires the people to take action
- leadership that acts on goals set by the people here
- leadership where the people start most things.

FIGURE 14.5: APPROACH TO LEADERSHIP	STRENGTH OF RELATIONSHIPS
	Leaders are seen as strong or inspiring
NEWCOMERS	✚ 0.9
YOUNG ADULT RETENTION	0.3
NUMERICAL GROWTH	✚✚ 2.8
SENSE OF BELONGING	✚✚✚✚✚ 15.8
COMMUNITY INVOLVEMENT	0.5
SHARING/INVITING	✚✚ 2.6
GROWTH IN FAITH	✚✚✚✚ 12.3

NB: Strength of relationship is the percent of variance explained after accounting for local context/faith type effects

SOURCE: 1991 National Church Life Survey

There is a positive link between leaders being seen as either strong or inspiring others to action and most measures of congregational vitality. As shown in Figure 14.5, this is particularly so in relation to a sense of belonging and growth in the faith of attenders, while such leadership is also of *some importance* in relation to numerical growth and attenders sharing their faith.

THE IMPORTANCE OF LISTENING

While strong or inspiring leadership is important, the NCLS also shows that congregations are more effective when leaders

- take the ideas of the congregation into account; and
- encourage others to use their gifts and skills.

Leaders taking attenders' ideas into account is critical

Leaders taking attenders' ideas into account is *critical* for developing a sense of belonging and *very important* in encouraging attenders' growth in faith. It is also *important* in relation to the flow of newcomers and of *some importance* in relation to most other aspects of vitality.

FIGURE 14.6: THE IMPORTANCE OF LISTENING		
	STRENGTH OF RELATIONSHIPS	
	Leaders take attenders' ideas into account	Leaders put a priority on attenders discovering gifts
NEWCOMERS	+++ 4.2	+++ 3.8
YOUNG ADULT RETENTION	0.0	0.0
NUMERICAL GROWTH	++ 2.7	+++ 4.2
SENSE OF BELONGING	+++++ 16.0	+++++ 20.9
COMMUNITY INVOLVEMENT	++ 1.8	++ 1.9
SHARING/ INVITING	++ 1.0	+++ 3.1
GROWTH IN FAITH	++++ 7.6	+++++ 14.1

NB: Strength of relationship is the percent of variance explained after accounting for local context/faith type effects

SOURCE: 1991 National Church Life Survey

Likewise, congregations where attenders feel their leadership puts a priority on attenders discovering their gifts tend to be more vital across a range of measures. The pattern parallels that for leaders taking attenders' ideas into account.

A wide range of writers recognise that it is imperative for attenders to discover their gifts for ministry. Effective leaders should not keep all tasks in their care, but should encourage people to develop their gifts and delegate tasks accordingly (Miller 1990, 56). Australian author Denham Grierson suggests that the test of effective leadership is whether attenders are strengthened and empowered in their witness; for this to happen leaders must develop the gifts of those in the congregation (1991, 107–110). Luecke encourages Lutherans in the United States to move towards leadership by 'personal gift' rather than just by 'office', if they are to be effective (1988, 136–138).

In *The Coming Church Revolution* Carl George places the issue of equipping others for ministry in clear terms: he sees the main role of the professional ministry as being to create 'volunteer ministers who are capable of being leaders of groups or teams' (1994, 117). George argues that the staff employed in a growing church should be people who can 'produce' ministers rather than who 'do ministry' (1994, 124).

DICTATOR OR TEAM PLAYER — STYLES OF LEADERSHIP

Christian congregations approach the task of outreach in many different ways — often reflecting the personality of the pastor. A Christian City Church (CCCI) congregation in a large industrial city has been growing numerically over the past five years through a program of outreach. Attenders reach out through many avenues — through social welfare outlets, such as sole parent groups, and through youth contacts in and around the beach, modern music events, competitions and other gatherings.

It has taken time to develop a vision for outreach among attenders at the congregation. The senior pastor imparted his own sense of excitement and vision to the leaders, who in turn have passed it on to the attenders.

Great care has been taken to equip outreach leaders. The pastor has also taken care to listen to the ideas of his congregation, and to nurture individual talent and initiative. A church member said: 'Everybody's ideas are considered important here — and we're promoting our church's vision at every opportunity. We think that's very important.'

'Our senior pastor is important too. But we still operate effectively and keep growing even when he is not here, because of the emphasis we place on training.'

The congregation illustrates how leadership can be strong and inspiring without being dictatorial. The result is a congregation that presents a broad and enthusiastic face to the wider community.

SO WHAT MAKES FOR EFFECTIVE LEADERSHIP?

Who would be the leader of a congregation? It is not an easy task to lead a group of people with different hopes and expectations. Many ordained clergy were brought up in an era when there were quite different expectations of clergy roles. Their training equipped them for ministry in circumstances far removed from those they face today.

It is liberating to realise that the demographic characteristics and background of ministers do not appear to be strongly associated with congregational vitality. Youthful enthusiasm and insights into their own generation make younger ministers an important resource for the growth of the church. Similarly, older ministers with their experience and greater wisdom have much to contribute. Neither group should be rejected out of hand on the basis of their age.

Clearly the background of ministers is much less important than what they do on the job. The same is true of other occupations which have been researched, such as those in the area of professional decision making (R. Homel, private communications).

So what makes for effective leadership? In the previous chapter the importance of leaders helping congregations to develop a sense of direction was highlighted. This chapter suggests some other key priorities:

- Leaders need to give priority to outward-focused ministry roles. This focus should not be forced out by other priorities, such as their pastoral, teaching and priestly roles, but should exist alongside of them. Outward-focused roles provide a model to attenders and help keep the congregation focused beyond itself.
- Leaders should seek to inspire others to action and offer direction where needed. This will be important if congregations are to move forward in relation to their goals.
- Leaders need to be able to discern the gifts and competencies of those in the congregation and to help them find a place in which to exercise and develop those gifts.
- Leaders need to listen to attenders' ideas.

This picture of leadership may be disturbing to some leaders. Clearly it is not enough to be a facilitator, enabling others to pursue their own goals. Nor is a dictatorial approach adequate. Effective leaders hold both of these aspects in tension, offering direction and taking the initiative while at the same time listening to the ideas of attenders and promoting other gifted individuals.

A survey of clergy and laity in Canada found similar tensions. Effective leaders focus on equipping others and seeking consensus and are ready to share authority. But visionary and pro-active leadership is also essential in fostering congregational effectiveness (Posterski and Barker, 1993, 171–187).

Australian church leaders need to rediscover their place in congregational life in an era of lay empowerment. As attenders take on

Effective leaders are one of the most important ingredients in developing vital congregations

roles that were traditionally the precinct of the ordained ministry, clergy will need to redefine their role. This is not a challenge Australian church leaders can afford to ignore. The NCLS makes it clear that effective leaders are one of the most important ingredients in developing vital and effective congregations.

There are many other aspects of leadership not explored in this study, for instance, personality traits, self-esteem, levels of stress, and personal spirituality. These and other aspects will be further explored in the 1996 NCLS.

CHAPTER 15

DIFFERENT AUDIENCES

With Whom Are We in Ministry?

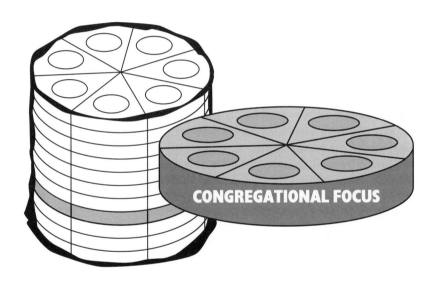

CONGREGATIONAL FOCUS

The rally call of 19th- and 20th-century church life was to the overseas mission fields. Today there is also a recognition of the need to relate to the range of cultural, socioeconomic, generational and interest groups that make up contemporary society. Mission has come home — into our own communities and backyards.

This chapter examines the relationship between vitality and the make-up of congregations, starting with an examination of the importance of the age, socioeconomic and ethnic profiles of congregations.

Some argue that a congregation should reflect the make-up and diversity of its local community. Others say that growing and effective congregations are primarily composed of the 'same kind' of people. This 'homogeneous unit principle' has generated both support and criticism. Congregation/community congruity and the homogeneous unit principle are discussed in this chapter.

The chapter also examines the place of the 'local church' in this changing environment. Today, people have far more access to transport, a factor which is reshaping our notions of community. How local or regional should congregations be and how specifically should they focus their ministry?

MINISTRY WITH WHOM?

Several studies have highlighted the fact that churches are significantly more involved with some sections of the Australian community than with others. The NCLS demonstrates that this is still true of the church today. There are different attendance levels between women and men, among those with different levels of education, those recently moving house, those from different age groups or generations and those from different ethnic backgrounds.

ATTENDERS AND THE WIDER COMMUNITY: A PROFILE

	Church attenders	In wider community
Men	38%	49%
People aged 15–40 years	37%	54%
People aged over 60 years	31%	19%
Public housing tenants	4%	7%
People with university degrees	16%	6%

SOURCE: 1991 National Church Life Survey adjusted for non-participants and 1991 Commonwealth Census

Does the make-up of a congregation have an impact on its vitality, and if so, in what ways? The results are shown in Figure 15.1.

• *Age differences:* One of the most significant challenges for many denominations is the relative absence of those under 40 years of age from their congregations. In some denominations, more than a third of attenders are aged over 60, while just 19% of the general community is in this age grouping.

In a study in the United States, C. Kirk Hadaway found that the age structure of a congregation has a major impact on growth — almost as great as that of evangelism (1991, 193). Further, he found that growing churches are primarily those which attract people aged 25 to 45. Churches with young married couples are also well placed for numerical growth through the addition of offspring to the congregation.

The NCLS supports these results. In general, congregations with younger age profiles are more likely to be attracting higher levels of newcomers, retaining young adults or growing numerically. However, they are less likely to be highly involved in the wider community.

FIGURE 15.1: MAKE-UP OF CONGREGATION

	STRENGTH OF RELATIONSHIPS			
	Younger age profile	Many families with children	Higher socio-economic status	Greater ethnic diversity
NEWCOMERS	++++ 7.0	++++ 5.2	– – 2.3	+ 0.6
YOUNG ADULT RETENTION	+++++ 10.2	++++ 9.3	+ 0.7	++ 1.2
NUMERICAL GROWTH	+++ 3.9	++ 2.7	++ 1.0	++ 1.2
SENSE OF BELONGING	– 0.8	– – 1.7	– – 1.5	+ 0.5
COMMUNITY INVOLVEMENT	– – – – 5.8	– – – 4.1	– – 1.2	0.4
SHARING/ INVITING	0.2	0.4	0.5	0.3
GROWTH IN FAITH	0.2	+ 0.7	– – 1.2	+ 0.8

NB: Strength of relationship is the percent of variance explained after accounting for local context/faith type effects
SOURCE: 1991 National Church Life Survey

Most newcomers to church life are under 40 years of age. The fact that they choose to attend congregations with people of a similar age does not bode well for older congregations wishing to attract younger attenders. Congregations with younger age profiles appear best placed to integrate newcomers.

A similar picture emerges in relation to young adult retention. Younger adults, moving from adolescence to adulthood and in the process of firming their identity, appear more likely to be retained in congregations where there are larger representations of young adults.

Congregations with younger age profiles appear best placed to integrate newcomers

Although not presented in Figure 15.1, congregations with high levels of wider community involvement tend to have higher levels of persons retired from the workforce, who may have more time for such commitment.

• *Stage in life:* There is also an important relationship between the presence of young families and newcomers. The tendency to go to church partly for the sake of the children has been well documented. A congregation that has young families may well put effort into ministry for children and adolescents, not only for the sake of these families but also for those currently outside of church life.

The presence of families with secondary or older children still at home is also strongly related to young adult retention.

• *Education and socioeconomic status:* There is some relationship between vitality and socioeconomic status, although this is not as strong as the age and stage in life effects. As can be seen in Figure 15.1, congregations with lower levels of education or social status are more likely to be effective, particularly in the area of attracting and integrating newcomers.

• *Ethnicity:* Similarly, the ethnicity of a congregation has some relationship to the vitality indicators in use in this study. Ethnic diversity is a characteristic of congregations that are growing numerically or retaining young adults.

• *New residents:* Congregations with high levels of new residents also tend to contain higher levels of newcomers. New residents are often looking for ways to make links in their new community. Congregations actively encouraging attenders to make contacts with new residents may be meeting a real need in their communities.

• *Gender balance:* The ratio of men to women generally does not make a great difference to the likely vitality of a congregation. In areas where a relationship does exist, these differences reflect age variations, ie older congregations will tend to have higher percentages of women.

BEING LIKE THE COMMUNITY

Few would disagree that, in principle, it is important for the church to relate to all sections of society. The reality is that most congregations are demographically different from the local community they seek to serve. Few have educational or age profiles which reflect that of the surrounding community. Does it matter?

Currie, Gilbert and Horsley (1977, 59) identified the need for a congregation to be of similar make-up (congruent) to its community. Often, congregations most adversely affected by local context are those that are very different in demographic make-up from their surrounding community. For instance, congregations which are struggling to survive in very multicultural communities are often comprised of older, Australian-born attenders. These congregations more closely reflect the make-up of the community a generation ago and have failed to attract new arrivals into their life.

There are relationships between a congregation's congruity with the community and its vitality. However, the results are mixed, as can be seen in Figure 15.2. Patterns in relation to urban congregations are shown, alongside the overall picture.

FIGURE 15.2: SIMILARITY OF CONGREGATION TO COMMUNITY

	STRENGTH OF RELATIONSHIPS	
	Urban congregations	All congregations
NEWCOMERS	+++ 4.6	+++ 3.6
YOUNG ADULT RETENTION	++++ 6.5	++++ 5.4
NUMERICAL GROWTH	++ 2.4	++ 2.2
SENSE OF BELONGING	− − − 3.6	− − 2.5
COMMUNITY INVOLVEMENT	− − 2.3	− − 2.4
SHARING/ INVITING	+ 0.8	+ 0.7
GROWTH IN FAITH	++ 2.2	++ 1.6

NB: Strength of relationship is the percent of variance explained after accounting for local context/faith type effects

SOURCE: 1991 National Church Life Survey

Congregations that have similar profiles to the wider community are more likely to be attracting and retaining newcomers, growing numerically or having higher levels of attenders experiencing growth in their faith. Such congruity is not a characteristic of congregations with high levels of belonging or wider community involvement.

HOMOGENEITY: THE WAY TO GO?

One of the most contentious issues of the last few decades has been what the Church Growth Movement has dubbed the 'homogeneous unit principle'. A homogeneous congregation is one where attenders are alike in some respect; for instance, they could be of a similar age, life stage, ethnicity or socioeconomic status. In contrast, a heterogeneous congregation is defined by its diversity, whether demographically or in some other way.

The homogeneous unit principle is based on the work of Donald McGavran. His interpretation of the phrase 'all the nations' contained in the Great Commission is to suggest that this includes tribes, castes, classes and subgroups in our society. From this he derives a 'people group' approach to evangelism. In his view a homogeneous unit is 'simply a section of society in which all the members have some characteristics in common' (McGavran, 1970, 85).

Homogeneity has been linked to numerical growth. Peter Wagner states that one of the seven vital signs of a healthy church is 'membership drawn primarily from one homogeneous unit' (1984, 37). McGavran and Arn say that growing congregations are primarily composed of the 'same kind' of people (1976, 76).

McGavran has been criticised for the vagueness of this concept and for the inadequacies of some of his sociology (eg McClintock 1988, 107). It is contended that he has given inadequate attention to what might be the boundaries of such a homogeneous unit, its interrelationship with other groups within highly diverse societies and how such groups may actually change over time.

Callahan argues against homogeneity as a desirable aim for churches. He states that a key to mission is reaching society's 'unacceptable' persons, not just those who are like the congregation (1983, 3). Others warn that striving for homogeneity can trap a congregation into a single, static identity (eg Carroll et al, 1986, 23). Others raise concerns about the theological propriety of a homogeneous approach, since the kingdom of God is about removing division between people. Congregations should, they believe, be as culturally diverse as possible, demonstrating the possibility of Christian unity and diversity.

Some argue a middle position. While the church needs to embrace all cultures, too many congregations are reaching the same segments of society. There is a need for complementary programs to reach a greater diversity of people than at present (Robinson and Christine, 1992, 40, 41). While striving for diversity, effective churches may need to provide homogeneous congregations *at some times* or groups within their life in order for people to worship and share with others of their own cultures.

Evaluating this concept is actually quite difficult, since what is meant by the 'same kind' of people may hinge on subtle cultural factors or the relative cohesion or insularity of particular interest groups. The NCLS cannot probe such subtleties; it can, however, make some broader observations. Using the demographic variables available in the NCLS, such as age, education, occupation, ethnicity and marital status, homogeneity measures were constructed and their relationship with vitality examined, both for urban areas and across all congregations.

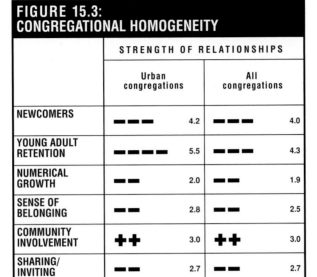

FIGURE 15.3:
CONGREGATIONAL HOMOGENEITY

	STRENGTH OF RELATIONSHIPS	
	Urban congregations	All congregations
NEWCOMERS	▬▬▬ 4.2	▬▬▬ 4.0
YOUNG ADULT RETENTION	▬▬▬▬ 5.5	▬▬▬ 4.3
NUMERICAL GROWTH	▬▬ 2.0	▬▬ 1.9
SENSE OF BELONGING	▬▬ 2.8	▬▬ 2.5
COMMUNITY INVOLVEMENT	++ 3.0	++ 3.0
SHARING/ INVITING	▬▬ 2.7	▬▬ 2.7
GROWTH IN FAITH	▬▬▬ 3.5	▬▬ 2.6

NB: Strength of relationship is the percent of variance explained after accounting for local context/faith type effects

SOURCE: 1991 National Church Life Survey

Little support for homogeneity can be drawn from these results (see Figure 15.3). Apart from wider community involvement, effective congregations are characterised by greater heterogeneity and a mix of people of different ages and backgrounds or at different stages of life. Each demographic dimension was also tested separately. In no case was homogeneity positively linked with vitality.

In an additional test on homogeneity, attenders were asked whether they felt their congregation was composed mainly of people with similar backgrounds or beliefs or whether it was characterised by high levels of diversity. Again, homogeneity was not linked with vitality, except in the area of belonging, where similarity of background seemed an advantage.

It is important to recognise the limitations of this analysis. This study is broad brush; there may be some cultural or interest groups who find diversity difficult or threatening. There may be some highly effective congregations relating intentionally to one cultural subgroup. The effectiveness of their strategy may be lost in the bigger picture.

Further, the 1991 NCLS was not translated into other languages, so non-English-speaking congregations were not included. This result cannot be taken as a reflection of the value of mono-ethnic congregations.

Nevertheless, these results place an important qualification on discussions about the value of homogeneity. Congregations with a healthy degree of diversity may be more adept at making new people feel as though they belong. Attenders may seek out others of similar backgrounds with whom they feel comfortable.

In a sympathetic analysis of the Church Growth Movement, Rainer acknowledges the level of criticism of the homogeneous unit principle and makes the following comment: 'With some valid points made by the critics, the principle was acknowledged as being descriptive rather than prescriptive. Little is said today about the homogeneous unit principle' (1993, 317).

Vitality is more related to the actual characteristics of people rather than the homogeneity of a group

This study suggests vitality is more related to the actual characteristics of people rather than the homogeneity of a group. For instance, the presence of higher proportions of younger people in a congregation is positively related to numerical growth and the flow of newcomers. Most homogeneous congregations would tend to have older age profiles, where young people have moved out of the congregation, leaving behind a homogeneous core of older attenders. Clearly it is not homogeneity that is the important factor but the presence of significant numbers of younger people.

LOCAL OR REGIONAL?

The church has often been slow to adapt to the city environment. Historically, most congregations have identified strongly with a local area. The parish structure of the larger denominations in Australia reflects this local focus; each congregational centre is geared towards meeting the spiritual needs of local residents. Some denominations have moved away from the local parish model by establishing congregations which are more regional in focus. Other congregations have developed an interest base, ministering to particular ethnic or subcultural groups.

Access to private transport has extended the catchment areas of congregations well beyond parish boundaries or the suburb within which a congregation is located. As denominations plan new congregations, they are being forced to rethink just how large a catchment area should be.

This question has been raised, in part, by the decline of many small, local congregations in urban areas. The apparent success of some larger, regionally based congregations has also placed the issue firmly on denominational agendas.

The catchment areas of urban congregations in Australia varies widely: 13% of congregations see their catchment as less than 2 kms, 54% see their catchment as within a 5 km radius, while only 15% consider their catchment to be larger than 10 km.

CONGREGATIONAL CATCHMENT: A PROFILE

Congregation leaders were asked the approximate catchment area of their congregation:

	Overall	Urban	Non-urban
Under 2 km	7%	13%	3%
2–5 km	23%	41%	11%
6–10 km	20%	20%	19%
11–20 km	18%	9%	24%
Over 20 km	23%	6%	35%
No area focus	9%	11%	8%
Total	100%	100%	100%

SOURCE: 1991 National Church Life Survey adjusted for non-participants

Attenders were asked how long it took them to travel to church. It could be expected that larger congregations would draw their attenders from further afield than smaller congregations. The time attenders in urban areas take to drive to church is shown in Figure 15.4 for congregations of different sizes.

FIGURE 15.4: ATTENDER TRAVEL TIME TO CHURCH BY CONGREGATIONAL SIZE

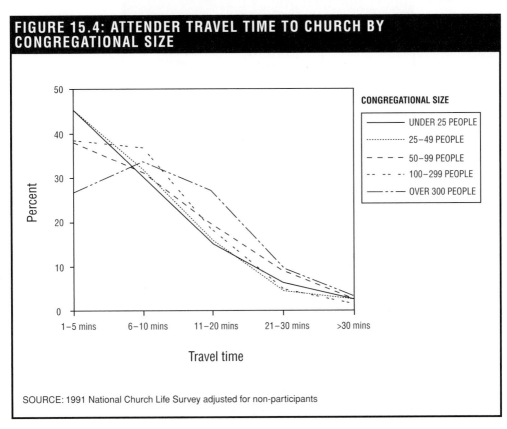

SOURCE: 1991 National Church Life Survey adjusted for non-participants

Perhaps the most surprising aspect of attenders' journeys to church is the similarity between congregations of different sizes. Congregations of more than 300 people have fewer attenders within five minutes of church and more 11 to 20 minutes away. The proportion of attenders travelling for more than 20 minutes remains relatively constant except for the largest of congregations. Apart from these differences, the profiles are remarkably similar.

Many small congregations draw their attenders from well beyond their local area

This indicates that, by and large, small congregations are drawing attenders from similar-sized catchment areas to those of larger congregations (*Winds of Change*, pp 96–103). Many of these small congregations would define themselves as 'local' congregations, yet they draw their attenders from well beyond their local area.

JOURNEY TO CHURCH AND CONGREGATIONAL VITALITY

Is there a relationship between catchment areas and congregational vitality? The results are shown in Figure 15.5 for congregations in urban areas.

FIGURE 15.5: THE IMPORTANCE OF A LOCAL FOCUS (URBAN CONGREGATIONS ONLY)

	STRENGTH OF RELATIONSHIPS	
	Short journey to church	Attenders know their neighbours well
NEWCOMERS	++ 1.3	▬ ▬ 1.1
YOUNG ADULT RETENTION	▬ ▬ ▬ 4.1	▬ ▬ ▬ 4.8
NUMERICAL GROWTH	0.0	▬ ▬ 1.6
SENSE OF BELONGING	▬ ▬ 2.9	+ 0.7
COMMUNITY INVOLVEMENT	0.4	+++ 4.8
SHARING/ INVITING	▬ ▬ 1.6	0.4
GROWTH IN FAITH	▬ ▬ ▬ ▬ 5.1	0.0

NB: Strength of relationship is the percent of variance explained after accounting for local context/faith type effects

SOURCE: 1991 National Church Life Survey

The NCLS shows there is a positive relationship between newcomers and a short driving time to church. This suggests that newcomers are more likely to go or be invited to a church which is close to them.

However, the opposite relationship exists with retention of young adults. Presumably young adults feel more comfortable in more regional congregations as they move from a locally focused life at school into a more broadly focused stage of life.

Similarly, congregations drawing from a wider catchment area tend to have higher levels of belonging, attenders willing to discuss their faith with others or invite them to church or feeling they are growing in their faith. These results cannot be explained by the younger age profile of more regional congregations. There is no relationship between the size of a catchment area and numerical growth or wider community involvement.

These results do not answer the question of whether a regional approach is better than a local one. This will depend on the particular context of the congregation, its sense of purpose and the hopes and passions of its attenders. Clearly regional congregations have a role to play in retaining young adults within church life. Denominations would do well to encourage the strategic development of regional congregations geared to the needs of young adults.

Many small, supposedly local congregations are already more regional, in terms of catchment, than their self-definition suggests. It is important that congregations recognise this, since promoting a strongly local focus may shape the mission outlook of the congregation.

ATTENDERS WITH A LOCAL ORIENTATION

As far back as the Industrial Revolution, social observers noticed that the social life of a city or large town was different from that of a small rural town. People in rural areas often spent their lives in one locality which formed the focus of their working and social lives. Relationships in the rural town were based on a set of agreed values, and the local institutions, such as the church, were an important forum for social interaction and maintaining these values. In a city or large town, the larger number and diversity of people reduced the importance of local community life.

Today, people develop networks and a sense of community in different ways. Some people retain a strong commitment to a local area. Many are part of social networks which are based on a common interest rather than a common locality. The social networks people select can vary at different stages within their life.

Social researchers have found that the shift away from local community involvement to involvement based on networks of common interest is reflected in people's orientation to the world around them. Wade Clark Roof (1976) has extensively explored the impact of a local versus cosmopolitan orientation on religious involvement among liberal Protestants in the United States. Alan Black has also explored the application of this concept in Australia (1991, 3). While this was not explored to the same depth in the NCLS, a single indicator was used to gain some idea of attenders' informal ties with their local community.

Attenders were asked if they knew their close neighbours well enough to be aware of some of their concerns. This is an indicator of a local orientation; it does not necessarily follow that those with little knowledge of their neighbours' concerns are necessarily more cosmopolitan in orientation. They may simply be uninvolved or unconcerned.

A 'local' orientation is indeed strongly related to stages in life among attenders. Around 13% of 15 to 19 year olds said they knew all or most of their neighbours well enough to be aware of some of their personal concerns. A similar figure is found among 20 to 40 year olds without children (11%), but the figure rises to 17% among parents with preschool-aged children, 22% among parents with school-aged children, 30% among 40 to 60 year olds with post-school-aged or no children at home, and 41% among those over 60 years of age.

The relationship between vitality and a local orientation is shown in Figure 15.5. As can be seen, there is a mixed relationship with congregational vitality. A local focus is *important* in relation to community involvement and *marginally* related to developing a sense of belonging. The link between a local focus and community involvement is partly related to the fact that older attenders (who tend to have a local focus in their lives) are also most likely to be involved in community groups. However, the link exists even after taking age into account.

As can be seen in Figure 15.5, there are other relationships between a local orientation and vitality, particularly a negative relationship with young adult retention. Further analysis suggests that these patterns are explainable by the age profile and stage in life of attenders.

> **A local focus is important in relation to community involvement**

WITH WHOM ARE WE IN MINISTRY?

The make-up of a congregation is related to vitality in many different ways. This study highlights the importance of a congregation's age profile or stage in life. A first response to these findings may be that having a full age range is important, but, it is difficult to attain. The many ageing congregations in Australia do not need to be reminded of this. The hard reality is that many congregations are caught in a self-perpetuating cycle. Having few younger people means that the congregation is less likely to either attract new younger people or retain those they have.

What are the options for such congregations? For some the path will be to take new steps of vulnerability, in order to pass on to a new generation what has been life-giving to them. For others it will be to recognise who they are and to seek to be effective in mission to the age groups with whom they are in contact.

In some ways, the make-up of a congregation is a given; it would be unhelpful for congregations to anguish too greatly over their profile. Rather, a reflection on their strengths may lead to creative initiatives.

At the same time, the make-up of a congregation can gradually change. Congregations need to be aware of how their profile is changing and need to respond in appropriate ways.

Congregations would do well to compare their profile with that of the wider community. Congregations often find it hard to keep up with the

IT WAS ONLY WHEN THE PASTOR STARTED MISSING SUNDAY SERVICES THAT THE CONGREGATION REALISED HE'D OVER-IDENTIFIED WITH THE NEW STREET MINISTRY.

social changes that are occurring around them. Social distance between attenders and local residents as the shape of the community changes will decrease a congregation's ability to draw in new attenders (Walrath, 1979, 264).

Yet, while it is a useful exercise to compare the profile of a congregation to that of the wider community it seeks to serve, it needs to be recognised that most congregations will not exactly mirror their communities. Congregation/community comparisons can be useful for helping congregations discover who they are and with whom they are in mission. As a congregation grows and develops it may wish to broaden its focus or develop ministry initiatives with other sections of the community.

DEALING WELL WITH DIVERSITY

Most congregations will not seek to be involved with one age, interest or ethnic group. For the majority, it will be a case of finding out how to affirm the place of different groups in their life. It may mean providing forums where those from similar backgrounds can meet and express their faith in ways that resonate with their culture. The congregation's corporate life will embrace and value each of these cultural components.

Congregations may use small groups as a place where attenders can meet with like-minded people. Cooperative activity with other congregations may enable larger groupings of some attenders, for instance youth or young adults.

Larger congregations may develop a range of activities or forums for different groups: youth fellowships, seniors activities, playgroups and so on. Worship services of different styles may be a significant step, with attenders coming together on occasions for larger celebrations. Mission activities with sections of the wider community under-represented in church life may need to be accompanied by careful reflection on appropriate styles of nurture.

In relation to a local or regional focus, congregations need to reflect carefully on their primary mission focus. Many congregations whose identity is 'local' may discover that they are far more regional in focus than they thought. Imposing a local focus on a group of attenders from across a region may inhibit the mission of a congregation. Attenders with a regional focus may be less likely to invite others if their congregation has a strong local focus.

CHAPTER 16

PROPERTY AND FINANCES

Do Buildings or Money Matter?

PROPERTY & FINANCES

Matters relating to money and buildings occupy a large amount of time in many congregations. Properties are often in need of repair and renovation. In some cases buildings need to be extended because congregations have grown; in many other cases congregations have decreased in size and find it hard to maintain their buildings. Pressures to change property to accommodate new styles of worship or new activities are often met with fierce resistance from attenders for whom the existing buildings have great meaning. Does the type of building a congregation uses matter? Should congregations be following the golden rule of real estate: location, location, location?

Financial matters can be an important litmus test of how attenders feel about their congregation and where it is heading. Finances can literally be 'the bottom line' for the viability of many congregations. How important are levels of giving and financial stability? Does financial stability enable congregations to get on with their business of mission and ministry? Or does it lead to complacency?

This chapter explodes some myths associated with church property and finances and their impact on congregational vitality.

MATTERS OF PROPERTY

Building churches was a major preoccupation in the 19th century for most denominations. As settlement spread across Australia new towns sprang up. New settlers arrived, bringing their culture and customs with them. Alongside the post office and town hall, church buildings became a prominent part of the landscape. They represented, in part, civilisation and heritage; they marked the centre point of community for new residents from different backgrounds.

As a result, the church today has a great many buildings dotted across Australia, ranging from large stone cathedrals to weatherboard chapels. Many would argue that they are a tremendous resource, the legacy of the history of Christian presence in this country. They consider church buildings to be an asset upon which the church can build . . . literally.

Others, however, see church buildings as millstones around the necks of the more established denominations. The cost of maintaining historic and possibly outmoded buildings is significant. Further, many old church buildings represent a bygone era, and the image they present appears culturally inappropriate to contemporary society. For those who want to see the church as a prophetic signpost to the future, it is sometimes frustrating to be trapped in a building that is an echo of the past.

If a church building possesses historical significance the tensions are further increased. Often there is huge pressure from the wider community to maintain such a building as a historic landmark, even if few in the community ever walk through its doors. Many church leaders find that the greatest hostility to the demolition and replacement of an old church building does not come from active attenders but from others in the wider community.

Modern church building design is quite different from that in times gone by. Traditional styles emphasising authority, awe and reverence have been replaced by designs that emphasise openness to the wider community, servanthood and functionality. 'Multipurpose' is a common theme around the design tables of church architects. Some of the larger church buildings in operation today have very little in the way of religious icons, and they resemble an auditorium more than a traditional church building.

Does the building in which a congregation worships have any relationship with congregational vitality? Are traditional church buildings an asset or a millstone? These are important questions for nearly all congregations, since the vast majority of congregations meet in a building they or their denominational body own.

The NCLS asked leaders a range of questions about

- the age of the church building
- the type of building
- available facilities
- building capacity
- visibility of the building
- ease of vehicle access to the site
- parking availability.

THE AGE OF CHURCH BUILDINGS

Apart from asking about the age of church buildings, the NCLS also asked congregational leaders whether their building was subject to Heritage Council or National Trust classification and when extensions or improvements were last carried out. The age of Anglican and Protestant church buildings in Australia is shown in Figure 16.1.

Nearly half of the buildings (46%) used by congregations in the survey have been built since 1950. Yet, if the images of church buildings which appear in the media were any indication, most congregations would be meeting in Gothic, sandstone buildings constructed in ancient history! This statistic shows just how misleading stereotypes can be.

Many commentators have argued for the importance of contemporary styles of church building. Some have suggested that the post-war generations in particular demand facilities that are contemporary in style and design. For these groups, older buildings and historic properties are likely to restrict rather than enhance ministry.

The results from this study suggest a small relationship between the age of a building and vitality (see Figure 16.2). Even after accounting for contextual differences (including population growth around the congregations), congregations with new buildings are more likely to be growing numerically. A Heritage Council or National Trust listing is not related in any way to any of the vitality measures.

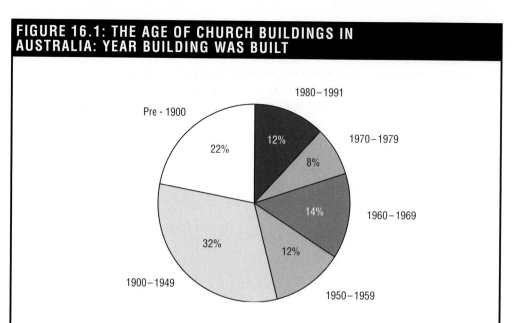

SOURCE: 1991 National Church Life Survey adjusted for non-participants

TYPE OF BUILDING

Most worship services are held in church buildings (82%) or church halls (5%). However, some services are held in non-church buildings: 3% meet in houses, 3% in schools, 3% in community centres, and 4% in other buildings. Partly this reflects the costs of establishing and maintaining church buildings. However, it also reflects the desire of many congregations to meet on 'neutral territory' that is not foreign to non-churchgoers.

Congregations meeting in non-church buildings are more likely to be growing numerically

The results in Figure 16.2 suggest a small relationship between use of non-church buildings and congregational vitality. Congregations meeting in such buildings are more likely to be growing numerically.

Not surprisingly, large congregations are more likely to provide special facilities for attenders. There is, however, no relationship between the provision of facilities and congregational vitality. For instance, congregations that provide schools or child-care centres are no more likely to be growing numerically than those which do not.

This does not mean that providing such facilities is not an important ministry. Churches should care for those who are hurting, marginalised or have some disability, regardless of the impact on congregational life. However, these facilities will not, of themselves, make a congregation more vital. And if congregational vitality is not addressed, the care givers can themselves be failing to be renewed.

BUILDING CAPACITY

SUITABILITY OF FACILITIES

The NCLS asked leaders about the suitability of their facilities for the ministry needs of their congregation. All in all, 60% of congregations in the study think their facilities are satisfactory; another 16% think their facilities more than meet requirements for their current needs. On the other hand, 24% think their facilities are inadequate, of which 17% feel there is space for expansion and 7% no room for expansion.

Perhaps not surprisingly, some relationship was found between facilities being seen as inadequate and vitality. Congregations where leaders feel facilities are insufficient for ministry needs are more likely to be growing numerically, drawing in newcomers or retaining young adults.

COMFORTABLY FULL OR UNCOMFORTABLY EMPTY?

Can a church worship centre that is too big or too small for its congregation impact on the congregation's life and vitality?

Kennon Callahan believes that ideally church buildings should be full to about 80% of their seating capacity in urban areas and 50–70% in rural areas. People prefer to worship in a building that is comfortably full but not overcrowded. Congregations which are consistently overcrowded should consider running additional services or extending their building (1983, 30).

Gordon Moyes found that as soon as a building becomes full, people cease attending as regularly as they once did. He suggests that churches

FIGURE 16.2: PROPERTY MATTERS

	STRENGTH OF RELATIONSHIPS			
	More modern church buildings	Use of non-church buildings	Facilities over-utilised	Services uncomfortably empty
NEWCOMERS	✚ 0.8	✚ 0.5	✚ 0.6	0.1
YOUNG ADULT RETENTION	0.1	0.0	✚ 0.6	▬▬ 1.7
NUMERICAL GROWTH	✚✚ 1.4	✚✚ 1.8	✚✚ 1.9	▬▬▬ 3.5
SENSE OF BELONGING	0.1	✚ 0.5	0.1	0.3
COMMUNITY INVOLVEMENT	0.2	0.2	0.1	0.2
SHARING/ INVITING	0.2	0.3	0.1	0.1
GROWTH IN FAITH	0.2	0.3	0.3	0.5

NB: Strength of relationship is the percent of variance explained after accounting for local context/faith type effects
SOURCE: 1991 National Church Life Survey

ought not to wait for their building to be filled. As soon as it is 75% full, congregations should start a new worship service or a new congregation (1975, 95).

The NCLS asked leaders to assess how full or empty their church building is at their largest worship service. Estimates of building capacity and service size were also used to create a ratio of attendance to overall capacity. From this data, the level of crowding was estimated to test the relationship with congregational vitality.

Nearly a third of leaders (31%) feel that their church buildings are comfortably full at their largest worship service. About 41% say their building is half full and 25% say it is uncomfortably empty. Only 3% report their building as being cramped.

There is some evidence that the extent to which the building is filled is related to numerical growth and young adult retention. Congregations with buildings described by their leaders as being uncomfortably empty are less likely to be experiencing numerical growth or retaining young adults. This result holds for congregations of all sizes.

SITE CHARACTERISTICS

VISIBILITY

The visibility of a congregation's property is assumed by many commentators to be significant. A church building that is clearly visible,

especially from major traffic arteries, is seen as advantageous to effectiveness (eg Schaller 1984, 190; Callahan, 1983, 78).

Some church buildings are highly visible, others less so. About a third of congregational leaders (32%) describe their buildings as highly visible. Some 28% say they are visible without standing out, 26% fairly visible and 15% easily missed.

Buildings belonging to larger congregations tend to be rated by the leaders as being more visible. However, there appears to be no relationship between visibility and vitality. While a highly visible building may make passers-by more aware of a congregation's existence, visibility does not necessarily translate into numerical growth or an inflow of newcomers into church life. Attenders' willingness to invite others is far more important than the visibility of the church property.

ACCESSIBILITY

A number of writers have argued that it is important for congregations to ensure that there is easy traffic access to their site (eg Schaller 1984, 191; Callahan, 1983, 72).

For most congregations access is not considered to be a particular problem. Only 3% of leaders consider traffic access a major issue. While in some congregations access difficulties may be a major source of dissatisfaction, the NCLS shows no overall relationship between traffic accessibility and vitality.

PARKING

Some commentators claim that people are no longer prepared to walk long distances to and from their cars. Moyes argues that one of the greatest needs for churches that want to grow will be for adequate parking space (1975, 101). C. Peter Wagner warns that people are deterred from attending church when car parks are full (1984, 184).

Only 2% of congregations have major parking problems. A further 14% have some difficulty and 84% no difficulty with parking at all. Again there is no relationship between vitality and parking, even in urban areas.

Do these results mean that visibility, accessibility and parking are always unimportant and irrelevant? The answer may be no for some congregations in major urban areas. Access and parking may be important issues for new church developments as well as established churches on busy roads and in congested inner-city areas.

Major problems in these areas will create dissatisfaction and frustration. But for the majority of existing congregations across Australia these issues are far less important than the people networks and relational contacts that attenders have with the wider community.

ATTENDERS' ATTITUDE TO PROPERTY

While it would appear that the type, age and characteristics of church property have little relationship with congregational vitality, a congregation's attitude to its property is significant. For some attenders, the nature of the church building is extremely important to their worship experience, while for others the building is purely functional and holds little direct significance.

In order to probe attitudes to property, the NCLS included the following question:

> **How would you describe the importance of this building to your worship experience?**
> a. Very important
> b. Of some importance
> c. Of little importance, but I feel comfortable in the building
> d. Of little importance, and I feel uncomfortable in it
> e. Unhelpful to me
> f. Don't know/not applicable

The older attenders are, the more likely they are to feel that the building is important for their worship experience. Some 81% of attenders aged over 70 years think the building has great or some importance to their worship experience, compared to just 46% of people aged 20 to 29 years (*Winds of Change*, p 176).

Many older attenders would have been involved in the construction or redesign of their church buildings. Over a long period, many memories, of events or perhaps of people no longer alive, would be attached to their place of worship.

A more functional approach to property where the building is of little importance to worship is positively related to some aspects of congregational vitality. It is of *some importance* in regard to numerical

A more functional approach to property is related to some aspects of congregational vitality

FIGURE 16.3:
ATTITUDES TO PROPERTY

	STRENGTH OF RELATIONSHIPS Attenders see the building as of little importance to their worship	
NEWCOMERS	++	1.9
YOUNG ADULT RETENTION	+	0.8
NUMERICAL GROWTH	++	2.8
SENSE OF BELONGING	– – – –	8.5
COMMUNITY INVOLVEMENT	+	0.5
SHARING/INVITING		0.3
GROWTH IN FAITH	– – –	4.8

NB: Strength of relationship is the percent of variance explained after accounting for local context/faith type effects

SOURCE: 1991 National Church Life Survey

growth and incorporating newcomers and *marginal* in relation to retaining young adults. On the other hand, congregations where attenders feel their church building is important to their worship experience are likely to have higher levels of belonging and growth in faith.

In part, this result is a function of the age profile of attenders, given that younger attenders appear to have less investment in the church building in which they worship. It also reflects different denominational traditions.

Congregational leaders would do well to do some careful listening and reflecting on this issue. As with styles of music, there appears to be some tension between drawing in new attenders and fostering a sense of belonging or growth in faith among attenders.

FINANCIAL ISSUES

In so much of what happens in the wider society it is the bottom line that makes all the difference. Initiatives are curtailed, needs left unmet, decisions made or expediency justified on the basis of available finances. Money is a central factor in many important decisions.

The bottom line can affect churches as well. Available finances can permit or limit what can be done. Finances can sometimes be found when there is enthusiasm and a moving of the Holy Spirit. Much generosity is shown by ordinary people in the face of a crisis or major needs.

In order to explore financial issues in the life of congregations, the NCLS asked a range of questions:

- *Level of giving*: attenders were asked their approximate level of giving as a percentage of their income. Leaders were asked whether financial giving had increased or decreased in the previous year.
- *Income from assets*: leaders were asked whether their congregation received income from any assets and how the level of such income compared to giving from attenders within the congregation.
- *Levels of debt*: leaders were asked about levels of debt within their congregation and how this related to giving from attenders.
- *Support from the denomination*: leaders were asked whether their congregation received any financial support from their denominational body.

ATTENDER GIVING

A third of attenders give 10% or more of their income to their congregation, and a further 44% give 5% or less, making a total of 77% who regularly donate a portion of their income (*Winds of Change*, p 125).

Many commentators have argued that an effective congregation will have a committed core of attenders at its heart who sacrificially give to allow it to grow and develop (eg Olson, 1993, 220; Pointer, 1984, 101).

The NCLS results support such a contention, although the relationships are not strong, as is shown in Figure 16.4.

High levels of giving may be seen more as a consequence of a vital congregation than as an ingredient in its formation. However, congregations would be well advised to examine levels of giving. Lower levels of giving may be an indicator of the lack of commitment to or enthusiasm for the directions of the congregation, or indeed of attenders' feelings about congregational life in general.

In contrast, high levels of giving are likely to indicate a commitment to and enthusiasm for the congregation's direction.

INCOME FROM ASSETS

Around 80% of congregations receive little or no income from assets such as properties and 20% do receive income from assets. Only 5% of

FIGURE 16.4 :
FINANCIAL MATTERS

	STRENGTH OF RELATIONSHIPS	
	High levels of attender giving	
NEWCOMERS		0.4
YOUNG ADULT RETENTION		0.5
NUMERICAL GROWTH		0.3
SENSE OF BELONGING	++	2.2
COMMUNITY INVOLVEMENT	+++	3.0
SHARING/INVITING	++	1.2
GROWTH IN FAITH	++	1.8

NB: Strength of relationship is the percent of variance explained after accounting for local context/faith type effects

SOURCE: 1991 National Church Life Survey

congregations have income from assets that is equal to or greater than income from offertories.

It is sometimes suggested that congregations with high levels of income from assets are likely to become too comfortable; in 'asset-rich' congregations, attenders may tend towards lower levels of giving. There is some evidence of this tendency. For instance, among mainstream denominations, some 36% of attenders in congregations with high levels of income from assets give 5% or more of their income, compared to 45% of attenders in congregations with no income from assets.

FINANCES: A PROFILE

- 20% of congregations receive income from assets; for 5% of these income exceeds offertories.

- Congregations belonging to mainstream denominations, which have long been established in Australia, are the most likely to have significant levels of income from assets. Some 26% of Uniting, 23% of Presbyterian and 22% of Anglican congregations have income from assets.

- 23% of congregations receive financial assistance from denominational bodies or other congregations.

- 21% of congregations have significant levels of debt on building projects; of these 10% have debts which exceed total yearly offertories.

SOURCE: 1991 National Church Life Survey adjusted for non-participants

However, this study does not reveal a relationship between levels of income from assets and any of the congregational vitality measures. This is perhaps not surprising given the small proportion of congregations with high levels of asset income.

INCOME SUPPORT FROM DENOMINATIONS

About 23% of congregations receive outside financial support from the wider church, mainly to support a minister or other staff. Some writers have been critical of denominational assistance within the life of the church. Lyle Schaller, for instance, observes that denominational assistance creates a sense of dependency and erodes the initiative of the congregation (1989, 162). Commenting on the United Methodist Church in America, Schaller sees denominational assistance as part of a system that rewards numerical decline (Wilke, 1986, 61).

However, this study did not detect a significant relationship — either positive or negative — between reliance on wider church support and vitality. No doubt there are times when support from the wider denomination may be helpful and times when it does allow congregations to become complacent. Denominations and congregations need to think carefully about how and why congregations are funded.

LEVELS OF DEBT

The pressures of making ends meet may be a barrier to growing effective ministry. Around 79% of congregations do not owe money on building projects, with a further 11% having debts that are less than the total offertories for the previous year. For another 10% of congregations, however, levels of debt exceed offertories for a whole year. This study does not reveal a relationship between debt and congregational vitality.

ON PROPERTY AND FINANCES

While financial matters are important, they do not appear to determine congregational vitality. Financial giving can be an important litmus test of how attenders feel about their congregation and where it is heading. However, other factors have a stronger relationship with the vitality measures used in this study.

Apart from levels of giving, other aspects of financial management are not related to congregational vitality in any clear-cut way. While individual cases of debt may be quite painful, across the church indebtedness or the need for assistance does not necessarily inhibit vitality.

In the same way, the NCLS suggests that many concerns about the significance of property may be overstated. The major concerns in growing vital congregations appear to relate to people, not property.

That is not to say that property issues ought to be disregarded. In some instances a new property can be the symbol of a new start and a new direction. When existing congregations are amalgamated, it may be important to start in a new property rather than one owned by either of the original congregations (Kaldor, 1994, 64,65). This makes it clear that it is a new venture and not the continuation of one or other of the founding congregations. Moving into the 'neutral territory' of a non-church building can be a significant step forward in ministries to particular subgroups within the community (Kaldor and Kaldor, 1988, 94–99).

In his analysis of the factors affecting congregational vitality, Callahan draws a useful distinction between sources of satisfaction and dissatisfaction. Sources of satisfaction, he suggests, are mainly relational. Functional characteristics, such as property issues, tend to be sources of dissatisfaction. The more the functional characteristics are present, the lower the level of dissatisfaction among attenders (Callahan, 1983, xiv). Property issues need not be an impediment to effective mission if other aspects of congregational life and direction are in place and moving forward.

*Taken overall,
property and
financial issues are
not major
determinants of
vitality*

Taken overall, however, property issues are not major determinants of vitality. The factors discussed in this chapter do not make the top of the list of key factors in any of the aspects of vital congregations considered in this study.

Congregational attitude to property, on the other hand, has differing impacts on congregational vitality. In the areas of numerical growth, retaining young adults, and drawing in newcomers a more functional attitude to property appears worth fostering. This reflects the attitudes to property of the post-war generations. Those with a strong attachment to a church building may lack some of the flexibility needed to relate to younger adults and those without a church background. Alternatively, those without a church background and younger adults may find it more difficult to discover spiritual significance in bricks and mortar.

Some writers point to the dangers of congregations being too attached to their church building or the building becoming a central part of congregational identity. Such attitudes may hinder the church's ability to adapt to new ways of mission in a changing society (Luecke, 1988, 27–29). They can bear witness to the church's inflexibility and repel newcomers to church life (Snyder, 1975, 52–71).

Yet a building which is seen by many attenders as unimportant to their worship experience may point to a different issue. Such congregations are also more likely to report lower levels of a sense of belonging or growth in faith. It could be that change is needed to a building so that it makes a positive contribution to the worship experience.

Viewing buildings as transitory or able to be modified can come more easily to denominations that do not possess historic buildings. Similarly, this attitude is natural and congruent with the cultures of the post-war generations. For other denominations and congregations with a large proportion of older attenders, wrestling with attitudes to property may be important. Encouraging changes in attitudes may in some cases be no easier than making changes to the bricks and mortar that have been inherited!

PART 3

MATTERS OF CONTEXT AND FAITH

Parts 1 and 2 focused on the characteristics of congregations and how these relate to congregational vitality. Throughout the analysis, relationships were shown after taking account of the effect of the context in which a congregation is located and the faith type of its attenders.

Both these factors were treated as givens. A congregation cannot change the nature of the community in which it finds itself, although it can do much to affect the ways in which it responds to it. Likewise, approaches to matters of faith and belief in a congregation usually develop gradually and are certainly not altered lightly.

Yet, both context and faith type are strongly linked to congregational vitality. Part 3 documents some of the impact of local context and faith type on congregational vitality. Chapter 17 examines context and Chapter 18 examines patterns of faith and the impact of denominational traditions.

Because of the way this study has been structured, the presentation of results in these final two chapters needs to be slightly different from that in the previous chapters. The rating system in Part 2 provided a measure of impact of various factors *after* accounting for the impact of context and faith type. The same ratings scale cannot, therefore, be used for these chapters. Instead, the tables simply show the total percentage of variance explained by context and faith type. Where the relationship is negative the percent of variance is shown in brackets.

Where the percent of variance is zero (0) there is no relationship between the vitality indicator and the factor under consideration. A percent of variance of one hundred (100) would mean the vitality indicator is completely defined by the factor.

CHAPTER 17

AS GOES THE COMMUNITY, SO GOES THE CHURCH?

The Effect of Context on Church Life

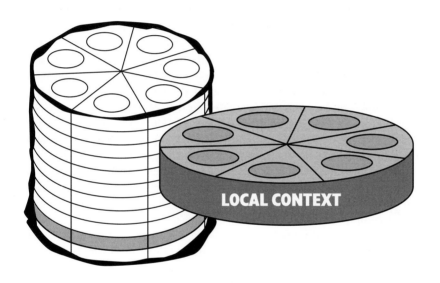

The conclusion was clear and categorical: where one church is failing nearly all the others are, because subjected to the downward pull of the common environment. Where one church is gaining nearly all the others are, because the common environment is on the side of all . . .

All told then, the conclusion 'like environment: like church' is abundantly demonstrated. 'As goes the neighbourhood so goes the church.'

— An early pioneer of church research in the United States, H. Paul Douglass (Douglass and Brunner, 1935, 254)

How much impact does context have on a congregation's vitality and effectiveness? Is it at all relevant? Or is it so significant that a congregation's future is totally defined by what is happening to its community? If so, there is little point in examining what makes for an effective congregation!

Clearly, H. Paul Douglass saw context as a critical factor. In the decades since Douglass made his observations, there has been a lot of research into church attendance in different communities. Most research has uncovered significant regional differences (eg Lenski 1953, Wuthnow and Christiano, 1979, in the United States and Martin, 1967, 47 in Great Britain).

There has been a considerable debate in the past few decades on the relative significance of contextual and internal congregational factors and which has the greater impact on church growth or decline. Indeed, a landmark publication edited by Hoge and Roozen entitled *Understanding Church Growth and Decline* (1979) invited a range of well-known writers to reflect on this question. Some, including Hoge and Roozen, suggest that local contextual factors are more important (1979, 326). Walrath demonstrated the relationship between changes in the nature of a neighbourhood and the fortunes of the local church. In his view, the context in which a church is placed has a great impact on likely attendance rates; internal factors may then determine whether that church performs at the top or the bottom of its context group (Walrath, 1979, 268).

Other writers in the book, such as Dean Kelley and Peter Wagner, felt that internal factors were more important. Internal factors include such things as the leadership style, theological orientation, sense of community, group processes, openness to change and so on.

In more recent times, the debate has recognised the importance of both contextual and congregational factors. Hadaway, for instance, observes that while churches may grow or decline in an urban location, in some areas the possibilities for growth are clearly better (or worse) than in others (1982, 372).

Other writers have taken a different perspective. Iannaccone, for instance, has claimed that some past research in the United States has over-emphasised the importance of context (1996, 197). He cites certain methodological issues to back up his claims.

Until the late 1980s, there was little research into regional fluctuations in church attendance in Australia. Indeed, while church planners and leaders referred colloquially to some areas as 'Bible belts', the standard research of the day emphasised the uniformity of church attendance in different communities (Mol, 1971, 109).

Such a finding was challenged by analysis in the late 1970s and 1980s (eg Langmead, 1977). *Who Goes Where? Who Doesn't Care?* (Kaldor, 1987) demonstrated what church leaders had suspected for a long time: church attendance in stable white-collar suburbs or new white-collar growth areas was many times higher than attendance in inner-city areas, blue-collar or multicultural communities. Church attendance in small rural communities tended to be higher than in larger towns.

DOES LOCAL CONTEXT MATTER?

The NCLS offers a unique opportunity to explore the impact of context on attendance rates. Estimates of attendance for all congregations participating in the survey were obtained from the congregations themselves, or from the leadership of their denominations, or were derived from other sources. This provided a comprehensive database of

attendance in Anglican and Protestant churches across Australia, regardless of their participation in the NCLS. When we connect Australian census data on local communities to the NCLS database, it is possible to examine the types of communities in which church attendance appears to be stronger or weaker.

Data was drawn for the local area around each participating congregation (see Appendix 1 for details). The census data includes factors such as the age profile of the community, its ethnic composition, socioeconomic make-up, family and household profile, growth in population, and the nominal religious affiliation of residents.

There are definitely Bible belts in Australia

There are definitely Bible belts in Australia. Levels of church attendance vary significantly between different communities. On average across Australia for every 1000 people in the population around 46 are estimated to be attending an Anglican or Protestant church on a given Sunday. But there are wide variations in attendance depending on the local area. Church attendance ranges from more than 100 people per 1000 in some rural areas to fewer than 15 attenders per 1000 people in other areas.

FACTORS AFFECTING OVERALL ATTENDANCE RATES

There are several factors affecting levels of church attendance in **urban areas** across Australia:

- Attendance rates are significantly higher in older, established areas with low levels of population turnover. Attendance is lower in growth areas or highly transient communities.
- Attendance rates are higher in areas where the average age of the population is older. Areas where there are younger adults under 40 years of age tend to have lower levels of church attendance. Not surprisingly, these are often growth areas on the edges of cities.
- Attendance rates tend to be higher in areas of higher socioeconomic status. Whether the measure of socioeconomic status includes levels of education, income or occupation, areas of higher status have significantly higher levels of church attendance.

Similarly, there are distinct patterns in **non-urban** Australia:

- Attendance rates are higher in stable communities with low levels of visitors or new residents. Such communities are less likely to have high population growth.
- Attendance rates are higher in older communities and communities with fewer 20 to 40 year olds.
- Attendance rates are higher in communities with a high level of involvement in farming and lower in communities with a high level of involvement in mining.
- Unlike the situation in urban areas, attendance rates in non-urban areas tend to be higher in areas with lower levels of education, income or occupational status.
- Attendance rates are lower in communities with higher levels of people born overseas.

SOURCE: Kaldor and Castle, 1995, 10.

The variations are even more clearly seen across Australian cities. In Sydney, for instance, a blue-collar, multicultural region such as Blacktown has an attendance rate of 27 people per 1000 and Fairfield a rate of 16 per 1000. In inner Sydney, Randwick fares not much better, with 17 people per 1000. Similar low levels of attendance appear in Melbourne in places such as Keilor (11 per 1000), Broadmeadows (14 per 1000) and Sunshine (15 per 1000).

In contrast, higher attendance rates are found in stable white-collar regions such as Ku-ring-gai in Sydney (78 per 1000) or in places such as Ipswich (93 per 1000) and Toowoomba (91 per 1000) in Queensland. In non-urban areas, attendance rates climb to more than 150 per 1000 people. Thus, attendance rates in some areas are more than ten times the rates in other areas. Variations in attendance rates in different communities are presented in detail in *Are There Bible Belts in Australia?* (Kaldor and Castle, 1995).

There can be no doubt that there are significant variations in overall attendance rates in different communities. Detailed regression analysis indicates that the nature of the local community could account for around 30% to 40% of the variation in levels of attendance in different areas.

It is therefore essential for congregations to understand the context in which they find themselves and to reflect on what are effective models of ministry in each type of community. Too often, books on church growth and planning make little mention of the community context in which the church is placed. Too often, leaders view successful models developed in quite different social contexts and seek to imitate them, without any translation to the situations in which they find themselves. Too often, such endeavours end up sinking without trace.

WHAT ABOUT CONGREGATIONAL VITALITY?

The fact that levels of attendance are different in different communities is sometimes used to gauge the relative effectiveness of traditional styles of church life. While differences may indeed be a reflection on styles of church life, it is important not to leap to simplistic conclusions.

Other factors may be at work as well, such as historical differences in new church development, the history of immigration of people from particular denominations to specific regions, or the attitudes of different sections of the community to the churches in times past.

Two examples may be illuminating. In fast-growing new housing estates, attendance levels may be low because fewer churches have been built. The scarcity of existing churches may make it easier to develop an enthusiastic, fast-growing congregation. Likewise, in a region with historically high attendance rates the decline of individual congregations may be masked by the high attendance levels across the region.

The NCLS can test not only the impact of local community make-up on attendance levels but also on congregational vitality.

FIGURE 17.1: THE IMPACT OF LOCAL CONTEXT

	STRENGTH OF RELATIONSHIPS		
	Local context overall	Urban	Non-urban
NEWCOMERS	12	15	11
YOUNG ADULT RETENTION	5	5	6
NUMERICAL GROWTH	8	9	8
SENSE OF BELONGING	8	7	9
COMMUNITY INVOLVEMENT	18	15	14
SHARING/ INVITING	9	9	10
GROWTH IN FAITH	13	12	14
SIZE OF CONGREGATION	28	14	30

NB: Strength of relationship is the percent of variance explained by contextual factors (adjusted R^2)

SOURCE: 1991 National Church Life Survey

Local context does have an impact on the various indicators of congregational vitality; the differences are, however, much less than the variations in overall levels of attendance discussed earlier in this chapter.

Levels of newcomers, community involvement and growth in faith are affected more significantly by the make-up of the local community than other indicators. A knowledge of the make-up of the local community in which a congregation is placed can account for between 5% and 18% of variation in the different indicators of congregational vitality. Young adult retention, numerical growth, belonging and sharing or inviting others to church are the least context dependent.

The relationship between the local community context and congregational vitality is complex. The relationships partly reflect similarities and differences in the demographic make-up of both congregations and their communities. This is explained further in the next sections.

A similar analysis of the importance of context on the likely size of congregations was also carried out. The context in which a congregation is placed is capable of explaining around 28% of the variation in the size of congregations. The same census data can account for only 8% of the variation in numerical growth. The size of congregations may be a function of recent growth or may be a legacy of history. There are other factors apart from growth at work.

Such a result underlines yet again the importance of not confusing the characteristics of numerically growing congregations with those of large congregations. This is a mistake made by commentators and denominational leaders far too often.

Clearly the context in which a congregation is placed does impact on its likely vitality. If other aspects apart from demographics could be taken into account, such as the presence of subcultural groups, local history and the impact of wider national trends, it is likely that context would be seen to be even more significant.

Clearly the context in which a congregation is placed does impact on its likely vitality

URBAN AND RURAL DIFFERENCES

The social life of a city or large town is different from that of a small rural town. People in rural areas often spend their lives in one locality, which forms the focus of their working and social lives. In a city or large town, the larger number and diversity of people reduce the importance of local community life. People tend to be part of social networks which are based on a common interest rather than a common locality.

Are city congregations more affected by the social make-up of their community than their non-urban counterparts? The results are also shown in Figure 17.1. Generally speaking, the answer appears to be no. While there are some slight differences, being located in the city or the country does not, in itself, make a great difference to likely congregational vitality.

POPULATION GROWTH

The NCLS suggests that both urban and non-urban congregations are more likely to be growing numerically in areas experiencing significant population growth. The results are shown in Figure 17.2. It also suggests that congregations in such communities are more likely to have high levels of newcomers. On the other hand, community involvement by attenders is likely to be lower in new urban areas; this result probably reflects the different age profiles and stability of new and older areas. Other factors are little affected by population growth.

AGE PROFILE

The NCLS suggests that the age profile of a community may significantly affect a congregation's fortunes. While involvement in wider community activities is more likely in older areas, on the other indicators effective congregations are more likely to be found in more youthful communities. In particular, congregations in younger communities are more likely to be drawing in newcomers. Further analysis suggests that these patterns hold in both urban and non-urban areas.

FIGURE 17.2: ASPECTS OF LOCAL CONTEXT

	STRENGTH OF RELATIONSHIPS			
	Higher population growth	Younger age profile	Higher levels of education or occupational status	Greater ethnic diversity
NEWCOMERS	3	5	7	5
YOUNG ADULT RETENTION	1	2	(1)	0
NUMERICAL GROWTH	4	3	(1)	1
SENSE OF BELONGING	1	2	(5)	1
COMMUNITY INVOLVEMENT	(1)	(8)	9	(5)
SHARING/ INVITING	1	2	(5)	2
GROWTH IN FAITH	1	3	(9)	3

1. NB: Strength of relationship is the percent of variance explained by contextual factors (adjusted R^2)
2. Where a figure is in brackets, there is a negative relationship with the vitality indicator
SOURCE: 1991 National Church Life Survey

SOCIOECONOMIC INDICATORS

Previous research on church attendance rates in urban Australia has suggested that there are higher levels of church attendance in areas which are better off or where there are higher levels of education. The pattern is, however, reversed in non-urban areas. Analysis of congregational vitality measures also reveals a mixed picture among urban and non-urban communities, highlighting the danger of a simplistic approach.

ETHNICITY

Congregations in more ethnically diverse communities tend to be more vital, particularly in relation to levels of newcomers. This may be partly due to particular congregations assuming more importance as a source of identity for those who attend in such areas. It may also reflect higher enthusiasm for church involvement among some ethnic groups.

As with other community characteristics, patterns in relation to wider community involvement among attenders are quite different, with lower levels of involvement more likely in more ethnically diverse communities.

WHAT WE DO DOES MATTER

Is the vitality or future of a congregation completely determined by the local context? To what extent can congregations affect their future by the way they respond to their context and by the priorities they set for their life and mission?

The NCLS provides an excellent opportunity to evaluate the relative importance of internal and external factors to congregational vitality. A selection of the strongest internal factors was used; internal factors do not include faith type or denomination, which are discussed in the next chapter.

The strength of relationship of internal factors with congregational vitality was then compared with that for contextual factors. The results are outlined in Figure 17.3.

FIGURE 17.3: HOW IMPORTANT IS LOCAL CONTEXT?			
	STRENGTH OF RELATIONSHIPS		
	Local contextual factors	Internal factors	Local context + internal factors
NEWCOMERS	12	33	39
YOUNG ADULT RETENTION	5	13	17
NUMERICAL GROWTH	8	24	29
SENSE OF BELONGING	8	56	59
COMMUNITY INVOLVEMENT	18	36	45
SHARING/ INVITING	9	68	69
GROWTH IN FAITH	13	68	69

NB: Strength of relationship is the percent of variance explained by contextual or internal factors (adjusted R^2)

SOURCE: 1991 National Church Life Survey

It would seem that a knowledge of the internal life of a congregation is more helpful in predicting congregational vitality than a knowledge of the community context in which a congregation is placed. Indeed, in this analysis, a knowledge of context adds little to the overall picture, given an understanding of the nature of congregational life and mission.

However, these results need to be interpreted with caution. The statistical techniques used reveal the strength of relationship, not causality or details about the nature of the relationship. The internal characteristics of a congregation may be in direct response to the nature of the community. A congregation seeking to minister effectively to a particular community may well tailor its ministry and priorities to the particular community for which it has a concern. Contextual and internal factors are not easily separated from each other.

So what do these results say? It is clear that internal factors can significantly affect the destiny of a congregation. While context can have a significant impact, it is not determinative of the likely fortunes of a church.

AS GOES THE COMMUNITY, SO GOES THE CHURCH?

This analysis points to some major issues for the churches. First, local context matters. Congregations ignore their context at their peril. If anything, this analysis probably underestimates the effect of local context, which can include unique cultural and historical aspects not represented in demographic patterns. Beyond the local context, there are a great many other, more national contextual forces at work, including wider cultural shifts, changing social and political values, changes in occupational structures, technological change, the media and so on (Hoge, 1979b, 94–100). While often not measurable in a way that could be included in the NCLS, they are significant in their impact.

Second, congregations can respond positively to the context in which they find themselves. Their futures are not completely determined by that context; rather their context creates an opportunity to respond positively to those around them. There is much a congregation can do to make itself more effective in mission in the particular context in which it has been placed.

> **Congregations can respond positively to the context in which they find themselves**

These two conclusions may seem to be contradictory. This is possibly because writers on context and internal factors often seek to champion the cause of one and deny the impact of the other. This creates the impression that any analysis of the church's place in the wider society is fundamentally in opposition to an examination of the internal factors in its life and vice versa.

This is a false dichotomy. Analysis of church life needs to be based on a premise that the patterns which emerge are not unalterable and that both contextual and internal factors can affect the future of a congregation.

SEEKING TO UNDERSTAND THE CONTEXT FOR MINISTRY

Congregations need to reflect carefully on what it means to be the church in their particular setting. Every social context is unique. Ray Herrmann, in reflecting on ministry in six coal-mining communities within 50 miles of each other in central Queensland, suggested that each required a different approach because of their nature and stage of development, the people and the company attitude: 'To have done the same in each place would have kept me busy, but not effective' (1983, 37).

Different settings pose different challenges and open up different possibilities. Churches can have a more pivotal role in the lives of smaller rural communities than they can in larger regional centres or cities. Clergy can have greater influence with a clearer social role. On the other hand, as observers such as Dempsey (1983b) have noted, they tend to come in as outsiders, generating distrust and uncertainty. Because of the small population base, many churches face financial difficulties in maintaining a church presence.

Churches in larger regional centres and cities must take into account the increasing diversity of their communities. Often these changing realities are obscured by the church's historical traditions as a village or small-town church.

White-collar dormitory suburbs more easily provide the churches with an accepted social role. This is far from the case in transient inner-urban communities which pose great challenges. Congregations developed when the area was a stable dormitory suburb are often in decline and culturally quite different from the population around them. Such contexts provide dramatic examples of how in so many places churches have lost their significance as centres of community life, just as the local community has ceased to have importance for people (Hughes, 1991, 101). People are tending to find their sense of belonging in communities of people with a common interest.

Yet the transient nature of inner-urban (and many other) communities also opens up possibilities. In such areas people tend to live in more regional interest-based networks. Congregations can develop significant ministries regionally to communities of people with common interests. (Bentley, Blombery and Hughes, 1992, 51). Examples in Australian cities include ministries among university students, ethnic groupings, social activists and bikers (Kaldor and Kaldor, 1988).

Multicultural communities present additional challenges. In some cases this is because of a declining base of nominal adherents; in others, questions of ministry involve accommodating the cultural diversity of attenders from different cultural backgrounds. Likewise, in growth areas, particularly blue-collar estates, difficulties are often presented by a lack of church plant, clergy or people resources.

So often congregations that developed at a time when the community was different, struggle in the new social reality, sometimes becoming refuges for a segment of the community. In more severe cases, the financial viability of a congregation comes into question, and it faces closure.

Congregations in communities experiencing certain types of rapid social change are likely to be most vulnerable. These include stable dormitory suburbs that become home to diverse ethnic groups, older areas in the process of decline due to expansion by industry, freeways or commerce, rural villages on the urban fringe rapidly moving towards an urban identity, suburbs experiencing large amounts of home unit development, and non-urban communities faced with large population turnover or growth.

Congregations that seek to hold on to a past identity when a community begins to change are likely to find themselves becoming increasingly redundant to their communities. They tend to become *closed systems*, defining their priorities only in terms of their membership, losing sight of the environment around them (Anderson and Jones, 1978). In this way, congregations become unaware of the changes taking place until the changes have proceeded far enough to be threatening. Once a group is threatened, they are more likely to react against the community than respond to it.

This issue is discussed in greater detail in *Who Goes Where? Who Doesn't Care?* (Kaldor, 1987). Responding positively to the community may require a change in mindset for many church leaders. Congregations wanting to develop a strong connection with a particular community may benefit from the following three prerequisites drawn loosely from the work of Currie, Gilbert and Horsley (1977, 59).

First, connection depends on **proximity**. A congregation needs to be accessible and available to the wider community. There need to be bridges between the congregation and sections of the community across which people and communication can flow. Such bridge building will require a good understanding of the community and its diversity, its past and its future, the networks, grapevines and gatekeepers.

Second, as was noted in Chapter 15, a **congruity** between church and community may be helpful. This picks up the issue of cultural appropriateness for the church in its life and expression. This may sometimes be a difficult issue, particularly in diverse communities where church life does not itself reflect that diversity. A congregation may need to take risks to develop culturally appropriate styles of church life and indigenous leadership. Congregations need to allow themselves to be affected by the diversity in the wider community, relating creatively to it rather than insulating themselves from it.

Third, congregations need to consider their **utility** to the wider community, what it is that they are actually offering. What are entry points for the gospel into the life of the community for which it is concerned? What are the community's hurts or its aspirations? How does the Christian faith relate to the community's situation? How ought the congregation be in mission with its community?

MOVING FORWARD

Most congregations consider that they are a part of the community they seek to serve. Such beliefs need to be backed up by quality action based on clear understanding. Understanding may only be a first step, but it is certainly a fundamental one. Some stress the importance of more training for clergy in the social sciences, to better understand their communities (eg Jackson, 1996).

Developing an understanding of the community requires contact with people with widely different views of the community: local government planners, teachers, kids on the street and so on. Different people provide different perspectives on the same community, which can help fill out the picture.

Such reflection is particularly important in areas undergoing rapid social change. Congregations which can recognise the signs of change in advance of their impact are likely to be more effective in responding to them.

Too often little thought is given to such issues by congregational and denominational leaders. The church needs to develop a wide vision for ministry that sees different types of ministries as appropriate in different social contexts. Different ministries in the same area can complement each other in relating to different segments of a society. And, as the results in this chapter show, while careful attention needs to be paid to the

context for ministry, that context need not be seen as overwhelming. If congregations have an understanding of the community with which they are in mission, there are creative ways forward for them if they have open eyes and hearts. There can be a creative future.

RESPONDING TO THE COMMUNITY CONTEXT

Questioning a church's role in its community can lead to some interesting discoveries — and send the congregation on a new and challenging journey.

Motivated by the question 'Who are the people in our area?', a Uniting Church congregation in the suburbs of Melbourne used the most recent government census to discover that two important groups of people lived and worked nearby. The census showed these 'peaks' as the elderly (already visible) and people aged 20 to 30 years.

It was assumed that the younger group was reasonably well educated, so the church committee tried to run academically oriented seminars in order to connect with them. The seminars did nothing to increase the numbers in the predominantly older congregation and were discontinued.

Five years ago, still determined to focus on outreach, the congregation tried again. This time it teamed up with other denominations in the area and opened a drop-in centre for students who attended a nearby university. The results have been more promising.

'Our centre offered the usual things, plus Bible study groups, discussion groups, and counselling', the minister said. 'It was terrific that our congregation supported the centre all the way, and even acted as volunteer staff. It was satisfying to see that many of the students who 'dropped in' on a regular basis became involved with its running, acting as treasurer, committee members, that sort of thing.'

Did the drop-in centre lead to an increase in numbers at church services? 'Yes, I think so', the minister said. 'The student population is very mobile, by its nature. We hope to instil some sense of curiosity and inquiry into the young people, so that they're tempted to drop in at a church — and it's there in our public image, the church service, that we need to change. We've realised this for some time.'

'That needs to be our next step. The question is, are we ready for it?'

CHAPTER 18

ARE THE CONSERVATIVE CHURCHES REALLY GROWING?

The Impact of Denomination and Approach to Faith

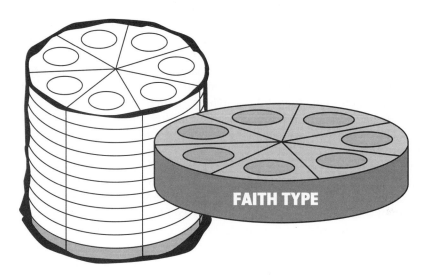

FAITH TYPE

Visit as many churches as you can in a day was the request. He wants to get a feel for church life in this city! And so it was organised. A rapid-fire trip into the back of as many worship services as possible on an overcast, drizzly Sunday morning, sometimes dropping into large traditional church buildings, at other times into little back rooms and halls.

The first visit was to a congregation of 100 or so, a congregation with well-dressed children sitting politely through the first half of a fairly traditional family service, with a sermon on Christian values.

Then it was down the road and into another traditional church building. Again a group of well-dressed people. Here, however, they were using choruses interspersed with some passionate talk of God's salvation and humanity's sinfulness. There were some references to the importance of not letting emotionalism overtake faith. Again we left in the early stages of the sermon, which seemed to be a fervent plea to attenders to get out and convert those they meet in their daily lives.

Our next stop was a local Pentecostal church. Interspersed among the songs at the end of the praise time were testimonies to what God had done for people in their lives. A young and enthusiastic band of guitars and drums, accompanied by clapping of hands and arm raising, created an often electric atmosphere.

The Anglican church just down the road was a contrast. Instead of the enthusiasm and celebration of the previous church there was quiet and contemplation, punctuated by carefully crafted liturgy. Candles and incense pervaded the atmosphere as the minister talked about the needs and rights of migrant women being abused in some of the factories in the local community.

As the day proceeded we visited a small house church meeting over brunch, a Fijian congregation, a fairly traditional Catholic mass, and a large regional Greek Orthodox church with its icons, candles and rituals.

All of these are expressions of contemporary Christianity — a variety of denominations with different emphases and styles, bringing rich traditions to a radically changing contemporary reality. And underlying the stylistic and cultural differences are often differences in beliefs.

To what extent are these differences important? What relationships are there between differences in beliefs and denominational traditions and the vitality measures used in this study? This controversial and difficult area is the subject of this chapter.

DIFFERENT FAITH STREAMS

Over the past two centuries the growing diversity of denominations and the possibility of choice has given rise to different theological and missional emphases. Some denominations have emphasised the importance of evangelism and the conversion of individuals in society, others the social responsibility of the churches in the wider community. The evangelical movement has emerged, and there have been many great mission endeavours. At the same time science, technology and social reflection have raised many questions for the churches, resulting in theological developments that seek to deal openly with such issues. More recently Pentecostalism and the charismatic movement have also had a dramatic impact.

During the 1950s and 1960s, an era when mainstream churches in the United States were experiencing numerical growth, it was believed that most denominational transfers of attenders were from theologically conservative to more liberal mainline churches (eg Stark and Glock, 1968, 183). It was felt that the latter were more in tune with contemporary life. In the radical theological ferment and questioning of the 1960s, attenders were asked to ponder *The Suburban Captivity of the Churches* (Winter, 1961) and *The Death of God* (Vahanian, 1961). Many assumed it was only a matter of time before more conservative, evangelical and fundamentalist churches would die out.

In 1972 Dean Kelley published a book that turned this assumption on its ear. 'In the latter years of the 1960s something remarkable happened in the United States: for the first time in the nation's history most of the major church groups stopped growing and began to shrink' (Kelley, 1972, 1). Kelley provided statistics on the decline in the mainstream denominations in the United States and noted significant growth among other conservative or independent denominations. 'These groups not only give evidence that religion is not obsolete and churches not defunct, but they contradict the contemporary notion of acceptable religion. They are not *reasonable*, they are not *tolerant*, they are not *ecumenical*, they are not *relevant*. Quite the contrary!' (Kelley, 1972, 25).

Kelley suggested that more conservative Protestant churches have grown because of their ability to provide a clear-cut message and set of behaviour codes and to meet the ultimate meaning needs of their constituents, while the more theologically diverse mainstream churches have lost some of their ability to respond to the basic human search for meaning. He argued that they had not grown because they had not imposed discipline on their members or expected as much from them, and, therefore, they suffered from 'the dynamics of diminishing demands'.

Kelley raised the possibility that the fortunes of churches are related to the nature of their beliefs. In a world of increasing religious plurality, churches that are not clear-cut on the nature and implication of their beliefs are less likely to be effective than those that are decisive. In a society with an increasing range of institutions and options for involvement, the churches must understand clearly their task and contribution or find themselves replaced by other options. Denominations most embedded in the surrounding culture will be the most subject to favourable or unfavourable shifts in that culture.

Needless to say, the Kelley thesis created heated argument and controversy. Mainline denominational leaders saw it as challenging their overall directions. Writing several years on, Kelley remained 'unrepentant and unreconstructed' (1978, 171).

Both Bibby in Canada (1978) and Bruce in the United Kingdom (1983) have suggested that declining church attendance has had a more damaging effect on the broadly based denominations than on conservative Protestant groups. However, both suggest that the effect is largely unrelated to people outside of church life. Rather they suggest that conservative churches have better rates of retention of their members than mainline denominations and they have, on balance, gained more members through inter-church transfer. The NCLS would support such observations on retention and denominational switching in relation to the Australian context, although it suggests mainstream denominations are also drawing in higher levels of newcomers.

The Kelley thesis raises a range of issues that we shall return to later in this chapter.

ARE CONSERVATIVE CHURCHES REALLY GROWING?

Evaluating the faith type of attenders in a survey such as the NCLS is not easy. The leaders of congregations were asked for the faith traditions that they considered to be the most significant to their congregation.

FAITH TYPE: A PROFILE

According to congregational leaders, the most significant theological traditions for their congregations are

• Anglo-Catholic/Catholic	20%
• Evangelical	46%
• Charismatic/Pentecostal	19%
• Reformed	13%
• Liberal	3%
• Traditions of their denomination	52%
• Traditions of a predecessor denomination	19%

NB: Leaders were allowed to select two options; percentages will not therefore add up to 100%.

- Some 21% of attenders believe the Bible to be the word of God, to be taken literally, while a further 48% believe it needs to be read in the context of the times to understand its implications for us today. Around 29% believe it is a valuable book, while 2% do not know.

- If they had to join a new congregation, 55% of attenders would choose one with a primary focus on evangelism and 19% with a primary focus on social action. Some 26% do not know.

- Regarding 'speaking in tongues' 37% of attenders approve of it as it is practised today, 31% disapprove and 32% have no opinion. Among those who approve, 20% have actually spoken in tongues.

SOURCE: 1991 National Church Life Survey adjusted for non-participants

---

In addition, attenders were asked three questions about matters of faith to be used as summary indicators: their attitudes to the Bible; whether they would prefer to join a congregation with an emphasis on evangelism or social concern; and their orientation to speaking in tongues. The questions are detailed in Appendix 1.

The first two questions were designed to give an indication of belief in relation to two issues which have been touchstones in theological debate within the churches. The last question was designed as an indicator of orientation to the charismatic renewal.

The NCLS also asked attenders some additional questions about specific beliefs, including beliefs about Jesus' person and resurrection, and attitudes to eternal life. Detailed exploration suggests that the responses to these questions add little to the overall predictive power of the core faith type variables already described (see Appendix 1).

There are many nuances and detail in this area that go well beyond the scope of the NCLS. Nevertheless, these indicators cover a great diversity of patterns of faith and are highly useful summary indicators in a study such as this.

Almost every aspect of congregational vitality is positively related to a conservative orientation to the Bible

The NCLS shows that attitudes to the Bible are significantly related to congregational vitality. Every aspect of congregational vitality, except for involvement in the wider community, is positively related to a conservative orientation to the Bible, although the level of impact varies for different indicators. The results are shown in Figure 18.1.

FIGURE 18.1: THE IMPACT OF FAITH TYPE

	STRENGTH OF RELATIONSHIPS			
	Conservative attitude to the Bible	Preference for evangelism over social action	Positive orientation to 'speaking in tongues'	Faith type overall
NEWCOMERS	5	1	4	11
YOUNG ADULT RETENTION	6	6	6	8
NUMERICAL GROWTH	3	2	6	6
SENSE OF BELONGING	8	10	13	16
COMMUNITY INVOLVEMENT	(12)	(16)	(13)	(21)
SHARING/ INVITING	35	42	53	54
GROWTH IN FAITH	23	27	38	40

1. NB: Strength of relationship is the percent of variance explained by faith type factors (adjusted R^2)
2. Where a figure is in brackets, there is a negative relationship with the vitality indicator
SOURCE: 1991 National Church Life Survey

A conservative orientation to the Bible is strongly related to a congregation's likelihood of having attenders willing to discuss their faith and invite others to church. It is also strongly related to growth in faith of attenders.

A conservative orientation to the Bible is also positively related to attenders feeling a strong sense of belonging to their congregation and the likelihood of young adults being retained within its life. The relationship between levels of newcomers and attitudes to the Bible as well as numerical growth is not as strong, although it is also positive.

In contrast, levels of involvement in the wider community are negatively related to a conservative orientation.

EVANGELISM OR SOCIAL CONCERN?

During this century there has been a lot of debate between Christians who place a strong emphasis on verbal proclamation and those who feel a strong commitment to social concern. This divide has been closely related to attitudes to the Bible. However, in recent decades the debate has also taken place within evangelical circles and is no longer just a division between evangelicalism and liberalism (Samuel and Hauser, 1989, 200–207).

Many writers on congregational vitality have seen an emphasis on evangelism as an important prerequisite for an effective congregation. Writers within the Church Growth Movement provide a good example of this. Observers of mainstream denominations have also developed such a perspective. 'We pass resolutions about the poor, but we do not invite them into our churches' (Wilke, 1986, 40).

Many have emphasised the importance of holding both dimensions together. As has been noted elsewhere, the NCLS suggests that the majority of Australian attenders would look for a balance of both social concern and evangelism.

The NCLS asked attenders whether they would prefer to be part of a congregation with a major emphasis on evangelism or on social concern. Not surprisingly, a preference for evangelism is strongly related to discussing faith and inviting others to church as well as growth in faith. However, a preference for evangelism is also an important factor in relation to a growing sense of belonging and in the retention of young adults.

Yet, in the area of newcomers and numerical growth a preference for evangelism is hardly significant. This lack of relationship between an orientation to evangelism and levels of newcomers is interesting.

Not surprisingly, in the area of community involvement the pattern is reversed. Congregations with high levels of attenders who favour a focus on social concern are far more involved in the wider community.

THE RISE OF THE CHARISMATIC MOVEMENT

A major change of the last few decades has been the growth of the charismatic movement across the church globally. In Australia it has moved from the fringe to being a major component of church life.

Pentecostal churches are perhaps one of the largest sectors of the Anglican/Protestant church in Australia, if attendance is used as the yardstick. The impact of the charismatic movement has spread far wider, with many congregations in non-Pentecostal denominations being charismatic in orientation. Around 10% of attenders in mainstream denominations speak in tongues (*Winds of Change*, p 75).

The NCLS also indicates there is a strong positive relationship between attitudes to 'speaking in tongues' and the congregational vitality indicators. As in previous sections, a positive orientation to the charismatic movement is strongly related to attenders discussing faith, inviting others to church and growth in faith. It is also important in the area of belonging, in retention of young adults, numerical growth and levels of newcomers. Again, a positive orientation to the charismatic movement is negatively correlated with involvement in the wider community.

A positive orientation to the charismatic movement is negatively correlated with involvement in the wider community

Some readers may be interested in the relative contribution of attitude to the Bible and orientation to the charismatic movement. Both are strongly inter-related. As can be seen in Figure 18.1, a positive orientation to the charismatic movement is more strongly related to numerical growth, a growing sense of belonging, growth in faith and a willingness to discuss faith or invite others to church than is attitude to the Bible. Both factors are of similar importance in relation to levels of newcomers and young adult retention.

HOW IMPORTANT IS FAITH TYPE?

So just how important is the faith type of a congregation in relation to vitality? Is it more important or less important than the local context in which a congregation finds itself or the nature and styles of congregational life discussed in Part 2? The relative contribution of faith type, context and internal factors to congregational vitality is presented in Figure 18.2. Again, the summary collection of internal factors discussed in the previous chapter was used.

Compared to the contextual factors, faith type appears to contribute more to a sense of belonging, discussing faith or inviting others to church, and growth in faith. This is unsurprising, given that these factors would be more influenced by the nature of the congregation than by its surrounding community.

In relation to numerical growth and wider community involvement, faith type and contextual factors appear to be of similar importance. Likewise, the differences are only small in relation to the level of newcomers and young adult retention.

Neither set of factors, however, has anywhere near the relationship with congregational vitality that the internal factors used for this test have. A more detailed analysis, summarised in Appendix 1, shows that internal factors account for a great deal of variation in congregational vitality, even after taking into account the effects of context and faith

FIGURE 18.2: HOW IMPORTANT IS FAITH TYPE?

	STRENGTH OF RELATIONSHIPS			
	Faith type	Context	Internal factors	Faith type + context +internal
NEWCOMERS	11	12	33	44
YOUNG ADULT RETENTION	8	5	13	19
NUMERICAL GROWTH	6	8	24	30
SENSE OF BELONGING	16	8	56	59
COMMUNITY INVOLVEMENT	21	18	36	52
SHARING/ INVITING	54	9	68	72
GROWTH IN FAITH	40	13	68	70

NB: Strength of relationship is the percent of variance explained by each set of factors (adjusted R^2)
SOURCE: 1991 National Church Life Survey

type. On the other hand, neither faith type nor context account for much variation in vitality after account has been taken of internal factors. The exception is wider community involvement, where both faith type and local context are significant predictors of patterns of wider community involvement even after accounting for internal factors.

To some extent such comparisons are artificial; styles of congregational life can be closely related to faith traditions. Many aspects of congregational life and expression flow directly from beliefs and traditions.

FAITH TYPE AND CONGREGATIONAL LIFE — TAKING IT FURTHER

There is value in seeking to understand better the connections between faith and congregational vitality described in this chapter. Why does a more conservative theological orientation have a positive effect on congregational vitality? In seeking to answer this, we return to Dean Kelley's work as a starting point.

Kelley identified several reasons why conservative churches are more effective, including the following:

- they present a clear-cut message that better meets people's ultimate meaning needs;
- they make higher demands on members in terms of commitment and behaviour;
- they exhibit greater zeal for evangelism;
- they are not affirming of culture.

A CLEAR-CUT MESSAGE

Kelley argues that conservative churches grow because they are able to provide clear-cut meaning systems for attenders. This is done in a social setting that demands commitment and conformity. Because such demands are made, lukewarm commitment and half-hearted acceptance of beliefs can be avoided (Hadaway, 1980, 303).

Gerlach and Hine (1968) suggest that features that have been important in the expansion of Pentecostalism include a belief system which offers a sense of identity, a strong sense of personal commitment, face-to-face recruitment by committed lay members, and a measure of real or perceived opposition from society. Such a list echoes almost point for point the issues highlighted by Kelley.

Alan Black's research on Pentecostalism in Australia highlights that Pentecostal attenders are more likely than attenders in more mainstream denominations to adopt absolute or rigid views on a wide range of theological, social and moral issues. (Black, 1988). Similar results have been found in the NCLS (see *Views from the Pews*).

The mainstream denominations, on the other hand, are more characterised by theological diversity. They are more likely to encourage questioning and reflection on matters of faith. There is less dogmatism and more of an emphasis on people finding a level of involvement with which they are comfortable.

No doubt many in non-conservative churches and in the wider community would be uncomfortable with the certainty and dogmatism of conservative groups. Some might quietly envy the security conservative faith can bring, but question whether issues of faith and life are capable of such clear-cut responses.

Because they are broader, the mainstream churches do not always provide such clear-cut meaning systems nor encourage such a strong sense of identity or commitment. Hadaway and Roozen suggest that these churches continue to 'cling to an establishment model of being *the* church, when in fact they no longer have the captive culture or subculture for such a model to work' (Hadaway and Roozen, 1995, 75).

Reflecting on survey results in Australia, Philip Hughes and 'Tricia Blombery draw a distinction between those seeing their faith primarily in terms of access to a loving God and those who see their faith primarily in terms of providing a set of values to live by (Hughes and Blombery, 1990, 37). The former group are more likely to take a literal view of the Bible and to be highly involved in church life and evangelistic activity. The latter group, termed 'principlists', are more likely to be liberal in theology and less involved in congregational life. As the social role of the churches has diminished, there has been less reason for principlists to be involved. It is this group, they suggest, that has been moving out of church life over the last few decades.

MAKING HIGHER DEMANDS

A major contribution to the study of religion that has generated much controversy has come from 'rational choice' theorists (eg Stark and Bainbridge, 1985; Iannaccone, 1992, 1994). Rational choice theory attempts to apply marketplace economic theory to churches. In an age where religious affiliation is increasingly a matter of choice, religious organisations must compete for members in the marketplace. The fortunes of religious groups and denominations will rise and fall depending on the value of what they offer to 'consumers'. Rational choice theorists argue that congregations which expect more of members are capable of offering and generating higher rewards for involvement. It is these congregations that will grow. Kelley's thesis becomes central to these people's understanding of the religious fortunes of congregations and denominations.

Further, they argue that clear boundaries in church life will be critical for effectiveness. Religious groups are always open to being used by people with little actual involvement with or commitment to them. As Hechter (1987, 27) explains: 'Truly rational people will not join a group to pursue common ends when, even if they do not participate, they can reap the benefits of the activity of others'. Finke and Stark note that mainstream denominations are plagued with members who draw upon the denomination for weddings and the like but give little back in return. In their opinion, such 'free riders' devalue the religious rewards of involvement for all (1992, 253). Iannaccone suggests strictness in conservative churches acts like an entry fee, discouraging those not seriously interested (1994, 1187).

Finke and Stark see the weakening of boundaries in church life and diminishing expectations about commitment as inevitable, because humans seem to have rather mixed motives when they make choices about religion (1992, 275). We want our religion to be sufficiently potent, vivid and compelling so that it can offer rewards of great magnitude — a religion that is capable of miracles and which imparts order and sanity to the human condition. The religious organisations that maximise these aspects also demand the highest price in terms of what the individual must do to qualify.

It is difficult, however, for people to be committed to meeting such costs over the long term. People begin to 'bargain' with their church for lower levels of commitment and fewer sacrifices. There comes a point, the authors argue, when a religious body has become so worldly that its rewards are few and lacking in plausibility. At this point people begin to switch away, either to other groups providing a more clear-cut message or out into the wider secular environment. In this way mainstream churches are always headed for the sideline (Finke and Stark, 1992, 275). Such comments echo sociological thinking on the differences between churches and sects.

GREATER ZEAL FOR EVANGELISM

A different orientation to the world will affect the mission orientation of a congregation. As a major study of a city in the United states noted: 'In fundamental ways each congregation's mission orientation is grounded in its understanding of the action of God in history' (Roozen, McKinney and Carroll, 1984, 263). Beliefs are likely to be critical to generating different styles of outward focus.

In the more evangelical or Pentecostal churches, a high premium is placed on the spreading of the gospel message and on eternal salvation as our greatest need. Organisations which strongly hold such beliefs are much more likely to be zealous in evangelism and missionary work. Consequently, part of the growth of such congregations will be through recruitment of new members from the wider community.

Some researchers see an outward evangelistic emphasis as more significant than the strictness of a congregation. Churches grow not by screening out 'free riders' for lack of commitment but rather by welcoming them to enjoy the benefits of involvement as 'free samples with the promise of even better things to come' (Hadaway and Marler, 1996, 220).

The NCLS results on the link between evangelistic activity, mission focus and the flow of newcomers into church life is dealt with in more detail in Chapter 11. It is sufficient to note here that engagement in such activity must work to the advantage of the more conservative groups in contrast to those congregations which eschew recruitment through such a process.

NON-AFFIRMATION OF CULTURE

Kelley argues that one of the characteristics of conservative churches is that they do not seek for 'relevance' or to be embedded in the surrounding culture.

Hoge suggests that the denominations that were hardest hit by the declines of the 1960s and 1970s were those that were highest in socioeconomic status and most affirmative of American culture: 'We believe Kelley is right when he says that denominations most embedded in the surrounding culture are most subject to favourable or unfavourable shifts in the culture' (Hoge, 1979c, 197).

Not all studies in the United States support this aspect of Kelley's work. While finding a link between numerical growth and conservative theology, Roof and his co-researchers found little relationship between growth and the extent to which denominations are embedded in or stand apart from the surrounding culture (1979, 216).

The NCLS tends not to support Kelley's thesis. The results in Chapter 9 in relation to worship style suggest that contemporary styles of worship have a positive relationship with numerical growth and other aspects of vitality.

NOEL HAD SEARCHED FOR YEARS BEFORE HE
FOUND A CHURCH WITH A TWIN EMPHASIS ON
NEW TESTAMENT GREEK AND HEAVY METAL MUSIC

Hughes attributes some of the success of Pentecostalism over the last
few decades to a congruence between Pentecostalism and contemporary
culture. The style of music in Pentecostal churches is contemporary, there
is strong encouragement to corporate participation in worship, and the
strong emotional content contrasts with a more propositional approach to
faith among mainstream churches (Hughes, 1996, 103).

It would seem important in discussing how churches strive to be
'relevant' or embedded in the surrounding culture to distinguish between
matters of style and content. The NCLS results and Hughes's comments
are more in the realm of style than content. They suggest the importance
of maintaining strength in commitment and meaning systems, yet
expressing them in non-alienating cultural forms. Alan Black has noted

that although Pentecostalism 'involves a deliberate rejection of some aspects of contemporary culture, in other respects it is closely attuned to that culture' (1991, 116). As Posterski comments from the Canadian context, effective churches will stay in touch both with the times and the truth (Posterski and Barker, 1993, 109).

LINKING FAITH TYPE AND VITALITY

A range of studies have been carried out that have sought to examine the links between faith, practices and vitality. Quite a deal of the United States research is documented in two edited volumes: *Understanding Church Growth and Decline* (Hoge and Roozen [eds], 1979) and *Church and Denominational Growth* (Roozen and Hadaway [eds], 1993). One study reported in the earlier volume found some support for a link between numerical growth and conservative theology and clear demands on members (Roof *et al*, 1979, 216).

Not everybody is in agreement with such theories (eg Thompson *et al*, 1993, 197). In an overview, Roozen and Hadaway suggest that the research provides little support for Kelley's ideas in relation to churches' organisational strictness. Rather, the growth of conservative denominations is, in their view, due more to a high commitment to evangelism and a lower level of secularism (1993, 42).

Using the NCLS database, it is possible to compare the relative contributions to vitality of faith type and two of the four aspects discussed above, namely, mission activity and levels of commitment. Aspects considered in relation to zeal for evangelism include the value attenders place on outward-focused activities and their openness to discussing faith or inviting others to church. Commitment is measured by level of attendance at worship and other activities, and levels of giving. While it is not an exact test of the Kelley hypotheses, the results can be illustrative of the links between faith and practice. The results are shown in Figure 18.3.

The explanatory power of the three categories of factors varies between vitality indicators. However, for all vitality indicators, faith type is less significant than either outward focus or commitment. In further analysis, the faith type of a congregation contributed little to explaining levels of vitality after accounting for a congregation's outward focus and the levels of commitment of attenders (see Appendix 1 for further details).

Faith type is less significant than either outward focus or commitment

Different patterns of faith result in different types of faith communities with differing levels of outward focus or internal commitment. The results here suggest that, in terms of congregational vitality, an outward focus or a strong sense of commitment appear to be more significant than the actual faith type, though of course the factors are strongly intertwined.

The result is an important one, because it suggests that it is not simply the adherence to a set of beliefs that is important to congregational vitality but whether those beliefs are acted upon. Believing in the importance of evangelism is one thing; carrying it out in sensitive and effective ways is another.

FIGURE 18.3: FAITH TYPE AND INTERNAL FACTORS COMPARED

	STRENGTH OF RELATIONSHIPS		
	Evangelism and an outward focus	Attender commitment (involvement and giving)	Faith type
NEWCOMERS	15	16	11
YOUNG ADULT RETENTION	9	11	8
NUMERICAL GROWTH	14	10	6
SENSE OF BELONGING	25	18	16
COMMUNITY INVOLVEMENT	28	29	21
SHARING/ INVITING	N/A	55	54
GROWTH IN FAITH	53	46	40

1. NB: Strength of relationship is the percent of variance explained by each set of factors (adjusted R^2)
2. N/A: Not Applicable

SOURCE: 1991 National Church Life Survey

The results also give some heart to congregations which do not affirm some of the more theologically conservative or charismatic beliefs which have been discussed here. As they seek to move forward, it will be important for them to reflect on how to grow commitment among attenders, and how to encourage an outward focus among attenders. There is much that congregations and denominations can learn from each other despite the different theological views they may hold.

IMPORTANCE OF DENOMINATIONAL TRADITIONS

Denominations and their traditions have been important carriers of the Christian faith through the centuries. In recent times there has been a high level of switching between denominations and an apparent loss of denominational loyalty. Writing of declining denominationalism in the United States, Anderson suggests that the churches that are mushrooming are frequently independent, fundamental, charismatic and non-mainstream. Further, within mainstream denominations he suggests that 'those denominational churches that have succeeded in attracting and keeping people often appear to be out of step with their denomination' (Anderson, 1990, 49).

The Australian context is in many ways different from that in the United States, yet similar patterns have been detected in the NCLS.

Extremely high levels of denominational switching are a characteristic of the post-war generations, who exhibit lower levels of denominational loyalty (*Winds of Change*, p 237).

This study reveals significant relationships between congregational vitality and denomination. The results are shown in Figure 18.4.

FIGURE 18.4: FAITH TYPE AND DENOMINATION

	STRENGTH OF RELATIONSHIPS		
	Denomination of the congregation	Faith type	Both denomination and faith type
NEWCOMERS	9	11	16
YOUNG ADULT RETENTION	9	8	11
NUMERICAL GROWTH	6	6	7
SENSE OF BELONGING	15	16	21
COMMUNITY INVOLVEMENT	18	21	26
SHARING/ INVITING	39	54	59
GROWTH IN FAITH	35	40	49

NB: Strength of relationship is the percent of variance explained by each set of factors (adjusted R^2)

SOURCE: 1991 National Church Life Survey

Denomination appears highly significant in relation to most aspects of vitality and, in general, is of a similar strength to the faith type effects. This is not surprising, in that denominational background embodies not only difference in practice and styles of church life but also differences in beliefs. The larger mainstream denominations are also more theologically diverse than the smaller denominations.

Which denominational background is positively related to vitality indicators and which has a negative relationship? With the exception of community involvement, congregations from mainstream denominations (Anglican, Uniting, Presbyterian and Lutheran) appear to be less effective than other denominations. Such a pattern holds true even after accounting for faith type differences between congregations. In other words, in two congregations where attenders have identical attitudes to the Bible or speaking in tongues or in regard to a preference for evangelism or social concern, the mainstream congregation is less likely to be effective. This suggests there are elements in the tradition and practice in these denominations that are less encouraging of vitality. These denominations would do well to reflect carefully on the results in Part 2.

On the other hand, mainstream denominations are more likely to have attenders involved in community groups or caring/justice activities sponsored by the congregation. This is true even for congregations from different denominations but with identical patterns of faith among attenders.

These denominational differences may be the result of different orientations to the world. The more theologically homogeneous denominations are, the less likely they are to engage in wider community-based activities. For instance, only 15% of Pentecostal attenders are involved in a community-based social welfare or action group, compared to 23% of attenders in large Protestant denominations and 32% of mainstream attenders (*Mission under the Microscope*, pp 20–22).

The denominational differences also partly reflect the differing age profiles of the denominations. Pentecostal denominations tend to have a younger age profile than mainstream denominations. As shown in *Mission under the Microscope*, young attenders are much less likely to be involved in wider community care activities than older attenders (p 19).

ON FAITH TYPE AND DENOMINATION

Are the theologically conservative churches growing? Yes, and not only in terms of numerical growth but also in regard to several other aspects of vitality. There are significant and sometimes dramatic differences in congregational vitality depending on their approach to matters of faith.

Most congregations do not develop their beliefs according to what is successful but rather seek to give expression to their beliefs in action. For most congregations, their approach to matters of faith and their denomination are unchangeable rather than something to be considered alterable in order to be more effective.

Accepting that patterns of faith and denominational background are largely to be treated as givens, the findings presented in this chapter will be of significant concern to large sections of the church in Australia and elsewhere. There appear to be significant differences in vitality between congregations with different patterns of faith. For the mainstream churches in particular there is much here to reflect upon.

Some will be unconcerned by these results, because they will not see some of the indicators of vitality used in this study as being important. Many mainstream leaders are suspicious of numerical growth for its own sake and are far more comfortable thinking about congregational vitality in terms of consequent action in the wider community. The results here in the area of community involvement should provide encouragement to such leaders.

At the same time, there will be many within the mainstream denominations who will feel that significant community involvement needs to be accompanied by a building up of the gathered body and a growing sense of belonging. If there is not a strong and committed community of faith there will be no wider community involvement.

There is an increasing level of reflection from within the mainstream denominations on the effectiveness of congregations from other traditions. The work of David Luecke in *Evangelical Style and Lutheran Substance* (1988) provides a good example of a writer from within a mainstream denomination reflecting on the style and substance of growing evangelical and charismatic churches in the United States. Much can be learnt from an examination of such churches and can be sensitively adapted to suit a particular denomination, as Luecke amply demonstrates. There is a need for leaders from within denominations to listen to and evaluate the experiences of those in other denominations.

Such a process of listening is not always easy. As Gary Bouma notes, those with a more absolutist theological orientation tend to feel they have a more encompassing faith and are suspicious of those with more relativistic views. Those who are more relativistic advocate tolerance but often have a blind spot in relation to those who are absolutist (Bouma, 1992, 60).

Listening and learning from each other may not always be easy, but that does not make it any less important. In different circumstances and cultural contexts, congregations may need to re-interpret or re-express denominational traditions and richness in ways that can be understood and that can give life to local communities rather than developing distance from them.

CHAPTER 19

SHAPING A FUTURE

Shelters or Windmills: Priorities for Growth

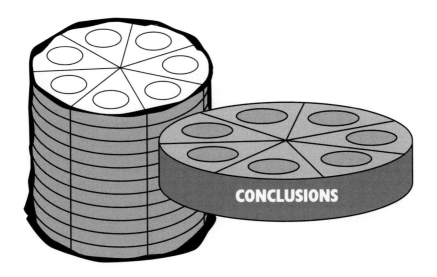

'When the wind of change is blowing some build shelters . . . others build windmills' (Moller, 1992, 137).

The west continues to develop technology at an ever-increasing rate, making startling discoveries in fields such as genetics and physics. Most discovery is greeted with enthusiasm, optimism and hope. Yet the art and literature of our society conveys quite a different message. One could well describe western society as containing technological optimism but literary despair (Robinson 1994, 16).

A theme for this age is finding strength to cope in an uncertain and ever-changing world and of finding values to live by. What do the churches have to offer in this search?

The fact that churches are in trouble in so many places is not just a concern for the religious community but has implications for the health of the entire society. Social institutions are struggling to define their place.

Writing about the churches in the United States, Loren Mead concludes that the churches face major problems which are not easily fixed or lived with, marking a need to rebuild the church from the ground up. It is no longer possible for churches to continue with 'business as usual' (Mead 1994, ix).

In part it is a matter of recognising that the churches are in a new mission era (Bosch, 1991). What is needed is more than superficial change. The churches need to engage in careful reflection on their purpose, place and priorities. Challenging? Certainly. But it is also a time of possibility.

Some may want to respond to the winds of change by building strong, weatherproof shelters. They may have been battered by the wind in the past or are afraid of its apparent force. They may feel a need to protect themselves from the uncertain squalls. They may be concerned about the impact of these winds on received traditions and accepted ways of doing things.

For others, the conditions create an opportunity to build windmills, to harness the wind to productive ends. They respect the wind and its force, but see its potential to provide energy and drive.

Creative churches will recognise the opportunities inherent in such challenging circumstances. Rather than lamenting the past, they will deal with how to live as a minority in a society whose dominant culture often lives in other ways. Instead of striving to reclaim what was, they will seek to give expression to God's creativity and work to translate what is into what can be (Posterski and Barker, 1993, 111).

Of all those seeking to give leadership within the churches we ask: when the winds of change are blowing, do you seek to build shelters or construct windmills?

SHAPING A FUTURE

This study has sought to bring more objectivity to the issues of congregational vitality. This enables the church to place the apparent 'success' of a particular congregation into a wider context. It is fair to say that without such research, some aspects of congregational life can receive too much prominence, while others are not given enough thought.

Shaping a Future is certainly not the first word, neither is it the last word, on issues relating to congregational vitality. There is a wide range of further work that can be done — on additional issues, on issues relating to particular denominations, or on social contexts. In the coming years it is our hope to further refine and develop our understanding of effective congregational life and ministry.

The research has important implications for all congregations. It has revealed some of the trends in church life and how aspects of church life relate to each other. More importantly, it points towards priorities and issues to be taken into account as congregations respond to their own particular situation.

Readers will no doubt respond to *Shaping a Future* in different ways. Those with a concern for received traditions will be wary. Of you we ask: please reflect on what is at the heart of the gospel and what is not. What is non-negotiable and what is in the realm of style, to be re-honed and reshaped in every context, culture and generation?

Readers will respond to Shaping a Future *in different ways*

There is a need to wrestle with the realities described in this book. For example, both newcomers and young adults within the church are more comfortable with contemporary styles of worship and are willing to switch congregations and denominations to find it. How is it best to respond to such realities?

Those concerned to relate more effectively to the wider Australian community, but who are dissatisfied with church life, may use this material in all sorts of ways. To you we say: be wary. Using this material as one might a marketing analysis can be dangerous. The Christian church is called to communicate its message in different cultures and contexts. Sometimes it needs to challenge the surrounding culture, not simply seek expression in it. As Rainer comments, 'Christians make decisions daily based on "what best works" without violating scriptural truths. The danger is replacing theology with pragmatism' (1993, 319). The more the church unthinkingly accommodates culture, the more it becomes secularised itself and therefore unable to challenge the failings of that culture (Hull, 1992, 145). We ask that you reflect prayerfully and carefully upon the value of what you have, particularly in the light of the survey results, and your own particular congregational history and sense of call.

Finally, there will be those who feel they are getting things right or doing well. To you we say: be encouraged but not complacent. In times of change it is always vital to reflect prayerfully on priorities and directions. As we all seek to discover the shape of church life into the next millennium, the garb of listening with humility is far more appropriate than a cloak of complacency.

MEASURING CONGREGATIONAL VITALITY

A vast range of different aspects of congregational life and community context have been analysed as part of this study. Part 1 of this book has shown which of these many aspects are most closely related to each of the seven measures of congregational vitality used in this study.

Many of the factors in Part 1 do not appear in more than one or two tables. The characteristics of congregations with high levels of belonging, for instance, are very different from those related to high levels of newcomers.

This diversity underlines the importance of multiple measures in order to understand congregational vitality. In future research we hope to develop and refine these indicators, possibly adding others seen to be important.

An important lesson from this analysis is the importance of defining what is meant by congregational vitality, effectiveness or growth. Too many writers in the past have been vague and in the process have created the possibilities for confusion.

The use of numerical growth as the indicator of effectiveness is a case in point. This study has demonstrated that the factors related to numerical growth are often quite different from those associated with either congregational size or the levels of newcomers without a church background in a congregation.

Numerical growth rates are actually measuring a range of issues: attraction of newcomers, additions from transfers and denominational switching, the stage in life of attenders (either for additions from biological growth or to be in a position to retain newcomers or young adults) and increases in the regularity of involvement of existing attenders. The factors in church life impacting on each may be very different. Separate analysis of each is necessary to understand numerical growth more fully.

THINGS THAT MATTER

The results summarised in Part 1 highlight characteristics of congregational life that are important for more than one measure of congregational vitality. While the exercise carries with it the dangers of reductionism and over-simplification, it seems useful to draw together some of these common characteristics of vital congregations.

There are a handful of factors, out of the hundreds examined, which are important across the range of congregational vitality measures in this study. These can be grouped under seven broad headings:

- having an outward focus
- high levels of involvement in congregational activities
- a strong sense of community within the congregation
- a clear sense of direction and purpose
- effective leadership

- a lively faith among attenders
- the age profile of the congregation.

1. AN OUTWARD FOCUS

Two important congregational characteristics related to vitality are the extent to which the congregation is outwardly focused and how comfortable attenders are to discuss their faith with others or invite them to church.

These two measures probe complementary aspects of an outward focus. The former reflects the extent to which congregations are concerned about wider issues and other people rather than the needs of attenders themselves. Such a focus is characteristic not only of congregations growing numerically or drawing in newcomers, but is also related to more internal measures such as sense of belonging and growth in faith. There is tangible evidence here that to build the inner life, congregations need to look outward and that 'in giving we shall receive'.

The latter measure is an indicator of attender openness about their faith in their daily lives. It is also strongly related to growth in faith among attenders, wider community involvement, numerical growth, young adult retention and the flow of newcomers.

Many newcomers initially join a congregation because of a personal invitation from another attender, an invitation from the clergy or through contact with a congregational activity. Attenders being willing to invite others is an important prerequisite for the arrival and retention of newcomers; it must also therefore contribute to numerical growth.

It could be that community involvement provides the opportunity for attenders to invite others to church, while growth in faith provides the continuing motivation to do so. It is likely that each factor reinforces the other. Mission becomes an ongoing orientation rather than simply being a one-off event.

2. INVOLVEMENT IN CONGREGATIONAL ACTIVITIES

It has been suggested that Pentecostal denominations are sustained by better socialisation of members and families through small group activities, by worship styles and by social arrangements which promote fellowship and community, producing high levels of commitment and participation (Bentley *et al*, 1992, 39). The NCLS suggests that this principle is true more generally; attender involvement is strongly related to congregational vitality regardless of denominational background.

The frequency of worship attendance and the proportion of attenders involved in small groups emerge as important factors across many of the vitality measures, including growth in faith, young adult retention, community involvement and inviting others to church or sharing of faith. However, involvement has less significance in relation to attracting newcomers or numerical growth. Congregations can have very positive nurture strategies without drawing in new people.

It is likely that high levels of involvement do provide important motivational resources for attenders. Those who are frequently involved are being exposed more often to worship, encouragement and the challenges of the faith in a corporate setting, leading to a greater involvement in the wider mission of the church. Intensive church involvement does not appear to reduce engagement with the wider world, but rather can be a necessary part of equipping attenders for community involvement.

3. A STRONG SENSE OF COMMUNITY

Several indicators in this study relating to positive group life and community recur as key characteristics in relation to most aspects of vitality. Attenders who feel positive about their congregation and have a strong sense of belonging tend to be in vital and effective congregations. Having close friends at church and open communication channels are also related to congregational vitality. On the other hand, high levels of conflict clearly have dramatic negative consequences for vitality in just about every possible way. The use of the term 'Christian communities' for congregations appears very apt.

Throughout this book, there have been references to the changing shape of people's networks and sense of community. Many would suggest that the importance of local community life has been declining. As people have found their sense of belonging and their social life in communities of interest rather than in local communities, church life has suffered (Bentley *et al*, 1992, 51).

This is not only a problem for the churches but for many other locally based organisations that function as 'mediating structures', linking individuals to the larger society and providing meaning and identity (Berger and Neuhaus, 1977).

Some have forecast the disappearance of the local community; others have said that it is being refashioned (eg Gannon 1978). Putnam suggests involvement in community groups and local institutions is declining and, in the process, reducing the 'social capital' available in communities. Social capital may include networks and values in society which promote trust between individuals and other collective benefits; various forms of voluntary associations and community groups would be part of this. In Putnam's view, strong trends are at work in contemporary society that are undermining this critical resource (Putnam, 1995, 65–78).

On the other hand, others feel that what is occurring are changes in how community is created and expressed rather than a decline in levels of expression. Wuthnow's study of small-group life across the United States — religious and non-religious — is a case in point (1994). People are expressing community in more flexible and informal ways.

Wuthnow considers small groups to be like glue holding society together, as well as being a social solvent: they provide a way out of traditional attachments that formerly bound people to their communities. Former church attenders may, when moving to a new area, not bother joining a church but become part of an informally arranged small group. Thus they never become fully integrated into or committed to church life. According to Wuthnow, such groups can help people slip out of previous forms of social organisation and, through people's lack of involvement in them, can weaken those organisations significantly (1994, 24).

In such a context, building community can be an important contribution the churches make to the wider society, if they are flexible enough to adapt their forms to reflect both contemporary reality and the particularities of their own situation.

Congregations will need to consider how this is to be done in their own particular situation. Some aspects of this are touched on in Chapter 15. At different stages in life, attenders are likely to value a local community attachment either more or less. Particular age, socioeconomic, ethnic or interest groups may fulfil a need for some to gather with like-minded people. Congregations may well need to foster opportunities within their life for people to spend time with other people like themselves, as well as occasions to celebrate unity in diversity.

4. A SENSE OF DIRECTION

Congregations that are moving in new directions, or where attenders believe that the leadership has a vision for the future to which they are fully committed, tend to have higher levels of congregational vitality.

It is important for congregations to define (or re-define) their purpose and priorities. While each congregation will need to do this in ways appropriate to their heritage and context, this study suggests some key principles to bear in mind.

It is clearly important for leaders to be able to articulate the vision for the congregation and model congregational priorities in their own ministry. Likewise, it is important for attenders to be fully committed to the vision.

Many congregations will need to be more intentional in the area of planning and direction setting. The 1996 congregational printouts can be a useful starting point. However, the process for planning beyond initial reflections is critical. Some important aspects of planning are touched on at the end of this chapter. There are many planning resources and consultants within denominations and beyond that may be helpful.

5. EFFECTIVE LEADERSHIP

Several aspects of the style of leadership in a congregation emerge as being significant.

As noted in the previous section, effective leaders will help congregations develop a clearly understood and well-supported vision for the growth of the congregation and its members. They will also strike a balance between being bold and directive, and taking into account attenders' ideas and affirming their gifts.

While preaching, teaching, pastoral and priestly functions may be foundational to ministry, leaders in effective congregations also have an intentional outward focus. Their concern is not just for the inward life of the congregation but also for people outside the congregation.

There has been great emphasis on the need for attenders to be given positions of leadership in congregational life. This study suggests that the spreading of roles across a wider range of people does not necessarily lead to greater congregational vitality. Of greater significance is the perceived level of support which those with roles are given.

Clergy and congregational leaders would do well to reflect carefully on the nature and style of their leadership. The congregational profile from the 1996 NCLS may be a useful starting point. Such reflection may suggest reorienting job priorities or augmenting congregational leadership with others who have complementary gifts and skills. It may suggest areas where leaders need to develop or receive further training.

The results are also significant for those in theological colleges. To what extent are they equipping future leaders for the realities of contemporary ministry and mission? The results of this study may suggest areas of training which need development.

6. A LIVELY FAITH

The private spiritual experiences and practices of attenders are important to vitality. High levels of attenders growing in their faith, making changes in their priorities as a result of their faith, experiencing moments of decisive faith commitment or the presence of God, or with active devotional lives, are all positively related to different aspects of congregational vitality.

This result underlines the importance of the spiritual dimension. While a study such as this cannot probe such matters in depth, it does highlight the centrality of faith to the purpose and life of congregations. 'Any religion which does not promote a hunger for the divine . . . is not religion at all, but mere philanthropy in fancy dress' (Rumi in Conway, 1994, 54).

7. AGE PROFILE

This study suggests that the age profile of a congregation is significantly related to congregational vitality in some quite different but important ways.

Figure 19.1: KEY FACTORS IN CONGREGATIONAL VITALITY

An outward focus among leaders and attenders, such as a concern for evangelism or wider community care. There is a readiness to discuss matters of faith with others and to invite others to church.

High levels of involvement, as shown by worship service attendance, small group and other group involvement.

A strong sense of community among attenders, as shown by high levels of satisfaction, a growing sense of belonging and low levels of conflict.

A sense of direction. Attenders perceive their congregation as having a definite sense of direction and purpose. Leadership has a strong sense of vision for the growth of the congregation, to which attenders are committed.

Effective leadership. Leadership is inspiring and directive, yet puts a priority on listening to attenders' ideas and encouraging them to use their gifts and skills. There is a sense among attenders that those with roles receive adequate levels of support.

A lively faith. Vital congregations tend to have higher levels of attenders growing in their faith, or experiencing moments of conversion or faith commitment. High levels of devotional activity among attenders, such as prayer and Bible reading, are also evident.

The age profile of attenders. Younger congregations are more likely to be attracting newcomers, retaining young adults and growing numerically. Older congregations with a stable base of attenders are more likely to be involved in service in the community.

Younger congregations are far more likely to retain young adults, to welcome newcomers into their midst and to be growing numerically. While it is to be expected that a congregation successfully retaining young adults would, almost by definition, have a younger age profile, such congregations also hold greater attraction to other young people. For younger adults it would seem to be a case of like attracting like.

For many congregations, these results are a source of despair rather than something upon which they can reasonably act. It could be that young attenders moved out of the life of the congregation many years ago. Attracting younger people may be a difficult if not impossible task.

Two important points should be made in this regard. First, it is very important that while they have young adults in their number, congregations should be very intentional about developing an outward focus among this age group and in seeking to nurture their faith. Too often congregations start to reflect on such matters only when they have lost almost all of their young adults, at which point they may lack a critical mass to move forward.

Second, for many congregations without a strong base of young adults, it may be far more important to develop mission priorities in other areas. This study shows, for instance, that congregations with high levels of wider community involvement tend to have a stable base of older attenders. Older attenders often have more time to be involved in congregational or community activities and are more locally focused in their lives (see Chapter 15).

These results in relation to the age profile of congregations suggest the need in congregational planning to consider the make-up of the congregation, as well as the aspirations of attenders. They also highlight the fact that there is often a time and a season for different priorities and, sometimes, moments not to be missed.

ON FAITH TYPE AND CONTEXT

LOCAL CONTEXT

The NCLS results show that the local context is particularly important in determining the size of congregations. This is an important principle for congregational leaders to grasp; the reason that their congregation may not be growing may simply be a reflection of the make-up of the surrounding community, while for other congregations significant growth may be as a result of a favourable demographic environment.

The realisation of the importance of local context is a freeing thing. A congregation of 200 people in one suburb may be the equivalent of a congregation of 400 people in another. In trying to work out what is effective in helping congregations to grow, church leaders should look carefully at the local context within which 'successful' congregations are located.

While context is not determinative of its future, a congregation will do well to carefully note what is happening around it in terms of changes to the demographic make-up of the community, identifying new challenges and possibilities for ministry.

FAITH TYPE

There has been a resurgence in theologically conservative groups in many different parts of the world. In Australia, the last 20 years has seen the growth and spread of the charismatic renewal and Pentecostal congregations. Denominations with a strong evangelical base often report patterns of growth.

The faith type of attenders is of great significance for other aspects of congregational vitality apart from numerical growth. Congregations with higher levels of attenders taking a more literalist view of the Bible or who are positive about speaking in tongues are also more likely to be drawing in newcomers, retaining young adults, have a growing sense of belonging, a willingness to discuss faith or invite others to church, and a sense of growth in faith among attenders.

Such congregations are, however, less likely to have attenders involved in wider community service or community care activities.

While theological orientation is of significance, the NCLS research also places it within a wider context. It is a key factor in relation to the retention of young adults, in community involvement, in sharing of faith and of growth in faith. Yet it is less important in relation to the remaining measures of vitality, where the nature of the internal life of the congregation appears to assume greater significance.

Further, the analysis in Chapter 18 suggests that, apart from providing a more clear-cut message, conservative beliefs may tend to generate vitality by encouraging an outward focus and higher levels of commitment among attenders. These are issues on which, no matter the faith type of the congregation, leaders can move forward.

THINGS THAT ARE OVERRATED

This research also points to some aspects of congregational life which appear overrated. However, an important dictum needs to be remembered here: 'Absence of evidence is not evidence of absence'. The lack of importance of a particular aspect may be due, in part, to how well that aspect has been measured in the NCLS. While every attempt has been made to examine the following areas from a number of different angles, further research would be required to establish any real links between these factors and congregational vitality.

PROPERTY AND FINANCES

For some congregations, owning a modern, multi-functional building seems important to their future. For others, their old church building is a burden and seen as a major handicap in reaching out to the community. Both perceptions may lead congregations to make expensive decisions in relation to church property.

The evidence of the NCLS suggests that such concerns may be overstated. While the need to upgrade property may become inevitable, there is little evidence linking it with the vitality of the congregation. In the same way, while in some cases financial matters may constrict or close a congregation, in the main they appear to have minimal impact across the range of measures of vitality used in this study.

Put simply, there are a great many congregations lacking in vitality that are blessed with more than adequate buildings and finances! Property may be a source of dissatisfaction and may limit options in some congregations, but generally it is unlikely to be the factor limiting vitality.

There are many congregations lacking in vitality that are blessed with adequate buildings

LEADERSHIP STRUCTURES AND BACKGROUND

The organisation of congregations and the deployment of staff is something which varies greatly from one denomination to another. Sometimes there is a belief that a particular approach to staffing is better than other approaches. No such patterns emerged in this study.

Leadership structures may affect vitality in particular contexts. Such patterns may involve the complex interplay of particular structures, congregations and personalities. Such complexity is beyond the NCLS. With little relationship found between structure and vitality, generalisations are dangerous.

Similarly, the background of ministers is often thought to be important. Some ministers are thought to be 'too old' while others are 'too young'! This study finds, however, that the background of ministers is of much less importance than what they do on the job.

CONGREGATIONAL SIZE

The size of the congregation makes less difference to congregational vitality than expected, once the faith type of attenders and the local community context are taken into account. Larger congregations are a little more likely to retain their young adults or grow numerically; these relationships are smaller than one might expect, and no relationship was found with other aspects of vitality.

The NCLS research has highlighted many ways in which large and small congregations differ in the way that they operate. The fact that size makes little difference to vitality reinforces the evidence of the NCLS that large and small congregations can have complementary roles to play in the mission of the church.

THE HOMOGENEOUS UNIT PRINCIPLE

The homogeneous unit principle has been a hotly contested concept in the life of the churches, particularly with the increasing social and cultural diversity of contemporary society.

This study does not provide support for general statements about homogeneity as a key characteristic of vital congregations. Indeed, socially diverse congregations appear more effective on a range of fronts.

Such results are very general; more detailed research would be necessary to determine the value of homogeneity in particular contexts or with particular subgroups. Further, many highly diverse congregations may organise themselves in terms of more homogeneous small groups, services of worship or other activities.

Nevertheless, most congregations would be well advised to reflect on how to be more open to different groups in the community.

FIGURE 19.2: TEN APPARENT MYTHS ABOUT CONGREGATIONAL VITALITY

1. **'We can just keep on going in the same way and it will make little difference to where we will be as a congregation in 20 years time.'**

    Unlikely. *Shaping a Future* suggests it is essential for congregations to reflect carefully on their future directions.

2. **'The local context pretty well determines the success or otherwise of a congregation.'**

    No. While congregations need to understand their community and respond in culturally appropriate ways, there is much that can be done to shape a creative future in most contexts.

3. **'Big congregations are always better than small ones.'**

    Not really. While larger congregations appear a little more likely to be growing numerically or retaining young adults, on most indicators of vitality size is of little significance. *Shaping a Future* suggests there is a place for congregations of all sizes.

4. **'If we could spread the workload across more of our attenders, the congregation will eventually be more effective.'**

    Not necessarily. High levels of attenders with roles, particularly of an administrative nature, do not appear to increase the vitality of a congregation. Better support for those with roles may be more important.

5. **'Being a leader who facilitates others is just as effective as being a strong directive leader.'**

    Shaping a Future suggests that leadership that inspires others is linked with effective congregations rather than leadership that is passive. At the same time, leaders need to empower attenders to use their gifts and skills.

6. **'Getting the pastoral and teaching roles right are the main priorities if leaders are to be effective.'**

    Effective leaders may need good pastoral and teaching skills. Yet *Shaping a Future* suggests an outward focus to leadership is critical. Without such a focus, pastoral and teaching skills may not be adequate to grow a vital congregation.

7. **'Ministers who are too old or too young will not be effective.'**

    Not necessarily. The study suggests leadership style and priorities are much more important than a leader's age or background.

8. **'Church buildings located on highly visible sites, with plenty of parking and easy traffic access, will draw a great many new people in.'**

    While a complete lack of parking or access may provide some limits to growth, *Shaping a Future* suggests relational networks are a far more significant aspect of visibility than physical location.

9. **'All we need is some lively worship and good advertising to get newcomers in.'**

    Again, attenders inviting newcomers along is far more important than advertising. Lively worship may mean attenders are more comfortable about inviting others, but it is one aspect to be considered among many.

10. **'Long church services will keep newcomers away.'**

    Not necessarily. *Shaping a Future* shows little overall relationship between length of service and levels of newcomers.

SOME ASPECTS OF WORSHIP STYLE

This study provides evidence that worship style is related to a congregation's ability to retain younger adults and those outside of church life more generally. An unthinking adherence to traditional worship forms may well be alienating to the post-war generations. On the other hand, satisfaction with music and preaching are important in relation to a sense of belonging and growth in faith. There are important issues here on which congregations should carefully reflect.

However, the impact of some other aspects of worship style appear to be overstated. For instance, the length of sermons or services of worship does not appear to be related to congregational vitality. Nor does the value of expository preaching over thematic preaching. There may be good and valid reasons to adopt one approach over another, but overall links to congregational vitality as defined in this study are not apparent.

MOVING FORWARD

How should a congregation respond to this material? Is it a matter of automatically seeking to duplicate as many as possible of these characteristics in their own life?

The real world is much more complex than that. Particular contexts generate particular priorities or issues. The processes of group life and of setting directions are complex and require great sensitivity.

This is not a book on congregational planning. However, because it will raise many questions for congregations about future directions, it seems important to conclude with some points for congregations to bear in mind

in relation to the process of direction setting. Those wishing to reflect further on these would be well advised to make use of planning consultants or their resources (eg Callahan, 1983; Grierson, 1991; Drayton, Kitto and Manton, 1992; Corney, 1991; Schaller, 1988).

• **There are often different types of change occurring at many levels in congregational life**. Some may be to do with changes in the community: the population may be growing or declining, or there may be major new developments in the area. Some may be changes within the congregation: new attenders or leadership, issues with the viability of certain activities and so on. Often changes are occurring at many levels at once; the presenting issues may be more a reflection of deeper concerns. Understanding the dimensions of change will be important if one is to help a congregation to move forward creatively.

• **Seek to be pro-active and specific**. Congregations simply feeling battered by continuous change may well become despondent or reactionary. A congregation with a vision for its future will be able to more readily adjust in response to new developments or opportunities.

If congregational goals or directions are too abstract, they may become hard to implement, resulting in confusion or their being discarded.

• **Planning should be planning for mission**. Congregations seeking to grow in vitality, whether numerically or in any other area, need to carefully evaluate why it is they wish to grow. This study suggests an outward focus is critical to congregational vitality in all aspects. In serving others we discover more clearly who we are.

Congregations need to reflect on how to grow forward in their mission. When they have identified their mission, it will be important for them to reflect on all aspects of their life and on how to develop each one to further their mission. This study will provide some valuable insights in this regard.

Congregations need to reflect on how to grow forward in their mission

Planning for mission often involves encouraging small groups of people with a particular passion to get on with it. Such mission teams may develop in many ways: through their longings to help a section of the community, through a sense of call that comes from shared times of listening to God, through involvement in the community or through unexpected opportunity or crisis (Drayton *et al*, 1992, 18).

ANALYSING THE PRESENT MAY NOT CREATE THE FUTURE ...

In working with a group of rural congregations the presenting problems were a shrinking population base and a non-viability due to lack of finances. Focusing on these problems in the past led to suggestions for closures and amalgamations, having less regular services or fewer or part-time ministers.

When asked the question 'What kind of future do you want for your church?', discussions centred on vital worshipping communities and making effective contact with people around them. Problems previously identified seemed no longer as relevant or as paralysing.

— from *Choosing Our Future*, David Merritt (1996)

• **Look beyond the 'problems' to hopes and yearnings**. Looking at current situations or problems may stimulate a desire to look at where a congregation is heading, but a way forward may be found through focusing on the future and building on hopes and strengths. What are the passions and deep yearnings of the congregation in regard to what they believe God is calling them to, the gifts and skills they would delight to use in the mission of God, and the dreams that bring them excitement (Carolyn Kitto, private communications)?

• **Planning needs to be realistic and ongoing, but not overwhelming**. Realistic planning may involve dealing with only one or two significant issues. Further issues can be placed on a timeline for consideration later.

Planning is not just a one-off exercise. Plans are meaningless if the process of implementation is not given sufficient energy and attention. Further, changes in direction may be needed in the light of attempts made to achieve goals that have been set or because circumstances have changed.

At the same time, it is important not to become obsessed with planning. Planning for mission may be more comfortable than actually doing mission. Callahan warns congregations of the dangers of 'analysis paralysis' (1983, xi).

• **Sometimes it is easier to develop a new project than reshape an existing one**. As Denham Grierson observes, fighting old battles can be exhausting, time consuming and unprofitable. A new initiative may tap present passions without people having to navigate pre-existing role patterns or ways of doing things (1991, 120).

• **All the mission 'needs' in a particular context need not be addressed by any one congregation.** A congregation that is excited by a new initiative in mission will find energy to move forward; if there is not a passion, it may not be appropriate to move forward in this area.

A good example is the issue of relating to younger adults. While it may be a priority in general to relate more effectively to the post-war generations, it may not be an appropriate priority for every congregation. One of the best gifts some rural congregations may be able to give to young adults in their community is to help them connect with another congregation in the city when the time comes for them to move. Other congregations may have different passions for mission that are also important. Still others may not be open to new initiatives in this area, to the extent that the perspectives of younger attenders would inevitably bring conflict with older attenders and be counter-productive to both groups.

• **Trust and ownership are critical**. As was detailed in Chapter 13, vital congregations are likely to have a vision for the future to which attenders are fully committed and which they believe is achievable. This will require trust in the congregation's leaders and ownership of the vision among attenders.

Achieving this means involving attenders in appropriate ways in the development of goals and directions. While this may not require all attenders to participate in all discussions or decision making, all need to feel that their ideas can be contributed and listened to. Too many direction-setting processes amount to leaders determining directions that they look to attenders to approve.

Approval does not necessarily imply ownership. Congregations where attenders are not committed or are only partly committed to the vision of the leaders are less likely to be vital or effective.

The importance of leaders listening to attenders has been affirmed throughout this study. Attenders feeling that they are heard is perhaps even more important than formally involving attenders in all decisions. Concerns about proposed new directions need to be acknowledged.

• **Changes need to be connected to the congregation's reason for being**. Because changes may be risky or costly, it is important for attenders to understand why such change is critical. New priorities need to be strongly based on a secure biblical and theological foundation and linked to a congregation's history and self-concept. Often a valued experience of a new direction in the past can help attenders understand the importance of new directions in the present.

It is important for attenders to understand why change is critical

• **New directions are not entirely within our control**. While Christians are called to make the most of their God-given wisdom and to prayerfully discern directions as a community, ultimately they must recognise that the future is in God's hands alone. In faithfully undertaking the journey, we may not be fully clear on the final destination.

IN CONCLUSION

This study has highlighted key characteristics of vital congregations as well as aspects of congregational life whose importance is overrated in relation to vitality. By using a range of vitality measures it has been possible for us to depict with greater sensitivity the nuances and textures of church life. However, a wide-ranging study of this kind augments but does not replace detailed case study analysis.

More detailed analysis for particular denominations or ministries in specific contexts may yield important new information. At the same time, it is vital for those involved in church life to reflect on what these results mean for their congregation or denomination. It will be important for congregations to step out in new directions in faith, exploring what it means to be the church in their own situation.

The prayer of the NCLS research team is that this material will be useful to congregations reflecting on their priorities and their future and that it will be used with wisdom and grace for the good of the whole church in a new mission era.

EPILOGUE

MAKING THE MOST OF NCLS RESEARCH

NCLS Research seeks to provide resources to the churches to assist them in planning for a creative future. The following resources are available from the NCLS offices:

MAJOR PUBLICATIONS

Winds of Change (1994)
A comprehensive analysis of congregational life which documents some of the major changes that are sweeping through the Protestant churches.
Mission under the Microscope (1995)
NCLS results illuminate ten vital issues congregations may need to address in developing a sustainable mission strategy for the 1990s.
Views from the Pews (1995)
A fascinating look at what attenders think and believe on social and church-related issues.
Several major publications are planned using data from the 1996 NCLS. Please contact NCLS Research for further information.

CONGREGATIONAL PRINTOUTS

Results from the 1996 NCLS for each participating congregation are available in the following forms:

Overview Printouts
These printouts give a demographic profile for each participating congregation. They detail the spread of ages, gender and marital status of attenders. This set of printouts also describes how often people in the congregation attend worship services, how far they travel to church, their church background, how involved they are in group activities, which church activities they most value, and attitudes to the Bible, the Eucharist and speaking in tongues.

Aspects of Vitality/Shaping a Future Printouts
These printouts examine each indicator of vitality in depth, reviewing the congregational characteristics which are most closely related to vitality. These printouts allow congregations to look at their own life in the light of the results in this book.

'Making the Most of Your Printouts' Resource Pack
This resource kit is designed to help congregational leaders look at their congregational printouts in a one-day workshop. It contains the set of printouts specific to each participating congregation plus a copy of the book *Shaping a Future*, a workbook and a video.

Detailed Congregational Profile
This contains a detailed report to congregations on all questions answered by their attenders, a breakdown by age, worship service and length of attendance and, where possible, changes between 1991 and 1996.

Looking at Your Community
Area profile sheets based on data from the 1996 Commonwealth Census can help congregations understand the nature of the community they seek to serve. This information will be available late 1997.

Denominational or Regional Reports
These provide information about each denomination or region, including cross-tabulated data by age, gender, education and ethnic background.

WORKSHOPS AND CONFERENCES

NCLS Research staff are available for workshops and conferences to help leaders and congregations understand the implications of *Shaping a Future* and the 1996 NCLS and how the printouts and results can assist their mission and planning.

'Making the Most of Your Printouts' Workshops
NCLS Research facilitators are available to run workshops with individual congregations to help them make the most of their printouts.

'Looking at Your Community' Workshops
Facilitators will be available in late 1997/1998 to help congregations look at the nature of their community using data from the 1996 Commonwealth Census.

For further information about these resources please contact one of the following addresses:

	Uniting Church Board of Mission	Anglican Home Mission Society
	PO Box A2178 SYDNEY SOUTH NSW 1235	PO Box Q137 Queen Victoria Building SYDNEY NSW 1230
PHONE	(02) 9285 4594	(02) 9261 9500
FAX	(02) 9267 7316	(02) 9261 9599
E-MAIL	ncls@ozemail.com.au	

WORLD WIDE WEB http://ncls.uca.org.au/

APPENDIX 1

ABOUT THIS STUDY

This appendix provides further detail about the NCLS, the methodology used in this study and technical details regarding the results presented in this book.

In August 1991, the National Church Life Survey (NCLS) invited attenders from around 8000 congregations in 19 denominations to complete a survey form during congregational activities (in fact one of 12 different survey forms). In addition, the leadership of each congregation completed a detailed survey of congregational life. The design of these forms was carried out by project staff in conjunction with contact persons from participating denominations, academics and church consultants both in Australia and overseas.

DENOMINATIONS INVOLVED IN THE 1991 NCLS

- Anglican
- Apostolic
- Assemblies of God
- Baptist
- Christian & Missionary Alliance
- Christian Revival Crusade
- Church of the Nazarene
- Churches of Christ
- Congregational
- Foursquare Gospel
- Lutheran

- Presbyterian Church in Australia
- Presbyterian Church in New Zealand
- Reformed Churches of Australia
- Salvation Army
- Seventh-day Adventist
- Uniting Church
- Wesleyan Methodist
- Westminster Presbyterian
- Some independent congregations, house churches and Christian communities

---

The National Church Life Survey has been an important example of interdenominational cooperation. It should be noted that an invitation was extended to the Catholic Church to participate in the 1991 survey. They showed considerable interest; however, several practical matters and time constraints ultimately created insurmountable barriers to their participation. The 1996 NCLS, however, has included a Catholic sample in conjunction with a large Catholic research project.

Twelve different versions of the 1991 NCLS attender survey form were designed to make the most of the survey opportunity. The first 35 questions were identical across all surveys. Most attenders (around 90%) in a participating congregation were given one of three primary surveys. The remaining 10% of attenders were randomly selected and given one of the remaining nine forms. In this way, random samples of between 2000 and 5000 attenders completed each of these smaller surveys. Overall, around 310 000 survey forms were processed.

Response to the survey was good: about 80% of the congregations which received forms participated.

ESTIMATES OF DENOMINATIONAL SIZE

Each participating congregation was required to supply an estimate of the number of attenders at worship services in a typical week. Where such data was not provided, estimates were made of the size of each participating denomination and the overall database was weighted to make it representative of the denominations that took part.

Details of how these estimates were derived are provided in Appendix 3 of *Winds of Change*.

MAKING THE MOST OF THE SURVEY

The National Church Life Survey is designed to assist congregations to reflect on their own life and involvement with the wider community and on mission directions for this decade and into the next century. For each participating congregation, data was collected on
- the congregation's relationship with the wider community;
- attenders' perceptions of their growth in beliefs, understanding and application of their faith;
- the social context in which a congregation seeks to minister.

The database is immense and is one of the most comprehensive databases on congregational life in any country. It has been set up to help congregations reflect on
- how to be creatively involved with the different groups that make up Australian communities;
- emerging styles of congregational life in this country;
- the extent to which attenders are growing in their understanding of their faith, in their beliefs/relationship with God, and in the impact that their faith has in everyday life.

CARRYING OUT THIS STUDY

Unlike that of previous publications, the focus of *Shaping a Future* is on the congregation rather than on individual attenders. The first step in the process of carrying out this study was to create a congregational database. This database was made up of data on each congregation provided by the congregation's leader, who completed a detailed congregational audit. In addition, all attender data from the main survey forms were aggregated to create congregational profiles.

When the survey was being designed it became evident that a huge range of issues about congregational life needed to be examined (see

Appendix 2 for details). In order to maximise the possibilities of the survey the sample of congregations was broken into three randomly selected groups as described earlier. Each group completed a common set of questions as well as another set only asked of their group. In this way a far wider range of data was able to be collected for analysis.

In the changing and diverse society that is contemporary Australia, the context in which a congregation seeks to minister is clearly important. For this reason demographic data on the local community around each participating congregation was drawn from the 1991 Commonwealth Census and added to the database. For urban congregations, a detailed profile was developed of the community within 1.5 kilometres of the worship centre. For non-urban congregations, those within a 5 kilometre radius were included.

In this way over 800 pieces of information were obtained about the life and mission of congregations across Australia.

While the response rate from congregations was generally good, for this study only those providing reliable and comprehensive responses were selected for analysis. This is particularly important in the case of the aggregated attender data. Where only a small percentage of a congregation actually completed attender forms, aggregated attender data would not be reliable.

According to statistical advice from Professor George Cooney of Macquarie University, congregations providing statistically reliable data were selected from the overall database. In addition, congregations with less than ten persons were excluded from the sample. In the end around 3500 congregations were selected from around 6700 to form the basis of this study. The denominational profile of selected congregations differed only slightly from that of all congregations in the participating denominations.

Because some attender questions were answered by all congregations and others by only a third of congregations, the sample sizes for analysis in this study range from around 900 to 3500 congregations.

It should be noted that, while the study on congregational vitality has been drawn from these 3500 congregations, the material included in profile boxes, which is based on leader responses, is drawn from the entire sample of congregations.

ABOUT THE VITALITY MEASURES

The congregational vitality measures developed in this study are described in detail in the early chapters of this book. Here is summarised some technical detail about each one.

• *Attracting and integrating newcomers*. The level of newcomers in a congregation was defined as the percentage of attenders who had joined that congregation in the last five years and previously were not attending church regularly anywhere else. The information has been drawn from two separate attender questions: one asking how long they had been involved with their congregation and the other inquiring about their previous church involvement.

How long have you been coming to worship services and/or activities run by this congregation?

a. Less than 1 year

b. 1–2 years

c. 3–5 years

d. I am visiting from another church

e. I am visiting and do not regularly go anywhere else

f. 6–10 years

g. 11–20 years

h. More than 20 years

Before you started coming here, were you participating in another congregation?

a. No, I've come here for most/all of my life

b. No, before coming here I had not been attending church for several years

c. No, before coming here I had never regularly attended a church

Yes, immediately prior to coming here I was attending a church which was:

d. Anglican

e. Apostolic

f. Assemblies of God

g. Revival Crusade

h. Foursquare Gospel

i. Other Pentecostal

j. Baptist

k. Catholic

l. Churches of Christ

m. Congregationalist

n. Lutheran

o. Wesleyan Methodist

p. Methodist

q. Missionary Alliance

r. Nazarene

s. Orthodox

t. Presbyterian

u. Reformed

v. Salvation Army

w. Seventh-day Adventist

x. Uniting

y. Other

• *Retaining young adults.* This aspect of congregational vitality is defined by the percentage of attenders with adolescent or adult children still living at home who still attend their congregation. Two attender questions were used. The first asked adult attenders whether their children attended church here, elsewhere, nowhere or a mix of these. The second asked attenders about the household in which they lived and the stage of life of any dependant children. Only those attenders with secondary or post-school-aged children living at home were included in the analysis.

Which statement best describes the level of church attendance of your children?

a. I do not currently have any children

b. Most of my children are involved with this church

c. Most of my children are involved with other churches

d. Most of my children are not attending church anywhere

e. I do not know whether my children attend church or not

f. More than one of the above

Which statement BEST describes the people who make up your household?
(NB: If your household is equally divided between two age groups, please select the youngest.)

a. I live alone

b. My household consists of some adults living together

c. A married couple without children

My household includes 2 parents and children living at home mainly of:

d. Preschool age

e. Primary school age

f. Secondary school age

g. Post school age

My household includes 1 parent and children living at home mainly of:

h. Preschool age

i. Primary school age

j. Secondary school age

k. Post school age

Several limitations of this index need to be noted. Many congregations have few families in them with secondary or post-secondary-aged children still living at home. Such congregations were omitted from the analysis. This reduced the sample size for this indicator to 3360 congregations.

Further distortion occurs where in some cases both parents are active in the same congregation and are both providing data on the retention or otherwise of the same children. In other cases only one parent is active in the congregation or the adolescent is part of a single-parent family. In the NCLS there is no way to overcome this discrepancy.

Finally, in some cases households will have one child still attending and another who has moved elsewhere or ceased to attend. Because of the limitations on survey size, multiple responses to this question were not permitted and a category was included which allowed attenders to respond that their situation was mixed. Such responses have been excluded from this analysis.

A more complete measure would require the exact tabulation of the number of young adults leaving a congregation as well as those being retained. Clearly this is beyond the scope of a study of attenders still active in the life of churches. It is our view that, despite its limitations, this indicator is useful in exploring what is an important aspect of congregational life.

• *Numerical growth.* This is based on overall estimates of attendance at church services for each year from 1986 to 1991, not on the number of attender responses or forms returned. For congregations which have commenced since 1986 a growth rate was calculated based on the number of years since their commencement. Overall, of the congregations in this study 3105 provided reliable growth data.

What is your best estimate of average weekly attendance at church services in each year? ie add average attendance for all services together.

Year	Usual Worship Attendance
1991	☐☐☐☐
1990	☐☐☐☐
1989	☐☐☐☐
1988	☐☐☐☐
1987	☐☐☐☐
1986	☐☐☐☐

• *A growing sense of belonging.* This indicator is derived from attender responses to a question on sense of belonging to their congregation (see Chapter 5). It is based on the percentage of attenders in a congregation who feel a strong and growing sense of belonging to their congregation and provides a good overall indicator of how attenders feel about involvement in their congregation.

• *Wider community involvement.* Responses to two different attender questions were used, one on attender involvement in congregational mission activities of various sorts and the other on involvement in wider community groups not connected with their congregation. The detail of these questions is given in Chapter 6. The index used comprises the percentage of attenders involved in community welfare or action groups and the percentage of attenders involved in congregationally sponsored social care/welfare activities.

• *Sharing faith and inviting others to church.* Again, this is an index derived from two attender questions, one on how attenders feel about discussing their faith with others and the other on whether attenders have invited others to congregational activities (see Chapter 6). The index is made up of the percentage of attenders open to discussing their faith with others or seeking opportunities to do so and the percentage of attenders who had invited someone to church in the last year.

• *Growth in faith of attenders.* Three primary questions covering faith exploration were included in the NCLS. From them a single *growth in faith* index was developed, comprising the percentage of attenders feeling they have grown significantly in their understanding of the Christian faith in the last year through their congregation, the percentage developing much stronger beliefs in the last year through their congregation and the percentage making major changes in their actions and priorities as a result of their Christian faith in the last year. The questions are detailed in Chapter 7.

ANALYSIS TECHNIQUES USED IN THIS STUDY

As has been noted in the early chapters of this book, a large number of multiple regressions were carried out in order to identify factors strongly related to each of the vitality measures.

In the preparation for this book a detailed review was also carried out of literature from Australia and overseas. Data from the NCLS was assembled to test as many hypotheses as possible that emerged from this review. Tests were carried out on each variable for normality of distribution and transformations were carried out where applicable. All results from regressions presented are significant to at least a 5% level.

In each case the contribution of the various internal factors was evaluated after accounting for contextual and faith type characteristics. These were entered first in the multiple regression prior to the entry of the internal variables in question.

Such controls were seen as important to assist congregations from all denominations and backgrounds to make the most of the study. As can be seen in Part 3, there are (sometimes strong) relationships between the vitality indicators and context and faith type. By first accounting for possible effects from these factors a more useful comparison can be made of the relative importance of different aspects of congregational life. Such controls 'level the playing field'.

In carrying out quantitative analysis on congregational life great care needs to be taken. There has been criticism of analysis techniques in some previous research in the United States (eg Iannaccone, 1996). Chapter 1 of this book outlines some reasons why we believe this study takes understanding of congregational vitality forward. From a measurement point of view it also has several strengths.

• *A wide range of denominations are involved.* A sample of one or a few denominations will understate the impact of internal characteristics. For this study the sample includes 19 denominations, which means that the study contains a high level of diversity, certainly more than has been available through previous work.

• *Attender data generates maximum sensitivity.* Research based only on leader responses will introduce measurement errors that can affect internal variables (data about the congregation) more than contextual variables (data about the community) and therefore understate the importance of internal factors. Estimates based on leaders' perceptions are highly prone to distortion because of the biases and perspectives of individual leaders. The use of aggregated attender data is, we believe, a vital step forward in establishing more finely tuned congregational data. Likewise the wider range of questions in use in the NCLS because of our use of multiple surveys also means that we are more able to measure the real impact of institutional factors by being able to ask more questions about different aspects of congregational life.

• *A large data base will reduce chance relationships.* A large amount of information on relatively few congregations can inflate the R^2 and invalidate significance tests. The issues related to searching over numerous variables and introducing chance relationships are important. In our analysis we have made use of adjusted R^2 values to account for degrees of freedom. Our large data set of between 900 and 3500 congregations also reduces dangers in this regard. A large sample size ultimately provides the best defence against chance relationships.

Further, while all tests have been done to a 5% level of significance, many were done to a more stringent 1% significance level. All results quoted in Part 1 meet this more demanding requirement as do most in Part 2.

• *Assumptions have not been made about prior effects.* Some studies in the literature have used stepwise regression to control for contextual factors and they assume that any capacity of the contextual factors to explain vitality is due to the contextual factors themselves. Such an approach may introduce a bias in favour of contextual factors.

The capacity of contextual factors to explain vitality measures may not always be due to the contextual factors themselves. A study seeking to compare the contribution of internal and contextual factors that overlooks this may understate the importance of internal factors.

However, our use in Parts 1 and 2 of contextual (and faith type) controls is not for the purpose of comparing the relative impact of contextual/faith type factors with other specific internal factors, but rather to level the playing field in comparing internal factors with each other. In these parts we are not looking for the exact R^2 value for each factor but are comparing their relative importance.

In Part 3, where we seek to evaluate the relative importance of contextual, faith type and internal factors, we have evaluated their contribution independently of each other as well as after accounting for the impact of each on the other. In these tests we have sought not to make assumptions about prior effects.

ADDITIONAL TECHNICAL DETAILS

The following section presents some results which were made use of in the text of *Shaping a Future* but which were considered too technical to be included in the body of the book.

1. DIFFERENCES IN THE CHARACTERISTICS OF DIFFERENT-SIZED CONGREGATIONS

In Chapter 8 some of the major differences in the characteristics of congregations of different sizes were summarised. These results were based on a series of multiple regressions. A similar procedure was used as was carried out for each of the vitality measures, with the difference being that in this case size was the dependent variable in question.

The results summarised in Chapter 8 are presented below in Figure A1.1.

FIGURE A1.1: HOW LARGER CONGREGATIONS DIFFER FROM SMALLER ONES		
CHARACTERISTIC	STRENGTH OF RELATIONSHIP	NO. CASES IN REGRESSION
More diverse profile	++++++ 19.2	1749
Similar social profile to community	++++++ 16.6	1749
A low ratio of staff to attenders	++++++ 14.2	3233
Many involved in decision making	−−−−− 10.9	979
Want congregation to get larger	−−−− 9.6	1093
Higher levels of conflict	++++ 8.2	1121
Involved in congregational activities	++++ 6.9	3336
Congregation is moving in new directions	++++ 6.8	1082
Attenders feel congregation is friendly to newcomers	−−−− 5.7	1130
Use contemporary music	++++ 5.6	865
Higher proportions of attenders in administrative roles	−−−− 5.5	3336
People before programs	−−−− 5.5	1130
Train attenders for mission and ministry	+++ 3.6	1015
Have directive and inspiring leaders	+++ 3.0	1059
Leader is less likely to be primarily a pastor	++ 2.4	914
Well-oiled channels of communication	−− 1.9	1130

NB: Strength of relationship is the percent of variance explained after accounting for local context/faith type effects
SOURCE: 1991 National Church Life Survey

2. ORTHODOXY OF BELIEFS

The main faith type variables used in Chapter 18 were attitudes to the Bible, a priority on evangelism or social concern, orientation to the charismatic movement, and the leader's assessment of the theological traditions most significant to the congregation.

Attenders were asked the following questions:

Which statement comes closest to your view of the Bible?

a. The Bible is the Word of God, to be taken literally word for word

b. The Bible is the Word of God which needs to be read in the context of the times to understand its implications for us today

c. The Bible is a valuable book, parts of which reveal God's Word to us

d. The Bible is a valuable book with much to teach us

e. Don't know

What is your opinion of 'speaking in tongues'?

Choose the sentence which is closest to your opinion.

a. Don't know or have no opinion

b. I generally disapprove of speaking in tongues as it is practised today

c. I generally approve of speaking in tongues in most situations, but do not speak in tongues myself

d. I approve of and have spoken in tongues myself

e. Speaking in tongues is necessary for all Christians

Suppose you had to join a new church. Which of the following would you be most likely to join?

a. One with a major focus on evangelism

b. One primarily concerned with evangelism that also demonstrated some concern for social action

c. One primarily concerned for social action that also demonstrated some concern for evangelism

d. One with a major focus on social action

e. Don't know/not applicable

In addition, congregational leaders were asked to respond to the following question:

There are many Christian traditions from which we may learn and grow. Circle up to TWO that are significant for your congregation.

a. Anglo-Catholic

b. Catholic

c. Charismatic/Pentecostal

d. Evangelical

e. Reformed

f. Liberal

g. Liberation theology

h. Eastern Orthodox

i. The traditions of our denomination

j. The traditions of our predecessor denominations

k. Other (please specify)

In order to assess the reliability of such measures, some additional orthodoxy questions were examined to ascertain whether they added significantly to the predictive power of the summary faith type variables.

The two orthodoxy questions involved attitudes to the person of Jesus and to eternal life. They are detailed in the question box below.

An important Christian belief is that Christ was fully God, fully human <u>and</u> physically rose from the dead. What do you think?

a. I have no doubt about it

b. I have some minor doubts

c. I have serious doubts

d. I don't believe it

e. Don't know

Another important Christian belief concerns eternal life. How do you think eternal life can be obtained?

a. I don't really believe in eternal life

b. Everyone will receive eternal life

c. I only need to try to be a good person

d. It comes by being good as well as faith in Jesus

e. Faith alone in Jesus is all that is needed

f. Don't know

In order to assess the additional impact of these two variables on the vitality measures, the additional variance explained after controlling for the summary faith type indicators was calculated. In addition, the total explanatory power of the faith type variables alongside these orthodoxy questions was determined. Both results are shown in Figure A1.2.

As can be seen, the orthodoxy measures do not contribute a great deal of additional explanatory power after accounting for the impact of the summary faith type indicators.

3. THE RELATIVE CONTRIBUTIONS OF ATTITUDES TO THE BIBLE AND ORIENTATION TO THE CHARISMATIC MOVEMENT

In Chapter 18 the relationships between the vitality measures and faith type variables are documented. Significant relationships were found with both attitudes to the Bible and orientation to the charismatic movement.

Further analysis has been carried out of the relative contributions of each of these variables. The results are shown in Figure A1.3.

Figure A1.3 shows the relative contribution of orientation to the charismatic movement after accounting for attitude to the Bible and vice versa. As can be seen, orientation to the charismatic movement contributes significantly more to explaining congregational vitality than does attitude to the Bible in the areas of growth in faith, discussing faith or inviting others to church, growing a sense of belonging, and numerical

FIGURE A1.2: ADDITIONAL IMPACT OF ORTHODOXY MEASURES — AFTER IMPACT OF OTHER FAITH TYPE VARIABLES

	ADDITIONAL IMPACT OF ORTHODOXY	OVERALL IMPACT OF FAITH TYPE (INCLUDING ORTHODOXY)
NEWCOMERS	3	21
YOUNG ADULT RETENTION	1	8
NUMERICAL GROWTH	0	6
SENSE OF BELONGING	4	20
COMMUNITY INVOLVEMENT	3	25
SHARING/ INVITING	1	54
GROWTH IN FAITH	2	42

NB: Figures in the first column of this table represent the percent of variance that can be explained by orthodoxy after taking account of the other faith type variables. In the second column are presented the total percent of variance explained by faith type and orthodoxy variables together

SOURCE: 1991 National Church Life Survey

FIGURE A1.3: FAITH TYPE — LOOKING MORE CLOSELY

	STRENGTH OF RELATIONSHIPS	
	Orientation to charismatic movement – after accounting for attitude to Bible	Attitude to Bible – after accounting for orientation to charismatic movement
NEWCOMERS	3	4
YOUNG ADULT RETENTION	0.5	1.6
NUMERICAL GROWTH	3	0.3
SENSE OF BELONGING	4	1.2
COMMUNITY INVOLVEMENT	0.5	8
SHARING/ INVITING	12	4
GROWTH IN FAITH	11	4

NB: Figures in this table represent the percent of variance that can be explained by the factor in question after taking account of the other factor

SOURCE: 1991 National Church Life Survey

growth. On the other hand, attitude to the Bible is more significant than orientation to the charismatic movement in relation to wider community involvement. Both aspects of faith type appear to have similar significance in relation to levels of newcomers. Although the predictive power of both is far less in relation to young adult retention, attitude to the Bible appears to be more significant than orientation to the charismatic movement.

4. EVALUATING THE CONTRIBUTION OF CONTEXT, FAITH TYPE AND THE INTERNAL CHARACTERISTICS OF CONGREGATIONS

In Chapter 18 the relative contributions to vitality of context, faith type and internal congregational life are evaluated. The results presented in that chapter are based on the analysis presented here.

First it is important to acknowledge some difficulties in this study in accurately assessing the overall significance of internal factors. Because questions used in this study were spread over three different survey forms, not all questions were asked of all congregations. It is not possible to establish an overall model for the internal life of congregations. Some of the most significant predictors in the 1991 survey were not part of the questions common to all congregations.

What has been pulled together for this test is a sample of significant internal characteristics. Models were developed that incorporated some characteristics common to all survey forms, such as levels of involvement in congregational activities, worship style and group life, as well as significant characteristics of congregations from questions specific to each of the three surveys. Comparisons were run of the relative contribution to vitality of each of the three models. From examination of these results it seemed that the most useable internal model was the one making use of the leadership style questions in survey B. This model has served as the basis of comparison in the tests in this area. In some cases higher levels of predictability of vitality may have been attainable from other models based on other survey forms; however, across all the measures of vitality the survey B model appeared to be the most predictive.

Use of this model means that these tests are based on a sample of around 900 congregations.

In order to evaluate the relative contribution of faith type, context and internal factors, the contribution of each was assessed after accounting for the impact of the other two sets of factors. These results are presented in Figure A1.4.

As can be seen, in some cases the impact of context is more significant than faith type — young adult retention and numerical growth provide examples. In others, faith type appears to be more significant — for example, discussing faith with others and growth in faith.

However, both sets of factors are far less significant on all aspects of vitality than is the summary set of internal factors.

While patterns of belief and congregational practice are highly related, as are context and practice, our study suggests that there is nevertheless much that congregations in any context or of any faith type can work on in order to increase their vitality.

FIGURE A1.4: THE IMPORTANCE OF FAITH TYPE

	STRENGTH OF RELATIONSHIPS		
	IMPACT OF FAITH TYPE– after accounting for contextual and internal factors	IMPACT OF CONTEXT– after accounting for faith type and internal factors	IMPACT OF INTERNAL FACTORS– after accounting for faith type and contextual factors
NEWCOMERS	4	4	13
YOUNG ADULT RETENTION	1	6	8
NUMERICAL GROWTH	1	8	16
SENSE OF BELONGING	0.4	4	39
COMMUNITY INVOLVEMENT	8	9	15
SHARING/ INVITING	2	1	17
GROWTH IN FAITH	2	2	25

NB: Figures in this table represent the percentage of variance that can be explained by the factor in question after taking account of the other factors

SOURCE: 1991 National Church Life Survey

5. THE LINK BETWEEN FAITH AND PRACTICE

In Chapter 18 the link between patterns of faith and practice within congregational life is explored in detail. It is suggested there that the link between conservative beliefs and congregational vitality could be partly explained by the fact that conservative congregations not only provide members with clear-cut beliefs but are also more likely to encourage high levels of commitment among attenders and to have a more clearly defined outward focus.

In order to understand these relationships better, summary measures of levels of commitment and outward focus were developed. The summary on levels of commitment is based on levels of involvement in worship and activities within the life of the congregation as well on levels of financial giving. The measure of outward focus is based on the extent to which attenders value the mission activities of the congregation and the extent to which they are comfortable to discuss their faith with others or invite others to church.

The questions on financial giving and on valuing the outward focus of the congregation are both part of the questions asked of one sample of congregations. This analysis is therefore based on around 900 congregations.

In order to assess the relative contributions of faith type, levels of commitment and outward focus to congregational vitality the contribution of each aspect was assessed after controlling for the other two sets of factors. The results are shown in Figure A1.5.

FIGURE A1.5: FAITH AND PRACTICE

	STRENGTH OF RELATIONSHIPS		
	IMPACT OF FAITH TYPE– after accounting for levels of commitment and outward focus	IMPACT OF LEVELS OF COMMITMENT– after accounting for faith type and outward focus	IMPACT OF OUTWARD FOCUS– after accounting for faith type and levels of commitment
NEWCOMERS	1	8	5
YOUNG ADULT RETENTION	3	3	2
NUMERICAL GROWTH	1	2	4
SENSE OF BELONGING	1	5	8
COMMUNITY INVOLVEMENT	3	10	7
SHARING/ INVITING	N/A	N/A	N/A
GROWTH IN FAITH	2	6	8

1. NB: Figures in this table represent the percentage of variance that can be explained by the factor in question after taking account of the other factors
2. N/A: Not applicable
SOURCE: 1991 National Church Life Survey

The contribution of faith type to explaining vitality is significantly reduced when account is taken of levels of commitment and outward focus. Further, in nearly every instance the contribution of faith type after accounting for the other set of factors is less than the contribution of levels of commitment or outward focus when similar controls are in place.

This suggests that a significant component of the contribution of faith type to congregational vitality can in fact be explained by differences in levels of commitment or outward focus. Again this suggests specific areas of congregational life on which congregations of all faith types and backgrounds can focus.

APPENDIX 2

FACTORS WORTH MEASURING
Looking at Congregational Life

DESCRIBING CONGREGATIONAL LIFE

The value of any research into factors affecting congregational vitality will clearly depend on the ability of the project to adequately examine the different aspects of congregational life. In a society that is becoming increasingly diverse and which is caught up in rapid social change, we can expect a range of styles of congregational life. The emergence of regional congregations, home churches, intentional Christian communities, mega churches, interest-based congregations, congregations without properties, workplace churches, ethnic congregations and so on highlights the complexity of establishing a framework that is capable of adequately describing such a variety of situations.

In developing this project we have made use of various theoretical perspectives; we have drawn ideas from the work of a range of congregational consultants and researchers. An important resource has been *A Handbook for Congregational Studies* edited by Jackson Carroll, Carl Dudley and William McKinney.

When examining congregational life one can identify a range of dimensions: the activities of a congregation, how it operates, patterns of leadership and direction setting, its resources and its identity as a congregation.

Within each dimension there are various aspects needing to be examined, as shown in Figure A2.1. In considering the activities of a congregation we can, for instance, examine worship, nurture and mission programs. Or, in looking at its resources we can consider its people resources, property and finances. Or we can talk about the background of staff, the structures in which they operate, or their style and priorities in leadership.

CONGREGATIONAL ACTIVITIES

We can define congregational activities as those organisations, structures, plans and programs through which a congregation expresses its mission and ministry, both to its own members and those outside its membership (Carroll, Dudley, McKinney, 1988). We can draw a distinction between those programs whose primary focus is on worship, those whose primary focus is on the nurture of existing attenders, and those with a primary focus on mission among people with little or no previous church connection. Some aspects of a congregational program will fit clearly into one category, while others will be serving more than one purpose at a time.

FIGURE A2.I: VARIOUS ASPECTS OF CONGREGATIONAL LIFE

CONGREGATIONAL SIZE

ACTIVITIES
CHURCH WORSHIP SERVICES
NURTURE ACTIVITIES
MISSION ACTIVITIES

HOW THE CONGREGATION OPERATES
GROUP LIFE
CONFLICT AND DIFFERENCE

LEADERSHIP/DIRECTION SETTING
PLANNING AND DECISION MAKING
STAFF BACKGROUND
LEADERSHIP STRUCTURES
LEADERSHIP STYLE

RESOURCES
PEOPLE RESOURCES
PROPERTY
FINANCES

IDENTITY
CHARACTER
HERITAGE
FAITH ORIENTATION
PERSONAL SPIRITUAL JOURNEYS

WORSHIP STYLE

Given the central place of worship in the life of congregations, worship services will say much about the nature and identity of a congregation. A fundamental principle of cross-cultural ministry is to encourage the emergence of indigenous forms of congregational life and expression. One key to that is likely to be the style of worship. The style of worship of a congregation says much about its cultural orientation. A congregation expressing its faith in cultural terms quite dissimilar to the culture of large sections of its wider community may well become cut off from that community.

Key issues may include length of services, styles of music, use of formal liturgy, attender involvement in services, use of symbols, and preaching length and style. These issues are dealt with in Chapter 9.

NURTURE STYLE

Some congregations place a stronger emphasis on participation in congregational life than others. It is important to understand the range of activities available within a given congregation and the levels of involvement of those in the congregation in each activity.

Congregations may run a wide variety of nurture activities. We need to know about the nature of a congregation's nurture programs and the percentage of the congregation involved in them. Some nurture activities involve formal teaching/discussion sessions, some have a strong social component, some emphasise a sense of intimacy in a small-group setting, and some have a focus on prayer or meditation. Congregational nurture activities are the focus of the first part of Chapter 10.

MISSION ACTIVITIES

Mission/service activities and emphases are a key aspect of congregational life likely to affect a congregation's openness to its community. Some congregations have a large array of mission/service activities structured into their lives. There are other congregations whose major thrust is to equip their members to 'bloom where they are planted' within their natural social networks. There are also congregations with little outward focus or contact with the wider community.

Chapter 11 looks at levels of outward focus and mission activities and their relationship with congregational vitality.

HOW THE CONGREGATION OPERATES

Congregational process is quite distinct from, though interrelated to, a congregation's activities. Process has to do with the underlying way in which relationships in the congregation are conducted. This will include various aspects of group processes including the nature of attender relationships and sense of community, histories of conflict and difference and how they are dealt with, and the flexibility of a congregation to move in new directions. Aspects of group life are the subject of Chapter 12.

GROUP LIFE

The nature of group life may significantly affect congregational morale, direction setting and member satisfaction. It may also influence the decisions about continued participation on the part of newcomers. In some congregations attenders are largely an 'audience', participating in an experience or activity but with little relationship to each other. By contrast there are congregations in which member interaction is a central theme – those involved share in depth with each other, learn from each other, and are accountable to each other. In some cases such a sense of community may be attractive to those outside who see the world as being hostile and impersonal. In other cases the demands of accountability may be far too rigorous for the outsider to contemplate.

We can measure the degree of interaction between attenders in a congregation – whether they have any contact with others and whether their relationships move to friendships or remain largely task-orientated. The extent to which those involved have their closest friends within the congregation may also be a significant measure of group life, as may forms of communication within the congregation, people's willingness to correct or confront each other when necessary, the congregation's friendliness to newcomers, and the degree to which the congregation addresses everyday issues in people's lives.

CONFLICT AND DIFFERENCE

A congregation with a history of conflict, particularly unresolved conflict, may not be a congregation that is very open to the wider community. A congregation that has worked through conflict constructively may have enabled many of its members to grow significantly. It is important in describing congregational life to gain a picture both of current levels of conflict and any history of conflict.

FLEXIBILITY

In a changing society congregations may need to be flexible to respond creatively to new circumstances. On the other hand, if flexibility means lack of clarity about a congregation's directions, this kind of flexibility may hinder its effectiveness.

LEADERSHIP/DIRECTION SETTING

Leadership and direction setting are critical aspects of any organisation, and congregations are no exception. There are many different styles of leadership and, particularly where paid staff are involved, questions of leadership can become highly complex. In studying this aspect of congregational life we can consider congregational planning and direction setting, staff background, leadership structures, and leadership style.

PLANNING AND DIRECTION SETTING

All congregations develop a set of priorities for their life and actions, whether consciously or unconsciously. They may have developed short- or longer-term plans. The level of intentionality of ministry development may be an important aspect of congregational vitality. The importance of planning and direction setting is dealt with in Chapter 13.

Having a plan is one thing; having achievable goals and concrete strategies to carry out the plan is quite another. It may also be important to know the level of congregational involvement in the planning process.

More generally, whether they formally recognise it or not, congregations make decisions in certain ways. Their method of decision making may influence their openness to sections of the wider community, who may feel more or less comfortable in congregations with different styles of decision making.

Some congregations see leadership in terms of 'offices', others in terms of the contributions of the gifts of individuals. The distinction is often drawn between hierarchical organisations and collaborative grass-roots movements — between 'organisations' and 'organisms'.

Much has been written on such issues. To a large extent, discussion turns on the degree of attender involvement in decision making and direction setting.

The role of leadership will also be important. Does the leadership articulate a clear consistent vision? Is the leadership able to set goals and achieve them? Do leaders take into account the ideas of others, assisting them to discover their gifts and skills? Do they help others to own a vision? Do there exist adequate competencies to move the congregation forward?

STAFF BACKGROUND

Just as those involved in a congregation are a significant resource, so too are any staff that are available to the congregation. It may be important to understanding the life of a congregation to know the number of staff involved as well as their background, the nature of their role and their call, and whether they are full-time or part-time. Important factors may also include their age, background, years of service, and orientation. These and the following aspects of leadership are the subject of Chapter 14.

STRUCTURES FOR LEADERSHIP

The addition of staff to the authority balance within a congregation adds a level of complexity. We may need to consider the relationship between staff and congregation as well as the relationship that staff and congregation have with the wider denominational structures. We may also need to consider, at least in the case of multiple staff congregations, the question of authority and decision making between staff. It may be important to know whether staffing has increased or decreased over the last few years and whether the staff also work with other congregations (eg in a multi-congregation parish).

LEADERSHIP STYLE

Leadership style can vary greatly from congregation to congregation. Indeed, leadership patterns may need to be very different in different kinds of congregations or in different contexts.

There can be many different styles of leadership: hierarchical or collaborative, authoritarian or non-directive, challenging or enabling, and so on. Styles of leadership have gone in and out of fashion over the years. The concern for empowering the laity in the 1960s sometimes resulted in role confusion for paid leadership. Some have found this threatening; others have embraced concepts of non-directive leadership. The Church Growth Movement has provided a reaction to such thinking, emphasising the importance of strong, directive leadership.

Describing leadership patterns will also involve discerning the priorities that leaders have for their roles. Some roles that may be seen as being important include:
- Priest – conducting worship and administering the sacraments
- Pastor – visiting, counselling and helping people
- Evangelist – converting others to the faith
- Educator – teaching people about the Christian faith
- Equipper – training laity for ministry and mission
- Social reformer – tackling social injustices
- Organiser – supervising the work of the church or parish
- Visionary – providing directions for the future.

CONGREGATIONAL RESOURCES

Congregations possess resources of various kinds: people resources, property resources and resources in terms of finance.

PEOPLE RESOURCES

Perhaps the most fundamental resource possessed by a congregation is the lives, activities, energy and commitment of those involved in its life. Furthermore, the attitudes, backgrounds and orientations of those involved may also significantly affect the openness of a congregation to the community around it. There are many aspects of the people resources of a congregation that may be worth measuring in a project such as this. These are dealt with in Chapters 8 and 15.

Congregational size is an obvious factor that impacts on the possibilities open to a congregation as well as on its style and ethos. Many observers have noted the effect of size on the internal structuring of a congregation's life. Large congregations function quite differently from smaller ones. Changes in size may create various stresses and tensions for a congregation. For example, a congregation that has declined in size may find that its program base is difficult to sustain with reduced numbers of people to do the work.

PROPERTY RESOURCES

Property resources may impact on congregational openness to its community. The location of any property, its capacity, accessibility (eg for cars, parking, wheelchair access), design, facilities and age may all be factors that will influence congregational vitality. Likewise, the visibility of congregational property may have an impact. Is it visually obvious to passers-by in cars, or to pedestrians on their way to shops, work or other community services? Chapter 16 deals with the results of this study in relation to property and financial resources.

FINANCIAL RESOURCES

The financial resources available to a congregation may significantly affect congregational life, either providing opportunities or imposing limitations. It is important to know the level of giving within a congregation (and any significant changes in recent years), income from assets and other sources, as well as any major debts that the congregation may be carrying.

CONGREGATIONAL IDENTITY

This final category of congregational life is quite elusive and often overlooked. There may be much about a congregation's identity that is seldom stated even by members to each other. Congregational identity is affected by many factors, including its character, denominational heritage, faith orientation, and the personal spiritual journeys of attenders.

CONGREGATIONAL CHARACTER

The character of a congregation is a product of many factors. The demographic character of a congregation may be of importance (see Chapter 15). Since contemporary society is characterised by increasing social diversity, it is important to know the backgrounds of those involved within a congregation. Key aspects of attenders' backgrounds may include their age, stage in life, gender, marital status, mobility, levels of education, occupation and ethnic background. It may also be valuable to identify attenders associated with particular interest groups or sectors of society (eg people involved in the farming community, union movement, academic world, etc).

There has been much recent debate about the importance of congregations being made up of people who are similar to each other in background (eg the Homogenous Unit Principle in Church Growth literature, cross-cultural mission principles, and anthropological insights). Does the degree of homogeneity of a congregation help or hinder its vitality?

The profile of a congregation may also be significant when compared with the profile of the community for which it has a concern. The degree of congregation/community congruity may impact on a congregation's effectiveness.

A fundamental aspect of a congregation's character relates to the purpose of the congregation and identifying the community for which it has a concern. Congregations can vary in regard to their focus: they may be highly local in orientation or they may conduct a more regional ministry. Congregations may have a primary concern for a local area or alternatively for a particular cultural, generational or interest group.

DENOMINATIONAL HERITAGE

Denominational traditions will affect the ethos and identity of a congregation. Congregations sometimes have their origins many centuries ago in quite different social contexts. The changes associated with modern technology, cultural diversity and contemporary thinking have created quite different contexts for these traditions to operate in today.

Denominational traditions include specific belief emphases as well as distinctive styles of worship and practice. Denominations may vary in regard to the way they are structured: some denominations have very little organisational infrastructure at a regional or state level while others have relatively large denominational organisations and/or centralised authority. The nature of a congregation's relationship to the wider denomination may also be significant. Such matters are examined in Chapter 18.

FAITH ORIENTATION

A critical aspect of congregational life must be the faith orientation of those involved, which is also covered in Chapter 18. This may include the theological traditions that have been most influential, attitudes to the Bible, the charismatic movement and speaking in tongues, and the relative importance of evangelism and social concern.

The faith orientation of a congregation may affect its life in many ways. There are strong links between faith and practice.

Faith orientation may also influence a congregation's perception of the boundary between congregation and community. Some traditions draw very firm distinctions between who is 'in' the congregation and who is not. Others see the entire community as part of the church, irrespective of people's levels of involvement. In such traditions the boundary does not exist; people simply have different degrees of involvement.

Faith orientation may directly affect the priorities of a congregation in terms of its mission. Some congregations and denominations have a heritage of strong personal evangelism, others of encouraging good citizenship, still others of struggling for significant social change, and others of providing a sanctuary from the struggles and tribulations of the wider world (eg Roozen, McKinney and Carroll, 1988). Faith orientation may therefore affect whether a congregation has an inward or outward focus, as well as its acceptance of people with different values and beliefs.

PERSONAL SPIRITUAL JOURNEYS

Most churches encourage attenders in their devotional life. Bible reading, personal prayer and experiences of the presence of God in everyday life are encouraged to a greater or lesser extent by the various Christian traditions. Does the personal spiritual journey of attenders make a difference to the vitality of a congregation? Chapter 10 covers such matters.

* * *

Understanding congregational life involves examining a wide range of factors that all contribute to defining the nature and future directions of a congregation. These factors are not independent of each other. Study of congregational life that does not cover the broad range of issues involved will be limited in its scope.

REFERENCES

The following references provide useful material on congregational vitality issues and/or are cited in the text.

ANDERSON, J D & JONES, E E, 1978, *The Management of Ministry.* San Francisco: Harper and Row.

ANDERSON, L, 1990, *Dying for Change.* Minneapolis: Bethany House Publishers.

ANDERSON, L, 1992, *A Church for the Twenty First Century.* Minneapolis: Bethany House Publishers.

ARN, W, 1986, 'How to Use Ratios to Effect Church Growth' in Wagner, C P (ed), *Church Growth: State of the Art.* Wheaton, Illinois: Tyndale House Publishers Inc.

ARN, W & ARN, C, 1982, *The Master's Plan for Making Disciples.* California: Church Growth Press.

BANKS, R, 1987, *All the Business of Life: Bringing Theology down to Earth.* Sydney: Albatross Books Pty Ltd.

BARNA, G, 1988, *Marketing the Church.* Colorado Springs: Nav Press.

BARNA, G, 1991, *User Friendly Churches.* Ventura, California: Regal Books.

BENTLEY, P, BLOMBERY, 'T & HUGHES, P, 1992, *Faith without the Church. Nominalism in Australian Christianity.* Melbourne: Christian Research Association.

BERGER, P L & NEUHAUS, R J, 1977, *To Empower People: The Role of Mediating Structures and Public Policy.* Washington DC: American Enterprise Institute for Public Policy Research.

BIBBY, R, 1978, 'Why Conservative Churches Really Are Growing: Kelley Revisited'. *Journal for the Scientific Study of Religion* 17 (2): 129–137.

BIBBY, R, 1993, *Fragmented Gods: The Poverty and Potential of Religion in Canada.* Toronto: Stoddart Publishing.

BLACK, A W, 1988, 'Pentecostalism in Australia: Some Preliminary Findings', paper prepared for the Conference of the Australian Association for the Study of Religion, Brisbane, September 1988.

BLACK, A W (ed), 1991, *Religion in Australia: Sociological Perspectives.* Sydney: Allen & Unwin.

BLACK, A W, 1991, 'Australian Pentecostalism in Comparative Perspective' in Black, A W (ed), *Religion in Australia: Sociological Perspectives.* Sydney: Allen & Unwin.

BLACK, A W & GLASNER, P E (eds), 1983, *Practice and Belief: Studies in the Sociology of Australian Religion.* Sydney: Allen & Unwin.

BLOMBERY, 'T, 1989a, *God through Human Eyes: Report from the Combined Churches Survey for Faith and Mission.* Melbourne: Christian Research Association.

BLOMBERY, 'T, 1989b, *Tomorrow's Church Today: Report from the Combined Churches Survey for Faith and Mission*. Melbourne: Christian Research Association.

BLOMBERY, 'T & HUGHES, P, 1993, *Faith Alive, an Australian Picture*. Melbourne: Christian Research Association.

BODYCOMB, J, 1986, *A Matter of Death and Life: The Future of Australia's Churches*. Melbourne: Joint Board of Christian Education.

BOSCH, D J, 1991, *Transforming Mission: Paradigm Shifts in Theology of Mission*. American Society of Missiology Series, No. 16. New York: Orbis Books.

BOUMA, G D, 1992, *Religion: Meaning, Transcendence and Community in Australia*. Melbourne: Longman Cheshire.

BOUMA, G D & DIXON, B R, 1986, *The Religious Factor in Australian Life*. Melbourne: MARC.

BROWNING, R, 1986, *Down and Under: Discipleship in an Australian Urban Setting*. Melbourne: Spectrum Publishers.

BRUCE, S, 1983, 'The Persistence of Religion: Conservative Protestantism in the United Kingdom'. *Sociological Review* 3: 453–470.

BURT, S E & ROPER, H A, 1992, *Raising Small Church Self-esteem*. Washington, DC: The Alban Institute.

CALLAHAN, K L, 1983, *Twelve Keys to an Effective Church: Strategic Planning for Mission*. San Francisco: Harper and Row.

CALLAHAN, K L, 1987, *Twelve Keys to an Effective Church — the Leaders Guide*. San Francisco: Harper and Row.

CALLAHAN, K L, 1990, *Effective Church Leadership: Building on the Twelve Keys*. San Francisco: Harper and Row.

CALLAHAN, K L, 1992a, *Effective Church Finances — Fund-Raising and Budgeting for Church Leaders*. San Francisco: Harper and Row.

CALLAHAN, K L, 1992b, *Giving and Stewardship in an Effective Church — A Guide for Every Member Ministry*. San Francisco: Harper and Row.

CALLAHAN, K L, 1994, *Dynamic Worship — Mission, Grace, Praise and Power: A Manual for Strengthening the Worship Life of Twelve Keys Congregations*. San Francisco: Harper and Row.

CARROLL, J W, DUDLEY, C S & McKINNEY, W (eds), 1986, *A Handbook for Congregational Studies*. Nashville: Abingdon Press.

CARROLL, J W & ROOF, C W (eds), 1993, *Beyond Establishment. Protestant Identity in a Post-Protestant Age*. Louisville, Kentucky: Westminster/John Knox Press.

CHANT, B, 1984, *Heart of Fire: The Story of Australian Pentecostalism*. Unley Park, South Australia: House of Tabor.

CLAYDON, D, 1993, *Only Connect: Sharing the Gospel across Cultural Boundaries*. Sydney: Lancer Books.

CONWAY, R, 1994, 'The Once and Future Church'. *Quadrant,* May 1994.

CORNEY, P, 1991, *The Gospel and the Growing Church*. Sydney: AIO Press.

CORNEY, P, 1992, *The Welcoming Church. How to Welcome Newcomers in the Local Church*. Sydney: AIO Press.

CORNEY, P, 1994, *Reinventing the Church: Key Issues Facing the Australian Church in the 1990s and Beyond.* Kew: Institute for Contemporary Christian Leadership.

CRABTREE, D F, 1989, *The Empowering Church — How One Congregation Supports Lay People's Ministries in the World.* Washington, DC: The Alban Institute.

CROUCHER, R, 1991, *Your Church Can Come Alive: Strategies for Church Leaders.* Melbourne: Joint Board of Christian Education.

CURRIE, GILBERT & HORSLEY, 1977, *Churches and Church Goers: Patterns of Church Growth in the British Isles Since 1700.* Oxford: Clarendon Press

DAVIS, N, KAVANAGH, B & McGUINESS, M, 1994, *An Introductory Myers Briggs Workshop, Presenters Resource.* Sydney: Institute for Type Development.

DEMPSEY, K, 1983a, 'Country Town Religion' in Black, A W & Glasner, P E (eds), *Practice and Belief: Studies in the Sociology of Australian Religion.* Sydney: Allen & Unwin

DEMPSEY, K, 1983b, *Conflict and Decline: Ministers and Laymen in an Australian Country Town.* Sydney: Methuen.

DIETTERICH, P M, 1993, *Strategic Questions for the Church Today: How Shall We Interact with Our Environment?* Chicago: Center for Parish Development.

DIETTERICH, P M & DIETTERICH, I T, 1989, *A Systems Model of the Church in Ministry and Mission.* Chicago: Center for Parish Development.

DOUGLASS, H P & BRUNNER, E de S, 1935, *The Protestant Church as a Social Institution.* New York: Russell and Russell.

DRAYTON, D, KITTO, C & MANTON, D, 1992, *Planning for Mission in Neighbourhood, Middle and Regional Congregations.* Sydney: Uniting Church Board of Mission.

EASUM, W, 1993, *Dancing with Dinosaurs: Ministry in a Hostile and Hurting World.* Nashville: Abingdon Press.

FINKE, R & STARK, R, 1992, *The Churching of America 1776–1990: Winners and Losers in America's Religious Economy.* New Brunswick NJ: Rutgers.

FINNEY, J, 1991, *The Well Church Book.* Worcester & London: The Trinity Press.

FINNEY, J, 1992, *Church on the Move. Leadership for Mission.* Cambridge: University Press.

FUNG, R, 1992, *The Isaiah Vision.* Geneva: World Council of Churches Publication.

GANNON, T M, 1978, 'Religious Tradition and Urban Community'. *Sociological Analysis,* Vol 30 (4) Winter 1978, pp 283–302

GEORGE, C F, 1991, *Prepare Your Church for the Future.* Michigan: Fleming H Revell.

GEORGE, C F, 1994, *The Coming Church Revolution: Empowering Leaders for the Future.* Grand Rapids, Michigan: Fleming H. Revell.

GERLACH, L P & HINE, V H, 1968, 'Five Factors Crucial to the Growth and Spread of a Modern Religious Movement'. *Journal for the Scientific Study of Religion* 7:23–40.

GIBBS, E, 1981, *I Believe in Church Growth.* London: Hodder & Stoughton.

GIBBS, E, 1987, *Followed or Pushed? Understanding and Leading Your Church.* MARC Europe: Bromley, UK.

GIBBS, E, 1994, *In Name Only: Tackling the Problem of Nominal Christianity.* Wheaton, Illinois: Bridgepoint Books.

GLOCK, C Y & STARK, R, 1965, *Religion and Society in Tension.* Chicago: Rand McNally.

GOODHEW, R H, 1990, *The Role of the Leader: an examination of the influence of ministerial leadership on the growth of six Australian churches from 1978 to 1989* (unpublished thesis).

GRIERSON, D, 1984, *Transforming a People of God.* Melbourne: Joint Board of Christian Education.

GRIERSON, D, 1991, *A People on the Way — Congregation, Mission and Australian Culture.* Melbourne: David Lovell Publishing.

HADAWAY, C K, 1980, 'Conservatism and Social Strength in a Liberal Denomination'. *Review of Religious Research* 21 (3): 302–314.

HADAWAY, C K, 1982, 'Church Growth (and Decline) in a Southern City'. *Review of Religious Research* 23: 372–86.

HADAWAY, C K, 1991, *Church Growth: Separating Facts and Fiction.* Nashville, Tennessee: Broadman Press.

HADAWAY, C K & MARLER, P, 1996, 'Is There a Method to this Madness?'. *Journal for Scientific Study of Religion,* Volume 35, No. 3 September 1996, 217.

HADAWAY, C K & ROOZEN, D A, 1995, *Rerouting the Protestant Mainstream: Sources of Growth and Opportunities for Change.* Nashville: Abingdon Press.

HAHN, C A, 1985, *Lay Voices in an Open Church.* New York: The Alban Institute.

HAN, G S, 1994, *Social Sources of Church Growth: Korean Churches in the Homeland and Overseas.* Lanham, Maryland: University Press of America.

HARRIS, D, HYND, D & MILLIKAN, D (eds), 1982, *The Shape of Belief — Christianity in Australia today.* Sydney: Lancer.

HARTMAN, W J, 1987, *Five Audiences — Identifying Groups in Your Church.* Nashville: Abingdon Press.

HARTMAN, W J & WILSON, R L, 1989, *The Large Membership Church.* Nashville: Discipleship Resources.

HECHTER, M, 1987, *Principles of Group Solidarity.* Los Angeles: University of California Press.

HENDRICKS, W D, 1993, *Exit Interviews.* Chicago: Moody Press.

HERALD, I J, 1989, *Conflict Management Ministry in the Church.* Katoomba: Berea Ministries.

HERRMANN, R, 1983, *Living Issues in Mining Towns.* Stanthorpe: International Colour Productions.

HESSELGRAVE, D J, 1980, *Planting Churches Cross-Culturally. A Guide for Home and Foreign Missions.* Grand Rapids: Baker Book House.

HEWETSON, D, 1991, *2001: Growing Tomorrow's Church.* Sydney: AIO Press.

HILLMAN, R, 1981, *The Church: Growing Up and Growing Out: A Discussion of Quality Church Growth in Australia.* Sydney: Unichurch.

HOGE, D R, 1979a, 'Why are Churches Declining?'. *Theology Today* 36 (1): 92–95.

HOGE, D R, 1979b, 'National Contextual Factors influencing Church Trends' in *Understanding Church Growth and Decline 1950–1978.* New York: Pilgrim Press.

HOGE, D R, 1979c, 'A Test of Theories of Denominational Growth and Decline' in *Understanding Church Growth and Decline 1950–1978*. New York: Pilgrim Press.

HOGE, D R & ROOZEN, D A (eds), 1979, *Understanding Church Growth and Decline: 1950–1978*. New York: Pilgrim Press.

HUGHES, P J, 1988, *The Church's Mission: Report from the Combined Churches Survey for Faith and Mission*. Victoria: Christian Research Association.

HUGHES, P J, 1989, *The Australian Clergy. Report from the Combined Churches Survey for Faith and Mission*. Melbourne: Christian Research Association.

HUGHES, P J, 1991, 'Types of Faith and the Decline of Mainline Churches' in Black, A W (ed), *Religion in Australia: Sociological Perspectives*. Sydney: Allen & Unwin.

HUGHES, P J, 1996, *The Pentecostals in Australia — Religious Community Profiles Series*. Canberra: Australian Government Publishing Service.

HUGHES, P J & BLOMBERY, 'T, 1990, *Patterns of Faith in Australian Churches: Report from the Combined Churches Survey for Faith and Mission*. Melbourne: Christian Research Association.

HUGHES, P J, THOMPSON, C, PRYOR, R & BOUMA, G, 1995, *Believe It or Not, Australian Spirituality and the Churches in the 90s*. Melbourne: Christian Research Association.

HULL, W, 1992, 'Is the Church Growth Movement Really Working?' in Horton, M S (ed), *Power Religion: The Selling Out of the Evangelical Church*. Chicago: Moody.

IANNACCONE, L R, 1992, 'Sacrifice and Stigma: Reducing Free-riding in Cults, Communes and Other Collectives'. *Journal of Political Economy* 100 (2): 271–91.

IANNACCONE, L R, 1994, 'Why Strict Churches are Strong'. *American Journal of Sociology* 99 (5): 1180–1211.

IANNACCONE, L R, 1996, 'Reassessing Church Growth'. *Journal for the Scientific Study of Religion*, Vol 35, No. 3 September 1996, 197.

JACKSON, W, 1996, 'Sociology: A Must in Training Tomorrow's Christian Leaders'. *On Being*. August 1996, Melbourne: 36 Media Ltd.

JENSON, R & STEVENS, J, 1981, *Dynamics of Church Growth*. Grand Rapids, Michigan: Baker Book House.

JOHNSON, D W, 1989, *Vitality Means Church Growth*. Creative Leadership Series. Nashville: Abingdon Press.

JONES, E E, 1976, *Strategies for New Churches*. San Francisco: Harper and Row.

KALDOR, P, 1983, *A Gulf Too Deep? The Protestant Churches and the Urban Working Class in Australia*. Sydney: Board of Mission.

KALDOR, P, 1987, *Who Goes Where? Who Doesn't Care?*. Sydney: Lancer.

KALDOR, P, 1994, 'Creating Regional Congregations by Amalgamation. Some Reflections on the Process' in Mavor, J (ed), *Creative Life Together: Ministry in Regional Congregations*. Melbourne: Uniting Church Press.

KALDOR, P, BOWIE, V & FARQUHAR-NICOL, G (eds), 1985, *Green Shoots in the Concrete*. South Australia: Pan Print.

KALDOR, P & KALDOR, S, 1988, *Where the River Flows*. Sydney: Lancer.

KALDOR, P, BELLAMY, J, CORREY, M & POWELL, R, 1992: *First Look in the*

Mirror: Initial findings of the 1991 National Church Life Survey. Sydney: Lancer.

KALDOR, P, BELLAMY, J, POWELL, R, CORREY, M & CASTLE, K, 1994, *Winds of Change: The experience of church in a changing Australia.* Sydney: Lancer.

KALDOR, P & CASTLE, K, 1995, *Are There Bible Belts in Australia?* Sydney: National Church Life Survey.

KALDOR, P, BELLAMY, J & MOORE, S, 1995, *Mission under the Microscope: Keys to Effective and Sustainable Mission.* Adelaide: Openbook.

KALDOR, P & POWELL, R, 1995, *Views from the Pews: Australian Church Attenders Speak Out.* Adelaide: Openbook.

KELLEY, D M, 1972, *Why Conservative Churches Are Growing.* New York: Harper and Row.

KELLEY, D M, 1978, 'Why Conservative Churches Are Still Growing'. *Journal for the Scientific Study of Religion* 17 (2): 165–172.

KLAAS, A C, 1996, *In Search of the Unchurched.* Bethesda: The Alban Institute.

KLOPP, H, 1982, *A Multiple Regression Analysis of Church Growth Principles* (unpublished thesis).

LANGMEAD, R, 1977, *The Western Suburbs Conference Report.* Melbourne: Baptist Union of Victoria.

LAWTON, W, 1988, *Being Christian, Being Australian: Contemporary Christianity Down Under.* Sydney: Anzea.

LEAS, S & KITTLAUS, P, 1977, *Church Fights, Managing Conflict in the Local Church.* Philadelphia: The Westminster Press.

LEE, H W, 1989, *Effective Church Leadership — A practical source book.* Minneapolis: Augsburg Fortress.

LENSKI, G E, 1953, 'Social Correlates of Religious Interest'. *American Sociological Review* 18, pp 533–544.

LENSKI, G E, 1961, *The Religious Factor. A Sociologist's Inquiry.* New York: Doubleday.

LUECKE, D, 1988, *Evangelical Style and Lutheran Substance.* St Louis: Concordia Publishing House.

MACKAY, H, 1993, *Reinventing Australia. The Mind and Mood of Australia in the 90s.* Sydney: Collins Angus & Robertson Publishers.

MACKAY, H, 1994, *The Australian,* 23/6/94.

MALLISON, J, 1996, *The Small-Group Leader: A Manual to Develop Vital Small Groups.* Adelaide: Openbook.

MARTIN, D, 1967, *A Sociology of English Religion.* London: SCM Press.

MAVOR, J E (ed), 1994a, *Creative Life Together: Ministry in Regional Congregations.* Melbourne: Joint Board of Christian Education.

MAVOR, J E (ed), 1994b, *Many Models One Aim: Mission Planning in the Australian Church.* Melbourne: Joint Board of Christian Education.

MAY, F J, 1986, 'Supernatural Anointing and Church Growth' in Wagner, C P (ed), *Church Growth: State of the Art.* Wheaton, Illinois: Tyndale House Publishers Inc.

McCLINTOCK, W, 1988, 'Sociological Critique of the Homogeneous Unit Principle'. *International Review of Mission* 77: January 1988, pp 107–116.

McGAVRAN, D A, 1970, *Understanding Church Growth*. Grand Rapids: Wm. B. Eerdmans.

McGAVRAN, D A & ARN, W, 1976, *Church Growth Principles*. Melbourne: Churches of Christ Federal Literature Dept.

McGAVRAN, D A, 1988, *Effective Evangelism, A Theological Mandate*. Phillipsburg: Presbyterian and Reformed Publishing Company.

McGAVRAN, D A & ARN, W C, 1977, *Ten Steps for Church Growth*. New York: Harper and Row.

McINTOSH, G & MARTIN, G, 1992, *Finding Them, Keeping Them: Effective Strategies for Evangelism and Assimilation in the Local Church*. Nashville: Broadman.

McSWAIN, L, 1980, *Critical Appraisal of Church Growth Movement*. Review and Expositor.

MEAD, L B, 1991, *The Once and Future Church*, Washington DC: Alban Institute.

MEAD, L B, 1993, *More than Numbers*. Washington DC: Alban Institute.

MEAD, L B, 1994, *Transforming Congregations for the Future*. Bethesda: The Alban Institute.

MERRITT, D, 1996, *Choosing Our Future: Options for the Church in the Riverina*. Melbourne: Uniting Church Press.

MILLER, C J, 1986, *Outgrowing the Ingrown Church*. Grand Rapids, Michigan: Zondervan Publishing House.

MILLER, H, 1990, *The Vital Congregation — Effective Church Series*. Nashville: Abingdon Press.

MILLIKAN, D, 1981, *The Sunburnt Soul: Christianity in Search of an Australian Identity*. Sydney: Lancer.

MOBERG, D O, 1962, *The Church as a Social Institution*. Englewood Cliffs: Prentice Hall

MOCK, A O, 1992, *Theological Perspectives and Involvement in Community Ministries: Exploding a Myth: Brief Paper*. Chicago: Centre for Church and Community Ministries.

MOL, J J (Hans), 1969, *Christianity in Chains*. Hong Kong: Associated Printers DNP Ltd.

MOL, J J (Hans), 1971, *Religion in Australia: A Sociological Investigation*. Melbourne: Thomas Nelson.

MOL, J J (Hans), 1985, *The Faith of Australians*. Sydney: Allen and Unwin.

MOLLER, C, 1992, *Employeeship: Mobilising Everybody's Energy to Win*. San Francisco: Time Manager International A/S.

MORRIS, L J, 1993, *The High Impact Church*. Texas: Torch Publications.

MOYES, G, 1975, *How to Grow an Australian Church*. Melbourne: Churches of Christ Federal Literature Department.

MULLER, R, 1993, 'How Are Churches Doing Evangelism?' in Patrick, B (ed), *New Vision, New Zealand*. Auckland: Vision New Zealand.

NICHOLS, A, 1984, *Reluctant Conscience. Closing the Gap between the Gospel and Reality in Australia*. Blackburn: Dove Communications.

NIEBUHR, H R, 1929, *The Social Sources of Denominationalism*. New York: Henry Holt.

NIEBUHR, H R, 1951, *Christ and Culture*. New York: Harper and Bros.

OLSON, D V A, 1993, 'Congregational Growth and Decline in Indiana among Five Mainline Denominations' in Roozen, D A & Hadaway, C K (eds), *Church and Denominational Growth. What does (and does not) cause growth or decline.* Nashville: Abingdon Press.

OSWALD, R M, 1992, *Making Your Church More Inviting*. Washington DC: The Alban Institute.

OSWALD, R M & LEAS, S B, 1987, *The Inviting Church: A Study of New Member Assimilation*. New York: The Alban Institute.

PATRICK, B (ed), 1993, *New Vision, New Zealand*. Auckland: Vision New Zealand.

POINTER, R, 1984, *How Do Churches Grow?* London: MARC Europe and the British Church Growth Association.

POSTERSKI, D C & BARKER, I, 1993, *Where's a Good Church? Canadians Respond from the Pulpit, Podium and Pew*. Canada: Wood Lake Books.

PUTMAN, R D, 1995, 'Bowling Alone: America's Declining Social Capital'. *Journal of Democracy,* Vol 6 No.1 January 1995, pp 65–78.

RAINER, T S, 1993, *The Book of Church Growth: History, Theology and Principles*. Nashville, Tennessee: Broadman Press.

RAUFF, E A, 1979, *Why People Join the Church: An Exploratory Study*. New York: The Pilgrim Press and Washington DC: Glenmary Research.

REEVES, R D & JENSON, R, 1984, *Always Advancing: Modern Strategies for Church Growth*. California: A Campus Crusade for Christ Book, Here's Life Publishers.

ROBINSON, I, KALDOR, P & DRAYTON, D (eds), 1991, *Growing an Everyday Faith: Effective Mission in a Changing Australia*. Sydney: Lancer.

ROBINSON, M, 1992, *A World Apart: Creating a Church for the Unchurched — Learning from Willow Creek*. Tunbridge Wells, UK: Monarch Publications.

ROBINSON, M, 1994, *The Faith of the Unbeliever — Building Innovative Relationships with the Unchurched*. Crowborough, UK: Monarch Publications.

ROBINSON, M & CHRISTINE, S, 1992, *Planting Tomorrow's Churches Today — A Comprehensive Handbook*. Tunbridge Wells, UK: Monarch Publications.

ROBINSON, M & YARNELL, D, 1993, *Celebrating the Small Church*. Tunbridge Wells, UK: Monarch Publications.

ROOF, W C, 1976, 'Traditional Religion in Contemporary Society: A Theory of Local-Cosmopolitan Plausibility'. *American Sociological Review* 41: 195–208.

ROOF, W C, 1978, *Community and Commitment: Religious Plausibility in a Liberal Protestant Church*. New York: Elsevier.

ROOF, W C, HOGE, D R, DYBLE, J E & HADAWAY, C K, 1979, 'Factors Producing Growth or Decline in United Presbyterian Congregations' in *Understanding Church Growth and Decline 1950–1978*. New York: Pilgrim Press.

ROOF, W C & McKINNEY, W, 1987, *American Mainline Religion: Its Changing Shape and Future*. New Brunswick, N J: Rutgers University Press.

ROOZEN, D A & HADAWAY, C K (eds), 1993, *Church and Denominational Growth. What does (and does not) cause growth or decline.* Nashville: Abingdon Press.

ROOZEN, D A, McKINNEY, W & CARROLL, J W, 1984, *Varieties of Religious Presence*. New York: Pilgrim Press.

ROSE, L L & HADAWAY, C K, 1982, *The Urban Challenge*. Tennessee: Broadman Press.

ROTHAUGE, A, (undated), *Sizing up a Congregation for New Member Ministry*. New York: Episcopal Church Center.

ROTHAUGE, A J, 1988, *A Diocesan Strategy for New Church Development*. New York: Episcopal Church Centre.

SAMUEL, V & HAUSER, A (eds), 1989, *Proclaiming Christ in Christ's Way*. Oxford: Regnum Books.

SCHALLER, L E, 1975a, *Hey, That's Our Church!* Nashville: Abingdon Press.

SCHALLER, L E, 1975b, *Growing Plans — Strategies to Increase Your Church's Membership*. Nashville: Abingdon.

SCHALLER, L E, 1979, *Effective Church Planning*. Nashville: Abingdon Press.

SCHALLER, L E, 1983, *Growing Plans*. Nashville: Abingdon Press.

SCHALLER, L E, 1984, *Looking in the Mirror: Self Appraisal in the Local Church*. Nashville: Abingdon Press.

SCHALLER, L E, 1986, *The Change Agent: The Strategy of Innovative Leadership*. Nashville: Abingdon Press.

SCHALLER, L E, 1987a, *It's a Different World. The Challenge for Today's Pastor*. Abingdon Press: Nashville

SCHALLER, L E (ed), 1987b, *Assimilating New Members*. Nashville: Abingdon Press.

SCHALLER, L E, 1988, *44 Ways to Increase Church Attendance*. Nashville: Abingdon Press.

SCHALLER, L E, 1989, *44 Ways to Expand the Financial Base of Your Congregation*. Nashville: Abingdon Press.

SCHUMACHER, E F, 1973, *Small Is Beautiful: Economics as if People Mattered*. San Francisco: Harper and Row.

SNYDER, H A, 1975, *New Wineskins: Changing the Man-made Structures of the Church*. London: Marshall Morgan and Scott.

STARK, R & BAINBRIDGE, W S, 1985, *The Future of Religion*. Berkeley: University of California Press.

STARK, R & BAINBRIDGE, W S, 1987, *A Theory of Religion*. New York: Peter Lang.

STARK, R & GLOCK, C, 1968, *American Piety: The Nature of Religious Commitment*. Berkeley: University of California Press.

SWEETSER, T, 1983, *Successful Parishes*. Minnesota: Winston Press.

THOMPSON, W L, CARROLL, J W & HOGE, D R, 1993, 'Growth or Decline in Presbyterian Congregations' in Roozen, D A & Hadaway, C K (eds), *Church and Denominational Growth. What does (and does not) cause growth or decline*. Nashville: Abingdon Press.

TILLAPAUGH, F R, 1982, *Unleashing the Church*. Ventura, California: Regal Books.

TILLER, J, 1983, *A Strategy for the Church's Ministry*. London: CIO Publishing.

TOWNS, E L, VAUGHAN, J N & SEIFERT, D J, 1981, *The Complete Book of Church Growth*. Illinois: Tyndale House Publications Inc.

TOWNS, E L, 1990, *10 of Today's Most Innovative Churches*. Ventura, California: Regal Books.

TROELTSCH, E, 1960, *The Social Teachings of the Churches*. New York: Harper Books.

VAHANIAN, G, 1961, *The Death of God: The Culture of our Post-Christian Era*. New York: George Braziller.

VAUGHAN, J N, 1985, *The Large Church: A Twentieth Century Expression of the First Century Church*. Grand Rapids, Michigan: Baker Book House.

VAUGHAN, J N, 1986, 'Trends among the World's Twenty Largest Churches' in *Church Growth: State of the Art*. Wheaton, Illinois: Tyndale House Publishers Inc.

VAUGHAN, E, 1988, *Change or Die: An application of church growth principles to the Anglican Church*. Unpublished thesis. Moore Theological College. Sydney.

WAGNER, C P, 1976, *Your Church Can Grow*. Glendale: G/L Publications.

WAGNER, C P, 1979, 'Church Growth Research: The Paradigm and Its Applications' in Hoge, D R & Roozen, E A (eds), *Understanding Church Growth and Decline 1950–1978*. New York: Pilgrim Press.

WAGNER, C P, 1984, *Leading Your Church to Growth*. California: Regal Books.

WAGNER, C P (ed), 1986, *Church Growth: State of the Art*. Illinois: Tyndale.

WAGNER, C P, 1990, *Church Planting for a Greater Harvest*. Ventura, California: Regal Books.

WAGNER, C P & SCHALLER, L (eds) , 1979, *Your Church Can Be Healthy*. Nashville: Abingdon Press.

WALRATH, D A, 1979, 'Social Change and Local Church: 1951–75' in *Understanding Church Growth and Decline 1950–1978*. New York: Pilgrim Press.

WARREN, R, 1995, *The Purpose Driven Church: Growth without Compromising your Message and Mission*. Grand Rapids, Michigan: Zondervan.

WHITE, J E, 1992, *Opening the Front Door: Worship and Church Growth*. Nashville: Convention.

WHITEHEAD, E E & WHITEHEAD, J D, 1982, *Community of Faith: Models and Strategies for Developing Christian Communities*. New York: Seabury Press.

WILKE, R B, 1986, *Are We Yet Alive? The Future of the United Methodist Church*. Nashville: Abingdon Press.

WILLIMON, W H, 1983, *What's Right with the Church*. San Francisco: Harper & Row.

WILSON, B, 1983, *Can God Survive in Australia?* Sydney: Albatross.

WINTER, G, 1961, *The Suburban Captivity of the Churches*. Garden City: Doubleday & Co.

WUTHNOW, R, 1976, 'Recent Pattern of Secularization: A Problem of Generations?'. *American Sociological Review* 41, 850–867.

WUTHNOW, R, 1994, *Sharing the Journey: Support Groups and America's New Quest for Community*. New York: The Free Press (Macmillan).

WUTHNOW, R & CHRISTIANO, K, 1979, 'The Effects of Residential Migration on Church Attendance in the United States' in Wuthnow (ed),

The Religious Dimension: New Directions in Quantitative Research. New York: Academic Press, pp 258–276.

THE NATIONAL CHURCH LIFE SURVEY TEAM

Peter Kaldor

Peter has had many years experience with mission groups and churches in different denominations. For the past 14 years he has been researching aspects of church life for the Uniting Church Board of Mission, providing congregations with information about mission possibilities. He is committed to helping churches relate more effectively to the many diverse groups in Australian society. Peter is the Director of the NCLS and has had a major role in all aspects of the research for this book, including the overall framework for the project, statistical analysis, and the writing and production of this book.

John Bellamy

John is the staff person from the Anglican Home Mission Society most involved in the NCLS. He has a background in town planning and is currently completing a PhD at Edith Cowan University, exploring the relationship between churches and the wider community. He believes that research has an important role to play in the mission of the church. John is a primary researcher and writer with the NCLS and has had a major role in the research, analysis, writing and production of this book.

Ruth Powell

Ruth has a background in psychology and statistics. Also a staff member of the Uniting Church Board of Mission, she has had previous involvement in welfare and experience with many different subcultures. Currently involved in post-graduate research (PhD) into age differences in the churches, Ruth is committed to ensuring that the church relates to all the different groups in society. Ruth is a primary researcher and writer with the NCLS and has had a major role in the research, the development of the model of congregational life and the statistical analysis underlying the results of this book.

Keith Castle

Keith has been employed by the Anglican diocese of Sydney as an urban planner for the past seven years to assist congregations and diocesan leaders. He believes that focused research is an essential component in helping the church to review the past and plan for the future. Keith has had an important and ongoing role in survey design, logistics and the production of resources for congregations.

Bronwyn Hughes

A member of the NCLS staff team from 1996, Bronwyn's media and communication skills have been a great gift to the project. Bronwyn has completed a Master of Management (Communications) degree and is planning further research to explore communication strategies and culture change in the church. Bronwyn has contributed to the production of this book, coordinating the design of graphical elements.

Joy Sanderson

Joy is employed by the Uniting Church Board of Mission and has provided administrative coordination over the past seven years for the NCLS team. Joy has had an important role in the administration of the project and production of this book.

Louise McLeod-Tollu

Louise is a member of the Home Mission Society and provides administrative support to the NCLS. Her previous experience has been in photography and film, and Louise is involved in the development of resources to assist churches in making the most of the NCLS.